The Men We Became:

More Echoes From the End Zone

Lisa Kelly

D1314670

Notre Dame alumna and author, Lisa Kelly (Photographer: Tracey Saraceni)

The Men We Became:

More Echoes From the End Zone

Lisa Kelly

Copyright © 2016 by Lisa Kelly

Content Editor:	Catherine Russell
Copyeditor:	Mary Ann Falkenberg
Front Cover Design:	Kenton Stufflebeam
Front Cover Photo:	Ryan Meyer
Back Cover Photo:	Lynne Gilbert

The author can be contacted by email at LisaKelly@TheMenWeBecame.com.

Published by Dog Ear Publishing
4011 Vincennes Rd
Indianapolis, IN 46268
www.dogearpublishing.net

ISBN: 978-1-4575-4804-8

This book is printed on acid-free paper.

Printed in the United States of America

Foreword

Every Saturday morning when I was six years old, I would watch those golden helmets on the television screen. I was determined, then and there, that I was going to go to school at Notre Dame. That was my dream as a little boy and one that I would fiercely pursue no matter what anyone said to try to discourage me. I was told over and over that I couldn't do it, so I just needed to give up.

I didn't give up, and their words only made me fight that much harder to achieve my goal. I worked and worked on my dream until the day that I opened my mailbox and, low and behold, there was the envelope with the iconic golden helmet on it. I couldn't believe my eyes. I couldn't hold back the tears of joy at knowing that I had made it. That all my hard work and perseverance paid off. I was going to the University of Notre Dame as I had stated so long ago as a six-year-old who had made up his mind that that is what he wanted.

Once you step foot on campus, you realize that there is no other place like it in the world. Coach Lou Holtz had brought me to this place, and I wanted to show everyone that I was deserving of being there. To say that studying and playing football was easy would be a lie because it was hard, and it was a struggle to keep up with all that is required of an athlete playing at a top-notch University. But I did it, and I did it in 3 ½ years.

Oh there were times when I just wanted to pack up and go home. I was from Southern California, and the weather in Indiana left a lot to be desired. I would call my mom and tell her I wanted to come home, but she always told me that was not an option. Staying true to your dreams and seeing them through was the ultimate goal.

While being a student in and of itself is very difficult, being an athlete along with that made for some trying times. Early morning practices and drills, classes during the day, and then back to practice in the afternoon. There was little time left for studying, so it was late nights, little sleep, and lots of hard work to make it all come together.

You become very close with your fellow teammates, as they are whom you spend most of your time with. You learn to count on each other, and in turn, this leads to being able to count on each other even more on the field. You always have each other's backs. I will never regret my decision to attend one of the top-notch Universities in the world. I know that the experience had a huge impact on my life, and I will cherish those memories always.

I want to thank the author of this book, Lisa Kelly, for including my journey in her book and allowing us to share some of our memories from our time at Notre Dame. Lisa, I value our friendship, and I hope everyone enjoys reading about our experiences as much as we enjoyed sharing them with you.

Thank You Lisa……

GO IRISH!!

Kory Minor
Linebacker
University of Notre Dame du Lac '99

a letter from this guy named Mike outlining academic expectations and what he and his team would do to insure our success in school."

Marv recalled, "I was a good student, studying theology which is a very tough major at a religious school like ND. Coach DeCicco (also the Notre Dame Fencing Coach) called me into his office and told me what it was going to take to be successful. He said 'Marv, this is how it's going to be. The minute I suspect you are not cutting it or you're having problems, we are going to reassess your major.' He said, 'I want you to meet with a graduate assistant every two weeks to assess your progress. Remember: you will get no breaks or special consideration.' I did what I was told and I was successful. Forty years later I saw Coach at a Notre Dame function and he still recalled that story. What made me feel great was when he said, 'I'm proud of you Marv and what you have accomplished.'"

Luther was focused on business as his major. He and Marv laughed at Luther's story of being called into Coach DeCicco's office for a chat, "You remember that fencing sword he had mounted over his desk? I walked into his office and sat down and all he said was, 'You see the sword behind me? If you don't get busy and study harder, you are going to find that sword up your ass.' Coach never minced words." Luther said, "I wasn't doing that bad in class, but he felt I wasn't working to my potential. He wanted our best just like Ara did on the field." Both Luther and Marv said what was even more important was if you weren't performing in the classroom you could bet Ara knew and it was likely Moose Krause the AD knew and you were going to hear from all of them.

The football players interviewed in this book all realize how they benefited from the evolution of the Notre Dame "student-athlete" concept. Notre Dame is not an easy place for any student, let alone for those who have the additional demands of athletics. Without this visionary program, many athletes would be left by the wayside, as they are at so many other schools. Today, thanks to the leadership of Mike DeCicco, Father Hesburgh and Father Joyce, Notre Dame consistently leads NCAA schools in graduation rates and overall academic performance.

Coach DeCicco passed away in the spring of 2013. His impact on Notre Dame and the NCAA schools will be a legacy for decades to come. Notre Dame student-athletes owe a debt of thanks to this Loyal Son.

Mike DeCicco was Notre Dame at its finest – he was the Notre Dame Value Stream at work.

Mike DeCicco quotes taken from: http://notredame.247sports.com/Article/Notre-Dame-Mourns-Death-Of-Mike-DeCicco-123852.

Quarterback John Huarte posed inside Notre Dame Stadium, c1962-1964.
(Photo courtesy of Notre Dame Archives.)

CHAPTER ONE

The Granite & Tile Specialist

John Huarte

*I*t's a run-of-the-mill Sunday afternoon when John Huarte emails me and says, "Today is a good day to do an interview. It's pretty quiet around here. Is today good for you?" I drop everything, quickly gather my questions and call Mr. Huarte at his home in Southern California. Mr. Huarte answers the phone and promptly tells me he'll be back in 20 seconds as he takes a moment to let his dogs, Dixie and Daisy (a golden retriever and a black lab), outside. He gets settled on his couch on the front porch on this lovely 70-degree California afternoon and our interview begins. You'd never know that this quiet, humble man was a Heisman Trophy winner, former NFL player and the owner of a successful tile and granite company for the past 40 years. Huarte is what you would call a true

"Notre Dame man." How does a modest, unassuming young man from Southern California rise to the challenges put in front of him and win a Heisman Trophy? This is John Huarte's story.

Notre Dame was pretty much the only school I was interested in. My brother David, who is five years older than me, attended the University of Notre Dame and majored in geology. My football coach at Mater Dei High School, Dick Coury, was a graduate of Notre Dame; so there were multiple influences in my life pushing me toward playing football at Notre Dame. I was raised on an orange and avocado ranch in Orange County, California, and I remember listening to Notre Dame football on the radio in the farm truck. I didn't really know much about Notre Dame; just that my dad put it on the radio and I sort of fell in love with it. I used to listen to names like Joe Heap, Ralph Guglielmi, Paul Hornung, and Johnny Lattner in the 1950s. Lindsey Nelson did the weekly broadcast, with that deep, rich voice of his, and I had this image in my mind of what Notre Dame was like even though I had no idea where Notre Dame was located.

I had this image in my mind of what Notre Dame was like even though I had no idea where Notre Dame was located.

The Notre Dame Years

I told the people on the plane on my first visit to Notre Dame (to see my brother graduate) that I'd never been "east" before, and they told me that I needed to keep flying past South Bend to be "east", but for me South Bend was east of California! When I arrived at Notre Dame as a student, being from Southern California I really had no idea what was in store for me as far as weather was concerned. I tried to get around campus in my high top tennis shoes, which were definitely much more suitable for a warmer weather climate. They were fine until the snow turned into slush, and then I had to go buy some snow boots. Looking back, I will never forget the day I received the letter from Notre Dame notifying me that I had received a full scholarship to play football at the University of Notre Dame. That moment changed everything for me. "Dear John, we are pleased to inform you that we are offering you a full scholarship to the University of Notre Dame ..." I still have it around here somewhere!

And before he even knew what had happened, the Notre Dame Value Stream had taken hold and set John Huarte off on his journey.

In order to succeed both academically and athletically at a school like Notre Dame you need to have drive, motivation, and a great deal of grit. While the Notre Dame Value Stream does a great job of guiding its student-athletes during their journey at Notre Dame, they still must have the internal fortitude to get the job done; and Huarte was a perfect fit.

> *I graduated from Notre Dame with a degree in business. In order to do that successfully and play football I went to summer school for three straight summers. I wanted to make sure I graduated from ND in four years. Attending summer school not only helped me academically but athletically as well. It gave me the advantage of spending time with my teammates and having impromptu practices, especially with a special guy named Jack Snow (one of Huarte's go-to wide receivers). Those extra summer practices allowed us to get our timing and coordination down which was important for a quarterback/wide receiver duo.*

I went to summer school for three straight summers. I wanted to make sure I graduated from ND in four years. Attending summer school not only helped me academically but athletically as well.

> *I came to Notre Dame with stars in my eyes, and thought I'd do a lot. I didn't play at all during my freshman year or my sophomore year, and I only played a few times during my junior year. I scrimmaged a lot during the week in my first three years, which helped me to continue developing my skills. I didn't even have a monogram letter going into my senior year. And then, as fortune would have it, Coach Ara Parseghian arrived. Paul Shoults also joined the staff that winter and by spring ball they had us looking pretty darn good, or so we thought. You never really know until you play that first game. I injured my shoulder that spring but it was healed and ready to go for fall practice. Our first game that fall, my senior year, was against Wisconsin and they were the heavy favorites. The heavens opened and the rain poured down in Madison that Saturday and we beat them by 24 points (Notre Dame 31-Wisconsin 7). Our offense was stout that day. It was good both on the ground and in the air. We went on to win nine games that season and only lost the last game (to USC) by 3 points in the last minute (Notre Dame 17- USC 20).*

Some coaches have a special knack of being able to recognize when their players are not being utilized to their full potential and to move them around to where they will shine the brightest. Ara Parseghian not only had that skill, but also was one of the best coaches in college football at getting the most out of his players.

Parseghian was very adept at evaluating players and making sure they were in the correct position for their particular strengths and weaknesses. He knew how to handle young college kids and he knew how to do it without over-coaching.

When Coach Parseghian arrived at Notre Dame, he moved a lot of guys around and into new positions. Parseghian was very adept at evaluating players and making sure they were in the correct position for their particular strengths and weaknesses. He was also very skilled at play selection, field position and knowing what risks to take as well as what risks not to take. Coach Parseghian is a great man and he was a tremendously skilled coach. He knew how to handle young college kids and he knew how to do it without over-coaching. He just told you what you needed to know and let you do the rest. He came to Notre Dame with a great supporting cast of assistants: Richard "Doc" Urich, Paul Shoults, and Tom Pagna (who was the backfield coach and worked very well with me), all of whom coached with Parseghian at both Miami of Ohio and Northwestern. His other five coaches: John Ray, Joe Yonto, Dave Hurd, George Sefcik, and John Murphy, were all former Notre Dame players. Parseghian and his staff really jelled well together and united our team into a cohesive group that became a very well-oiled machine.

A good coach will make his players see what they can be rather than what they are. ~ Ara Parseghian

It was pure luck for me that Coach Parseghian came along my senior year and that we had such a big year that season. I set 12 new records that year, and that was after not playing at all my first two years and only playing a few times during my junior year. The opportunities that Parseghian gave me that year gave me the chance to go pro. Parseghian brought a lot of little things to the table that, as a combined whole, made us into a successful team. When Ara first met with the team, he announced to us that everyone was going to get a chance to play, and that he was not going to pick favorites. My class-mates and I were seniors, and he still played us even though we'd be leaving after the season was over and the younger guys would be with him for a longer period of time. I respected him for giving each and every one of us an equal chance. Coach Parseghian also had a remarkable attention to detail. He would give us very clear instructions as to what he wanted both on offense and defense. He always made sure you knew exactly what he wanted from you. In any sport and on any team, during most games, at some point you will have a mental lapse and this is where penalties occur. Coach Parseghian would gently remind us in his pre-game speeches that we needed to be fundamentally sound, to work very hard at being penalty-free, and to be conscious of taking care of the ball in order to prevent fumbles and interceptions. He would drill into each and every one of us the details of what he expected us to do on both offense and defense. When he was done with you, you knew exactly what he wanted.

When Ara first met with the team, he announced to us that everyone was going to get a chance to play, and that he was not going to pick favorites.

When Coach Parseghian arrived at Notre Dame he took over a team that went 2-7 in the fall of 1963 and took them to a 9-1 record in 1964. Quite a dramatic turnaround. How did Parseghian take the same group of guys who had only won two games the year before and turn them into true college football contenders?

Parseghian did a great job at making sure we were very well prepared for game day. When you are prepared, you make fewer mistakes, and when you make fewer mistakes you win. We also had some very good talent on that team, and he knew how to bring the talent out of guys. We had a tremendous group of guys on offense. We also had Kevin Hardy, Tom Regner, Alan Page, Pete Duranko, Tom Rhoads and Don Gmitter anchoring our strong sophomore defensive line. And we had a great kicking game with our kicker Kenny Ivan. When Parseghian took all of these components and put them together and had us concentrating on not making mistakes, the end result was pretty good; we won. Our defense was quite disciplined in doing their job and we (the offense) got the ball handed back to us a lot.

Coach Parseghian was an extremely talented college football coach and knew exactly what was required to get his men prepared for game day, but he still had a little bit of fun with them.

On the 1964 football squad we had a guard named John Atamian from Niagara Falls, New York. He was my offensive guard and I was the quarterback running plays. We were in practice one day and Atamian had instructions to block one specific person and he blocked the wrong person. Parseghian noticed the error and said, "Gosh darn it, I've never met a dumb Armenian before!!" (Both John Atamian and Coach Parseghian were Armenian). We all just died laughing. Atamian went on to play offensive guard in the Canadian Football League for the Hamilton Tiger-Cats, Toronto Argonauts, Saskatchewan Roughriders, Winnipeg Blue Bombers and Calgary Stampeders. He won the Grey Cup with the Tiger-Cats in 1965 and with the Stampeders in 1971. He was one tough guy.

Huarte's four years at Notre Dame were filled with countless memorable experiences; but his senior year was truly the pinnacle of his career at Notre Dame. The Notre Dame Value Stream and the vision of Coach Parseghian helped Huarte reach his full potential which included leading his team to a magical nine wins that season. It also allowed him to win the Heisman Trophy that year, with his go-to wide receiver Jack Snow finishing in fifth place.

My favorite moment at Notre Dame was probably when Michigan State came to Notre Dame during my senior season. In the years prior to that meeting, Michigan State had beaten us quite a few times. We beat them that day by three touchdowns, with a final score of 34-7, on national TV, and we showed the nation how great we really were. Everything just went right for me that day, so that is definitely my favorite memory at Notre Dame.

Huarte's road to the Heisman trophy was quite unusual.

Never before had an unknown player, a player who had not even earned a monogram yet, come out of nowhere to have a truly remarkable, rags-to-riches season, and become one of the greatest Heisman trophy surprises of all times.

There was a phone down at the end of Walsh hall on the second floor. It rang, George Keenen went down there to answer it and then he shouted down the hall "John, you got it!" I walked down, took the phone, Charlie Jones our PR man said, "John, you won the Heisman trophy, you have to go to New York." I later called my parents. It was very exciting.

Professional Career

Following an electric 9-1 senior season, Huarte:

- set 2 NCAA and 9 Notre Dame offensive records
- threw for 2,062 yards and 16 touchdowns
- had a career passing efficiency rating of 144.7 (which still ranks third all-time in the Irish record book behind Kevin McDougal and Jarious Jackson)

Huarte was an in demand commodity and excited about his future pro football career.

In the 1965 pro football draft, I was drafted by the New York Jets into the American Football League (AFL). They drafted me because they knew a Notre Dame Heisman Trophy winner would be instrumental in helping them sell tickets as so many Notre Dame fans and subway alumni would want to see me play. I never played one minute during my time with the Jets, though. I sat on the bench behind Joe Namath. Then, following the 1965 season, I was traded to the Boston Patriots and was there for one season. At the end of the 1966 season, there was a contract dispute with the Patriots and I became a free agent and signed with the Philadelphia Eagles where I played for two years (1967 and 1968). Following the 1968 season, I was cut from the Eagles and got signed by the Kansas City Chiefs.

The year that I was with the Chiefs we went on to win the Super Bowl. I sat on the bench behind star quarterback Lenny Dawson, and ended up with a Super Bowl Ring and a bonus. I stayed with the Chiefs as their backup quarterback for three years (1969, 1970 and 1971) and then I spent one year with the Chicago Bears. I spent a total of eight years in the AFL and NFL and never had one start.

I spent a total of eight years in the AFL and NFL and never had one start.

In 1973 I was no longer playing football. Right about that time a new league was forming, the World Football League; I got picked up by the Memphis Grizzlies to be their starting quarterback and I played with them in 1974 and 1975. I played a lot of football and had a great time. Halfway through the 1975 season the league went bankrupt and we all had to go home. That was my 10 years of playing professional football. It was a lot of moving around, but it was a lot of fun as well.

The Notre Dame Value Stream helped Huarte make the decision that although playing professional football was fun, it was time to venture onward into the next phase of his life.

Today

John Huarte and his wife Eileen.

At that point I knew it was time to go home. I moved back to Southern California and got into the tile and granite business with my brother Gregory; our business was called Arizona Tile Company (www.arizonatile. com). My wife, Eileen, and I started with a small tile store in San Diego in 1977. Since then, our little tile and granite company has turned into quite a big deal. We now employ 700 people who staff 23 branches in 7 western states. We are an import and distribution company, and our products are distributed to both residential and commercial customers. Since our doors opened in 1977, we've always searched the globe in the pursuit of truly extraordinary surfaces. Through relationships with select quarries and suppliers, our company offers a vast selection of granite, travertine, onyx, slate, marble and limestone, including stunning tile and stone you won't find anywhere else. Our treasury of surfaces also includes beautiful and unique medallions, porcelain, tile and other design creations and applications that bring drama and enchantment to any space.

My wife, Eileen, and I have five children and 12 grandchildren, so that's pretty much our life right now; spending time with the grandkids and trying to stay fit and healthy. Three of our daughters live within a mile of our house, and our two sons live within an hour drive of us, so we really enjoy having the family so close. Our oldest grandson plays baseball (pitcher/first base) at Denison University in Granville, Ohio.

John Huarte's Lessons from the Notre Dame Value Stream:

- Academically, major in a degree that you can really do something with; take classes that have a strong economic value so that when you get out of college you will have a degree that has a high market value. Don't major in something that no one cares about; you don't want to waste your time.

- Athletically, concentrate every day on staying healthy. A lot of people get hurt which oftentimes ends their careers. Practice and play smart. You have to be very alert and aware of what's going on while at practice and during games so that you can reduce your chances of being injured. I've seen a lot of excellent players get injured by being careless and end their careers that way.

- Be prepared. Prepare yourself during the week and in the offseason; practice, condition, and work on your skills in order to be your best on game day. Work especially hard on the skills needed for your specific position. Be sure to master those.

Notre Dame Football Media Day – Terry Hanratty (#5), Coach Ara Parseghian,
and Jim Seymour (#85), 1968.
(Photo courtesy of Notre Dame Archives.)

CHAPTER TWO

The Financial Quarterback

Terry Hanratty

*T*erry Hanratty grew up in Butler, Pennsylvania, a steel mill community where the boys were raised big and strong and all of the top colleges headed to recruit the next crop of football superstars. As a four-sport athlete at Butler Senior High School (football, basketball, baseball and track), Hanratty was a hard worker and was not afraid to face any challenge placed in front of him. Following his athletic career at Butler Senior High School, Hanratty went on to attend the University of Notre Dame where he was a three-year starter and two-time All-American, as well as a Heisman Trophy candidate. Hanratty and wide receiver Jim Seymour formed a dynamic passing/receiving duo, which led Notre Dame to the national title in 1966. In his career at Notre Dame Hanratty completed 304 of 550 passes for 4,152 yards and 27 touchdowns, and carried the ball 181 times for 586 yards and 16 touchdowns. He then went on to play football in the NFL with fellow Notre Dame teammate, halfback Rocky Bleier, in Pittsburgh with the Steelers. But that is only part of the story! This is the rest of Terry Hanratty's story.

Recruiting today is much more complicated than it was 50 years ago due to the emergence of the internet and social media. There was a time when recruiting wasn't a complete media circus, and all colleges wanted were smart, talented, strong young men with solid family values. Terry Hanratty fit this bill.

I grew up in Butler, Pennsylvania, 25 miles north of Pittsburgh, and back in the 1960s recruiting in Western Pennsylvania was equivalent to recruiting in Florida, Texas and California today. If you wanted quality football players, Western Pennsylvania was where you went. The whole area was producing talent left and right. My high school football coach, Art Bernardi, produced over 60 Division I football players in 20 years of coaching high school football. Western Pennsylvania was filled with lots of ethnic groups: Polish, Irish, German, Italian; we worked in the steel mills and were raised to be big, tough kids. I was fortunate in that I had a lot of college offers, but my high school coach was really good at guiding me and helping me make a smart, educated decision. Coach Bernardi told me that I wasn't going to go to USC because it was simply too far away. At that point in my life I hadn't even ever been on a plane yet. My first plane trip was to Michigan State University for my official visit. He told me, pick a few schools that you really want to go to, make your visits and be honest with all of these people. Don't take a visit to Miami just to get a free trip to Florida if you're not serious about going to Miami. When I sat down and went over all of my options, it came down to Michigan State and Notre Dame, and once I met Ara (Coach Parseghian), my decision was made.

Football was my least favorite sport. I loved baseball, basketball, track and then football. ~ Terry Hanratty

My junior year of high school was when this all changed. I decided that I wanted to play football and discard the other sports, but at that point everything had been developed and I never had any of the injuries that these kids have today. You can go to the NFL right now and pick out 10 players and come up with a great basketball team because these kids played multiple sports at a very high level. Basketball is probably one of the best sports for developing the whole body. When I was a kid, my generation was the first ever to go to college in my family. These days, everyone goes to college so you need to really look at the quality of the degree in addition to the quality of the athletic program.

When Coach Parseghian came to Pittsburgh to recruit Hanratty he may not have been a Notre Dame legend yet, but he certainly did know how to sell Notre Dame. The Notre Dame Value Stream swiftly picked up Hanratty and carried him toward his future in South Bend, Indiana.

Ara came to Pittsburgh to meet me and we met at a hotel in downtown Pittsburgh. I remember looking at the menu and a steak sandwich was $3.50. In my mind I was thinking, "If I get a steak sandwich (we didn't have real steaks at my house) instead of a club sandwich (which was $1.75), will he be thinking that I'm gouging him?" One club sandwich and a few hours later, I drove home and told my mother that I was going to the University of Notre Dame. Ara was one amazing coach. Normally with most head coaches, you'll find some second or third team guys who will bad mouth the coach for something he did wrong or someone he mistreated, but not Ara. Everybody loved him, from the starters all the way to the guys riding the bench. He had such a dynamic personality, everyone wanted to be around him.

I don't believe in team motivation. I believe in getting a team prepared so it knows it will have the necessary confidence when it steps on a field and be prepared to play a good game. ~ Tom Landry

The Notre Dame Years

There are good college football coaches, there are great football coaches, and then there are coaches that are on a level all their own. Coach Ara Parseghian is definitely in this latter elite group.

Ara's ability to have us 100% prepared for anything we could possibly face on Saturday was what made him such a talented head football coach. Back when I played at Notre Dame in the mid 1960s you couldn't play your freshman year, so I was a starter for the next three years. I was never once surprised by anything I faced during a game. We won a lot of games but we lost a couple as well. Our losses were usually the result of a bad performance. The losses, however, were never from being unprepared or from not knowing what Ara expected of you. He had you completely ready with a phenomenally constructed game plan, and you felt 100% comfortable going into every game. You were extremely prepared for anything that was headed your way.

Quite honestly I think Ara Parseghian is a one-of-a-kind guy. You will not find anyone like him ever again. He was such a dynamic recruiter. He had this personality that was so magnetic; you just had to play for him. It's truly something you can't read or learn in a Coaching 101 book on "how to become Ara Parseghian," it's just not that simple. He had this honesty and fairness about him. I haven't seen those qualities in a coach anywhere else.

Yes, Ara may have been dynamic, magnetic, fair and honest, but when it came time to get down to business, he was just that: all business.

> *When you'd screw up at practice, Ara would tell you to bend down and touch your toes and then he'd literally kick you in the butt. One day Ara came to practice and he was really upset. He said, "Dushney, get over here and bend down and touch your toes," and then he kicked him in the butt. Then he said, "I know you're going to screw up today so I'm going to go ahead and kick you in the butt now!"*

Most of us feel pretty lucky just to be able to attend a school like Notre Dame. To be able to play football at Notre Dame, that's even more special. But to win a national title, that's the pinnacle of any Notre Dame football career.

> *Winning the national championship in 1966 has got to be up there. What Ara did, coming in to Notre Dame and completely turning the team around, it was a remarkable thing to witness. They probably should have won it in 1964 (the year John Huarte won the Heisman Trophy). In 1965 they were very good but they just didn't quite have the right quarterback to lead them to a championship. In 1966 we pretty much had the same guys from the year before, but Ara was finally able to get us over the hurdle and win the national title. It was really neat. Jim (Seymour) and I probably knew each other better than anybody else on that team. We worked out together all winter long. We used to go into the field house and work on our moves. It was just an automatic feel I had for Jim. I knew exactly when he was going to turn and he knew that when he turned around the ball would be there. It was a great chemistry we had.*

How do two guys develop the kind of connection that Hanratty and Seymour had? You only get that by going that extra mile; by going above and beyond what everyone else was doing. And that's exactly what Hanratty and Seymour did.

> *If you remember the old field house, or if you've ever seen photos of the old field house, the ceiling was constructed with visible rafters. It was a great place to practice throwing the ball because you had to put it over the rafters in order to throw it more than thirty yards. It was a great place to practice throwing it high and dropping it right in where you wanted it to be. Jim Seymour and I spent a great deal of time in the field house practicing our connection.*

All of the hard work and perseverance paid off for Hanratty, but life at Notre Dame (and beyond) wasn't all work and no play. His Notre Dame head coach, Ara Parseghian, did a great job of recognizing that Hanratty and his fellow teammates were still developing young men. Ara always kept a watchful eye on his players to make sure the balance between work and play didn't tip to one extreme or the other.

> *Coach Parseghian had been notified by a few professors that some of his players were skipping class. As a result of this, Parseghian put Coach Boulac in charge of following these football players and making sure that they actually made it to class. One of my classrooms had a door into the class from the hallway. It also had another door which led out of the room from the back of class. We would go into class through the front door (while Coach Boulac was watching us) and then out the back door and over to "The Huddle." This worked for a few days until Coach Boulac got wind of what we were doing. One day we did what we usually did and were sitting in The Huddle when in walked Coach Boulac. He caught us.*

The Notre Dame Value Stream always gets us on the right track, even when we occasionally stray from our course.

At so many schools you have students and you have athletes, but often times the two do not mix. At Notre Dame, their athletes are student-athletes. They are expected to perform well both on and off the field, not just in one area but in all areas.

> *You just hit it on the head right there, "student-athlete." A lot of schools give "attendance" diplomas, but at Notre Dame you have to do the work. Football was a full time job, but so was school. You really had to buckle down in order to get everything done. Coach Parseghian and his staff kept track of each and every one of his students. If you missed classes he would call you into his office. He wanted you to get that diploma more than he wanted to win on Saturday.*

Professional Career

The Notre Dame Value Stream always seems to understand what we need, and for Hanratty it began his post-graduation journey by taking him home.

> *It was nice to be able to essentially go "back home," being drafted by the Pittsburgh Steelers. To this day (I'm in my late 60s), the two best decisions I ever made were:*
>
> 1.   *Going to Notre Dame, a decision made by me.*
>
> 2.   *Going to play for the Steelers, a decision made by the Rooney family.*
>
> *You could not have asked for two better places to "work". I was drafted by the Steelers in 1969 and then Terry Bradshaw was drafted the next year. It wasn't the best of working conditions, having two young quarterbacks on the same*

team, but we worked very well together. We won two Super Bowls during the time I was with the Steelers and it was a great experience. The guys I played with at the Steelers, we still keep in touch and get together for reunion golf outings. It was a tremendous experience, it really was.

Hanratty is the kind of guy who brings laughter with him wherever he goes. His time with the Steelers was no different.

Jack Lambert was a middle linebacker for the Pittsburgh Steelers and was one of the meanest guys in the NFL. No one would mess with him ... well, except for me! When I'd go into the locker room before practice, I'd go early enough so that I could place two cups of water underneath his shoulder pads, which were sitting on the top shelf of his locker. When he'd arrive to the locker room, he'd pull down his shoulder pads and the water would spill all over his face. I did it to him three days in a row. And for three days in a row he had water spill all over his face. Finally I told him, "You big dummy! Tomorrow morning, get up on your stool and look under your shoulder pads and if there's water there, move the cups of water before taking down your shoulder pads." The next morning, Jack gets up on his stool and looks underneath his shoulder pads, and there's no water. He was so very proud of himself; he was strutting around the locker room as proud as a peacock. The next day, he comes to practice, pulls down his shoulder pad and water pours all over his face. I was 25-0 with different tricks on Lambert and he never got me once!

One of the wonderful things the Notre Dame Value Stream does for Her Lady's students and student-athletes is to show them their strengths and weaknesses early on. This guides them through the journey of life and helps them navigate the forks in the road as their journey changes course, which it often does.

I was used to making quick decisions on the field, because let's face it, if you take too long to make a decision as a quarterback, the next thing you know you're flat on your back.

I majored in economics at Notre Dame and always enjoyed finance and how the financial markets worked. While I was still playing for the Steelers I began dabbling in the stock market, so transitioning into a profession as a stock trader on Wall Street was a natural fit for me. I worked for a few firms before I found the right fit and then found my place at Sanford C. Bernstein in New York City where I worked as an institutional trader for about 24 years. My time playing football for Notre Dame and the Pittsburgh Steelers prepared me well for my career in finance. I was used to making quick decisions on the field, because let's face it, if you take too long to make a decision as a quarterback, the next thing you know you're flat on your back. This quick decision making skill was very useful as a stock trader when your goal is to get the best possible price on a stock when it becomes available. You have to be confident in your decision-making skills to succeed on Wall Street. For the past seven years I have been working out of my home in Connecticut putting together hedge funds for top-tier investors with Cross Shore Capital Management LLC.

Today

Terry sent five children to college following his successful careers in the NFL and the financial industry: three to Notre Dame, one to Indiana University and his youngest daughter Erin is currently attending USC.

While it is fun to look back on his successful career at Notre Dame, Terry was also blessed to be able to enjoy his son Conor's time at Notre Dame as a football player.

Terry Hanratty

It was really neat. Watching him on the team has been a very proud moment for me. He's undefeated in all of the games he's started in. I've always told him football isn't a profession. First and foremost, get your degree from Notre Dame. You have to be ready for that 40-year experience because you never know when football is going to end and that degree is going to kick in. Conor was a fifth year senior in 2015 and because of an injury was on a medical scholarship for the year. He stayed at Notre Dame for his fifth year in order to finish his MBA (Conor graduated with his undergraduate degree in May of 2015). He walked out of Notre Dame with two degrees!

Terry Hanratty's Lessons from the Notre Dame Value Stream:

- Make smart decisions about what you study in college. For an athlete, it is the degree that is going to give you an edge. Football only lasts so long, so choose a school that's going to educate you and set you up for the next forty years.

- One percent of college athletes make it in the pros. That's a tough statistic to overcome. You need to take the 99% in that bet and go to a university that is going to give you an education and get you a job when you graduate.

- We put these kids on a pedestal when we give them three, four or five stars. As a student-athlete you need to think about the forty-year decision and not just the four-year decision.

Player Ken MacAfee (#81) running with the ball, fall 1975. Dome yearbook staff photographer. (Photo courtesy of Notre Dame Archives.)

CHAPTER THREE

The Oral Surgeon

Ken MacAfee

*K*enneth Adams MacAfee, Jr. started his journey in Brockton, Massachusetts, the hometown of Rocky Marciano. His head football coach at Brockton High School, the Brockton "Boxers," was married to Rocky's sister and so MacAfee not only played football but also pursued his interest in boxing. At 6'5" and 225 pounds, MacAfee had the breaking speed of a tailback and the sure hands of a wideout, and began to excel for the Brockton Boxers as a sophomore. In both his junior and senior seasons MacAfee led the Boxers to the scholastic "Super Bowl," the state championship game, where they won two consecutive state titles. MacAfee finished his high school football career with 23 touchdown receptions and in his four years at Brockton high school, the Boxers were 33-3-1 and MacAfee was selected as a first-team All-American. And this was just the beginning of MacAfee's tremendous football journey. He went on to play football for both Ara Parseghian and Dan Devine at the University of Notre Dame, played alongside two outstanding quarterbacks in Rusty Lisch and Joe Montana, won the national title in 1977 and went on to play football in the NFL for the San Francisco 49ers. How did this outstanding football player from Brockton, Massachusetts, go on to become an oral surgeon with his own practice and also lecture at Harvard University? This is Ken MacAfee's story.

It's not where you start, it's where you finish.

I was recruited by quite a lot of schools. I kept a file of all the schools that were recruiting me; 205 schools in all sent me letters while I was in high school, trying to convince me that I should play football for them. And of course back then you were allowed to make unlimited college visits, which isn't the case today. You could spend an entire year visiting schools if you wanted to. I scheduled 20 visits and ended up visiting 12 schools in total. Once I visited Notre Dame, it became the benchmark. Every school I visited before or after Notre Dame was compared to the visit to ND. Finally it occurred to me, if I'm comparing all of these schools to Notre Dame, I should just go to Notre Dame. I was using Notre Dame as my benchmark and nothing else could compare to what Notre Dame had to offer.

It did not take the Notre Dame Value Stream long to rise to the top and emerge as the clear path for MacAfee.

Notre Dame had won the national title in 1973 and my freshman year was the following year. ND winning the national championship was certainly a factor when it came to making my decision. I knew that ND was going to win and I wanted to win in college. Academically, no other school could compare to Notre Dame. I was interested in pursuing dentistry or medicine and a lot of schools were not supportive of a football player who wanted to study premed in college. Notre Dame was in a class all its own in that respect. I looked at Notre Dame, USC, Rice, Alabama, Tennessee, and North Carolina: a lot of schools in the SEC. I didn't want to be at a school that had athletic dorms because you'd never get any time away from the athletic culture. Notre Dame distributed the athletes evenly in every dorm on campus as opposed to putting all of the football players in a football dorm. That was very appealing to me. USC and Rice didn't have athletic dorms either, but they couldn't compare to ND.

My host during my visit to ND was tight end Mike Creaney. My recruiting visit to Notre Dame was the worst trip of them all. There were 20 – 25 recruits visiting campus that weekend. A bunch of us got stranded in Chicago and couldn't make connecting flights to South Bend because it was foggy, raining and snowing; so they put us on a bus and we got to campus around one in the morning. The coaches met us at the bus station and took us over to the Morris Inn. The next day we got to go to a Notre Dame Hockey game and ND beat Michigan Tech, who was the reigning national champion in hockey. ND beat them twice that weekend. On Saturday night we went to the ND men's basketball game, where they beat UCLA and snapped the Bruins' 88 game win streak; and Mike Creaney looked at me and said, "Multiply this by at least 10 and you have a Notre Dame football game." On Sunday, all of the flights were still cancelled so we got to stay an extra night at Notre Dame. On that particular Sunday, the Notre Dame football program was holding their national championship banquet, which we got to attend since we were still there. My conversations with Ara that weekend were pretty eye opening for me. He said he'd be more than happy for me to pursue medicine or dentistry, and that he already had several football players who were pursuing similar paths. He told me that if I had to miss practice in order to complete my class work or prepare for a test that was no problem. Academics came first at Notre Dame. It was so amazing to speak to Ara like that. He was such a legend. You just wanted to fold yourself under the table.

The Notre Dame Years

Most football players feel extremely fortunate to have the opportunity to play under one legendary coach during their time in college, but MacAfee had the opportunity to play under two Notre Dame legends, Ara Parseghian and Dan Devine. Although each coach had their own coaching style, the Notre Dame Value Stream showed MacAfee the benefits of each and allowed him to grow and learn under each man's guidance.

My roommate freshman year was Harry Woebkenberg from Archbishop Moeller High School in Cincinnati. He ended up leaving after our sophomore year. When we were freshmen, Ara announced that he was going to retire. Our first inclination was that we should transfer. Then we thought, what are we talking about?! This is Notre Dame. We're not going to transfer anywhere better than this! We didn't know much about Dan Devine when he came in. We knew he had been a head coach with the Green Bay Packers and the University of Missouri, but we also knew that he hadn't had much success at Green Bay so no one really knew what to expect out of him.

Parseghian was a very forceful head coach who had control of everything. Devine was a very soft-spoken guy who deferred a great deal of the day-to-day coaching to his assistants. Parseghian called all of the offensive plays and was very much involved in the week's preparation while Devine sat in his tower and watched practice from above. But in the end they both won national championships. Parseghian had an infectious personality and the guys really enjoyed being around him. Devine was reserved and soft spoken and wasn't very popular among the players but his assistant coaches were great and we responded very well to them.

Part of what draws you to play a sport like football is the competition. There is the competition that occurs against other teams, and then there is also the competition that occurs within the team to win a starting position in the various positions. The latter can either bond you as a team, or it can become divisive as it did during MacAfee's time at Notre Dame. But no matter what challenge the game threw at them, the Notre Dame Value Stream was always there to help them work through it and overcome adversity.

There was a great deal of separation among the team. A lot of guys thought Joe Montana should be the starter and some thought Rusty Lisch should be the starter. There was a great deal of controversy around the quarterback position, even within the team. Joe came in on three separate occasions during his sophomore year when we were losing in the fourth quarter and we won each one of those games. Most notable was the Air Force game; we were down 30-10 with 10 minutes left in the game and he brought us back to win 31-30. Then against North Carolina, we were losing 14-3 and Montana threw an 80-yard touchdown pass with a minute left. Everyone knew what his abilities were, unfortunately he got hurt in spring practice (before his junior year season) and had to sit out a year.

When he came back everyone was confident in his ability but the coaches were unsure as he had been out a year. Instead of giving him an opportunity they started Rusty Lisch. Lisch was a great athlete but he was not a good quarterback. He ended up playing for the St. Louis Cardinals as a defensive back. Montana was just a better quarterback and most people were of this same opinion, but Devine thought Lisch should get the starting nod. When we were losing 10-0 to Purdue in the first quarter, Devine put in Gary Forystek. Forystek was known for his passing game and so he came out passing. Then he took this really awful hit that ended up breaking his neck. It was the first time I had ever seen an ambulance come out onto the field. After they took Forystek off the field Devine put Lisch back in but we were still in the same quandary that we were in before and so then he went to Montana. Montana's first pass was to me. He threw this wounded duck of a ball to me. A Purdue linebacker stepped in front of me with 60 yards of green grass in front of him and snatched the ball but he ended up dropping the ball. After that Joe settled down. We came back to beat Purdue by a score of 31-24 with 17 unanswered Notre Dame points in the fourth quarter. After that win, the rest is history; we didn't lose another game the rest of the year. He proved his abilities that year, which gave him great opportunities moving forward into the NFL.

In any collegiate football career at a school like Notre Dame there are always one or two games that you will talk about for the rest of your life. One of those games for MacAfee was the game against USC in 1977, a game that will forever be remembered in Notre Dame tradition and lore.

On game day I had one ritual or superstition that I always followed.

We went out in our blue jerseys and warmed up as always. No one had any inkling of what was going to occur. On game day I had one ritual or superstition that I always followed. I had to be the last one into the locker room after warm-ups and the last one out of the locker room at game time. As I was coming towards the locker room I heard this commotion that was getting louder and louder the closer I got. As I walked up the stairs from the tunnel into the locker room it sounded as though we had just won the game. I walked into the locker room and everyone was taking off their blue jerseys and putting on these green ones. It was utter chaos in the locker room; everyone was jumping around. It was pretty impressive I must say. It was remarkable what happened after that. Whether or not the green jerseys were a significant factor in that win, they certainly did have an impact. The aura surrounding that game with the addition of the green jerseys, we were more pumped up than you can even imagine. The coaches had to actually come into the locker room to settle everyone down. It was an enjoyable experience, but winning the game was even more enjoyable. We were just going to wear the green jerseys for that game and then someone said, "why don't we wear the green jerseys for the rest of the year? Use them as our trademark and potentially win a national title." And the rest, as they say, is history.

Even in a national championship winning season such as the one MacAfee experienced in 1977, there will always be the naysayers and those individuals who don't respect your accomplishments or the hard work that you've put in to get there. This is when the Notre Dame Value Stream shows you how to walk the straight and narrow path and to hold your head up high.

The best award I could receive would be the opportunity to play Texas for the national championship.

A few things had happened leading up to that game (January 2, 1978 Cotton Bowl, Notre Dame vs. Texas). I was in New York for the Heisman Trophy presentation with Earl Campbell and Terry Miller at the Waldorf Astoria Hotel, and it was the first time that the presentation had been televised. They asked me if I thought I had a chance to win the Heisman Trophy and I said, "Of course not. I'm a tight end/glorified lineman!" During the awards presentation they also awarded positional awards such as "best lineman." I was voted the best receiver and when I went up to accept my award they gave me a minute to speak. I commented that while this award was nice the best award I could receive would be the opportunity to play Texas for the national championship. Hopefully, the game would be the epitome of every player's career. The next day I started getting death threats from Texas fans, "If you come down here to play you're going to get shot; we're going to kill your family." I thought my comment was pretty benign but they took it to the next level.

We went down to Texas to practice and on the fourth or fifth night a rock came through my window with a note attached to it, "If you play during the Cotton Bowl we are going to kill you." I went to the last two practices in a police car and not on the bus with the team. The night before the game they took us to a hotel about 20 miles outside of Dallas and brought us back into town the next morning for the game. One of the coaches asked me if I was nervous and I said, "What's really going to happen? If they want to shoot me, fine. Who cares? We're going to win the game and win the national championship." Having to play Texas in Dallas was basically like giving them home field advantage; and to beat them the way we did was fabulous. They only scored one touchdown at the very end of the first half, which was the result of a defensive penalty we received. There was no time left on the clock and the penalty gave them an extra play.

Leading up to the game, a couple of our teammates had been pretty outspoken. Bob Golic had said, "It's going to be no contest. We're going to beat them." There was a sense of over confidence and Devine finally had to bring the team together and tell us to be quiet. He told us that all we were doing was giving Texas fodder and that we were not allowed to speak to the press any more. He told us to get ourselves together; no game is won in the newspaper. The Texas players were a pretty arrogant bunch themselves. They thought they were going to run all over us with the home field advantage. The tickets for the Notre Dame fans started on the 50-yard line and went to the corner of the stadium and the rest of the place was filled with Texas fans. With 10 minutes left in the fourth quarter all of the Notre Dame fans were still there and the rest of the stadium was practically empty. It was a great feeling to see that the Texas fans had given up and left.

The day after the game Luther Bradley, Ross Browner and I got on a plane and flew to Hawaii because we were playing in the Hula Bowl the next week.

Who was in the seat next to me but Brad Shearer from Texas. He was sitting there reading the headlines in the paper and said, "Oh well, we're ranked number four, I guess that's not too bad." He smiled at me and said, "What can I say, you killed us." At that point I knew there weren't any sour grapes. We ended up having a nice conversation on the plane. He was a good guy and a gentleman, but what could he really say? They got beat. It was awesome because we beat them right in their backyard. They were the only undefeated team that year and it was the perfect storm for them and they couldn't pull it off. Playing and beating Texas was the only way we could be named national champions that year. All four teams above us (we were ranked number five) that year lost their bowl games so it worked out perfectly for us.

In addition to playing football for the University of Notre Dame, MacAfee also dabbled in a little boxing during the offseason and participated in Notre Dame's boxing competition called the "Bengal Bouts."

Basically I just wanted to stay in shape during the offseason and that's why I decided to train for the Bengal Bouts. I first got involved during my freshman year. I was supposed to fight Doug Becker but he ended up getting pleurisy in his lungs. Since we were the only two heavy weights they ended up cancelling the fight. The next year I did it again. Doug Becker beat Jim Browner for the heavy weight title and I lost to Ross Browner by a split decision in the super heavy weight title fight. It was less of a competitive thing for me and more a great way for me to stay in shape during the offseason. However, I wasn't completely new to the sport. I had done some boxing in high school. My hometown, Brockton, Massachusetts, was also the hometown of Rocky Marciano. My head football coach in high school was married to Rocky's sister; and so I had always been interested in boxing. But after that fight against Ross Browner I decided that was enough boxing for me. It was fun, and his win was a worthy call. Ross and I had a pretty good rumble that year in the final. Preparing for the Bengal Bouts took a lot of hard work and dedication from a lot of people.

I did the worst thing you could possibly do as a boxer; I knocked him down in the first round. He got up at the count of nine and I expended too much energy attempting to finish him off. I had worn myself out. By the third round I could barely breathe because I had overdone it in the first round. He definitely got some good licks in during that fight but he didn't knock me down. Win or lose it was helpful for keeping in shape and staying prepared for football. Boxing is such a taxing sport. In professional boxing they fight for 15 three-minute rounds. In Bengal Bouts we would fight for three two-minute rounds. I can't imagine fighting for 45 minutes. I have a great respect for professional boxers. They are in phenomenal shape to be able to fight like that.

You never know when a seemingly minor disruption in your life will end up being a very important detail in the success of your future. The Notre Dame Value Stream always seems to know what you need and just when you need it.

The best thing that could have happened to me personally was when they changed the Pitt game my senior year. The game was originally scheduled at the beginning of October. They moved it to the first weekend of the season and set it as a nationally televised game. That created a bye on that first weekend in October, and that was also when the dental achievement test was given. If the Pitt game hadn't been moved, I wouldn't have been able to take my test, and I would not have been able to pursue my dental education following graduation from Notre Dame. Who knows where my career would have gone. I took the test, got into dental school and pursued my career as an oral surgeon and was able to do everything that I wanted to do professionally.

When Ara recruited me he told me, one, he would give me the opportunity to play for a national championship.

As far as favorite on the field memories go, the first game that I started as a freshman was pretty memorable. Playing against Alabama in the Orange Bowl my freshman year was pretty special to me because my Dad went to Alabama. And my senior year was such a tremendous season. We didn't start out too well but we built it into something amazing. The green jersey game against USC and beating Texas in their backyard were experiences I will never forget. All of these experiences gathered together tell the story of a great experience at Notre Dame. When Ara recruited me he told me, one, he would give me the opportunity to play for a national championship. And two, that I would have the opportunity to get one of the greatest educations in the country. He told me if I was not interested in those two things, good luck. I took his offer and I did both; I won a national title and got an outstanding degree. I don't think I could have done that at any other school.

Professional Career

Following his national championship winning senior season, MacAfee decided to enter into the 1978 NFL draft.

I told Bill that the team was going nowhere.

I was the 7th pick in the 1978 NFL draft by the San Francisco 49ers. Ross Browner went as the 8th pick to the Cincinnati Bengals and Luther Bradley went as the 11th pick to the Detroit Lions. I was hanging out in Sorin Hall when I got a call from a reporter from the Boston Globe asking me how I felt about my draft pick and I said, "What are you talking about?" The 49ers hadn't even called me at that point. About an hour later I received a call from the 49ers and they did a press conference with me via speakerphone. I played in the NFL for three years. Then Bill Walsh came in and wanted to move me from tight end to guard. I lost more games in my NFL rookie year than I did in high school and college combined. We were 2-14, 2-14 and then 6-10. I told Bill that the team was going nowhere and that I had decided to go back and finish dental school. Of course, the 49ers ended up winning the Super Bowl that very next season.

Playing in the NFL was initially fun, but it doesn't matter what level you're playing at, when you're losing it's not that much fun. Especially coming from the programs I came from. I was part of a high school team that won three state championships and then the national championship at Notre Dame. Then I was drafted into the NFL, which should have been the pinnacle of my career, made decent money, but only won two games my rookie year. There's nothing quite like winning, it's motivating, and if you're not winning, playing the game just isn't much fun. Every week it was misery. Half of the games we lost were by less than five points. We were so close but we just couldn't convert opportunities into wins. For me, playing in the NFL was a way to pay for dental school. I graduated from dental school debt free. It took many of my classmates 25 years to pay off their school debt.

Today

The Notre Dame Value Stream does a great job of redirecting our path when it sees we've run out of road. When MacAfee realized he was no longer enjoying playing in the NFL he refocused his passion and set out to accomplish his goal of completing dental school and embarking upon his next career.

I went to dental school at the University of Pennsylvania in Philadelphia and also did my residency there in oral and maxillofacial surgery. I did four years of dental school and four years of residency in four different hospitals. I worked in the academic community for eight years at the University of Pennsylvania and had a faculty practice at the hospital. In 1994, when my son was born, we moved back to the Boston area. My wife was also from Massachusetts so I told her if we were going to make the move back home, we better do it now before the kids begin school; so that's what we did. It was well worth it. I lectured at Harvard and taught at Massachusetts General Hospital for a few years and now I have my own private practice. It was nice to be 18 years old and know what profession I wanted to pursue. It's also nice when it all works out for you. I believe that everything happens for a reason and all of the dominos definitely fell in the right direction for me.

MacAfee always knew that he wanted a career in dentistry, but reaching that goal was sometimes challenging and early on he wondered if he was on the correct path. The Notre Dame Value Stream, through the guidance of Emil T. Hofman, answered MacAfee's doubts and prepared him for a successful future and rewarding career.

Trying to combine athletics with academics was quite a challenge for me. The pre-professional program is difficult enough without adding football into the equation. It took a tremendous amount of discipline. When I started pre-professional at Notre Dame, the first science course I had to take was chemistry. I had Emil T. Hofman for chemistry my freshman year. His name became an adjective, "I have an Emil on Friday." It seemed like the whole campus was studying for that class on Thursday nights. He gave a seven-question quiz every Friday. I took the first three quizzes and then I got moved up to second team on the football team. At that point I lost interest in the academic side of school and dropped chemistry. I thought, to heck with pre-professional, I'm going to play football. I got more and more playing time and then half way through the season I was bumped up to be a starter.

Ken MacAfee and his family.

I went home the summer after my freshman year and was completely disgusted with myself because I had a goal to become an oral surgeon and I let football get in the way of that goal. I worked a job that summer for a few weeks and flew back to Notre Dame in June specifically to meet with Dr. Hofman. I went directly to Emil's office and told him that I wanted to get back into the pre-professional program. He gave me the thickest chemistry book from his bookcase and told me, "Read this and if you still want to re-enroll in the pre-professional curriculum, come back and see me in September." I'm sure he thought he'd never see me again. On the first day of classes I showed back up at his office and told him that I wanted to become an oral surgeon. "Here's your book back, I read the whole thing." He let me back into pre-professional on a semester-by-semester basis and monitored my progress. As a result, everything worked out for me and I was able to accomplish my goal of becoming an oral surgeon. Emil was a big factor in my life as far as the academic side of Notre Dame was concerned. I gave the Emil T. Hofman lecture about 10 years ago before the first home football game. It was awesome and humbling that he invited me back to give a lecture to the physicians at Notre Dame.

Ken MacAfee's Lessons from the Notre Dame Value Stream:

- Keep the hyphenated name "student-athlete," student first and athlete second. Athletics is short lived and you never know what is going to happen. I saw so many guys who thought they were going to have long football careers and with one injury their careers were over.

- One thing that you have to keep intact is your mind and your ability to think. You have to maintain good academic standing. You have to put academics first; there is no two ways about it.

- Make sure your academic accomplishments speak for you long after your sports career is over. It's all about thinking about your future and planning what you're going to do after athletics. In my first year in the NFL I made $60,000. After paying my dental school tuition and expenses I had $1,300 left in my bank account. But that tuition money was spent on my future, for when football was over.

It's awful to watch these kids today become academically ineligible. Notre Dame has such a great academic support system, there is no way you should get bad grades or fail a class. Your career is based on what you accomplish in college. Those academic accomplishments, in particular, will propel you for the rest of your life. Athletics is a "here today gone tomorrow" type of culture; "what have you done for me lately."

Portrait of Notre Dame football player Tom Galloway, 1983.
(Photo courtesy of Notre Dame Archives.)

CHAPTER FOUR

The Asset Manager

Tom Galloway

*T*om Galloway grew up in Albany, New York. He was the youngest of seven children and the only one to follow in his father's footsteps and attend the University of Notre Dame. Tom had no intention of playing Division I football; he was accepted to Notre Dame based on academic merit and had not been pursued by the University to play football. Unbeknownst to him, Tom's high school football coach sent his stats and game films to Notre Dame head coach Gerry Faust and staff. Shortly thereafter Galloway received an offer to try out for a walk-on spot on the Fighting Irish football team as an outside linebacker. Little did Tom know what an amazing future was ahead of him at Notre Dame. Galloway currently sits on the ND Monogram Club Board of Directors, and the

Lou's Lads Foundation. How does a young man from Albany, New York, who never even intended on playing Division I football, end up becoming the epitome of a Notre Dame man? This is Tom Galloway's story.

It is extremely difficult to describe the Notre Dame mystique to someone who has never been through it. But as a Domer, when you encounter another Domer there is an undeniable bond. That bond holds the Notre Dame family together and creates a network like no other. And when a child decides at a young age that Notre Dame is his ultimate collegiate destination, the Notre Dame family does everything it can to help make that happen, as in the case of Tom Galloway.

The Notre Dame Years

I was the youngest of seven children, five boys and two girls: Matthew, Mark, Luke, John, Anne, Mary, and little Tom. Ever since I was in the first grade, I wanted to go to the University of Notre Dame. By the time I got to high school, after I had been talking about it for so many years, my classmates just stopped asking me where I wanted to go to college because they already knew the answer. I was recruited to play football at some local Division III schools: Ithaca College and Holy Cross. I also took a football visit to Boston College and Doug Flutie was my host for the weekend. However, my dream was always to go to Notre Dame. When I was accepted into Notre Dame based on my academic merit, I had no idea that my high school football coach was sending my stats and game films to Coach Gerry Faust. That was, until the day I received a letter from the Notre Dame Athletic Department saying that while they did not have any football scholarships available, that they'd love to have me try out for a walk-on position on the football team; and so it began.

I received a letter from the Notre Dame Athletic Department saying that while they did not have any football scholarships available, that they'd love to have me try out for a walk-on position.

Never having been to Notre Dame in my life, I was a very nervous and anxious eighteen-year-old young man. I did not know what to expect when I arrived two weeks early with the other freshmen athletes, which was two weeks prior to the rest of the student body. And there I was, saying goodbye to my parents one minute, and trying out for the Notre Dame football team the next! Despite being invited out, there were no guarantees of actually making the team as a walk-on. It was different for the scholarship players who had been recruited with high expectations of someday making a significant contribution to the team. If either during or at the end of the double session practices your gear was gone from your locker, that was a message that you had been dismissed from the team. There weren't any notes explaining what had happened or why the coaches had decided what they did, which also meant no more housing, no more meal plan, and for the remaining sessions, you were done. Goodbye. After two weeks my gear was still in my locker and I (along with several fellow walk-ons, including my eventual roommate Mike Seasly and NFL Pro Bowl kicker and Super Bowl winner, John Carney) was on the team. Once you are on the team, you pretty quickly start to fall into your role as a prep team player at practice.

When your dream is something that an elite few actually get to pursue, the road is often rocky and the cuts can be deep. But when you are carried on your journey by the Notre Dame Value Stream, the road inevitably becomes smooth and the cuts heal and make you stronger. Galloway talks about his journey as a Notre Dame football walk-on.

It was quite a humbling experience. I was just a walk-on from upstate New York. Tony Furjanic (outside linebacker) was two years older than I was and he and Mike Golic were our captains in 1984. Every Saturday on game day I'd write Tony a note and leave it in his locker because I looked up to him so much. I had never done anything like that before in high school, but at the time, he was the captain, he was a fellow linebacker, and extremely talented. I just couldn't believe what I was experiencing and going through, and felt I wanted to express my enthusiasm and best wishes for a good game.

As a freshman walk-on I bought my own tickets to the football games.

As a freshman walk-on I bought my own tickets to the football games because unless you were chosen to dress for the home game, or you were on scholarship, if you wanted to attend the game you were responsible for getting yourself into the game and watching the game with the rest of the student body. At the time the coaching staff would dress the entire team for just one home game a year. It was humbling when your friends would say, "I thought you were on the football team" and then having to explain that there were 120 players on the team, only 80 players dressed for every home game, and only 60 players were able to travel. The first goal then was to make the cut of those 80 players that were chosen to dress for the home game. The next goal was to make the cut of the 60 players chosen to make the travel team. Each week you'd rush in to see if you made the dress list or the travel list for that week.

The walk-ons got dressed in the rifle range.

As a sophomore most of the walk-ons dressed for every home game. Not many people know this, but there is a room that was located down the hall from the traditional locker room, and it was actually a rifle range that was used for target practice when the stadium was built. Given the size restrictions of the locker room and the challenges that present themselves when 120 guys are trying to fit into a relatively modest locker room, the walk-ons got dressed in the rifle range. It was about 300 or 400 feet from the regular locker room, where the rest of the team dressed. Walking from the rifle range to the regular locker room, we would see fans staring at us and trying to figure out who we were and if they knew us. It was quite comical!

Just when you start to think your dreams are out of your reach, the Notre Dame Value Stream has a way of lifting you up and giving you a renewed sense of purpose. Spring ball at Notre Dame did just that for Galloway.

One thing I always enjoyed as we moved through the season and into spring practice was when the Notre Dame Alumni Club of St. Joseph County would sponsor the annual Blue Gold Spring Game, and allow neighboring children to come out on to the field and watch us practice. After we finished practice they would get to stay after and get our autographs. I loved that. When I signed autographs I would try to ask the child or fan what their name was and would address my autograph to them personally. I wanted to make sure they felt special, to feel that we were happy to have them there.

As a junior not only did the walk-ons get to dress for every home game, if we had earned it, we might make that travel list of 60 players and travel to an away game. I made the travel team for the Navy game when we were playing the Naval Academy at Giants Stadium. My parents, siblings, my girlfriend (and now wife of 27 years) and lots of neighbors came to Giants Stadium to see me on the sidelines. I didn't actually get to play in the game, but I was there on the sideline in the group of 60 players who traveled that day. There were lots of photos, a spray-painted banner hung from the railing that they had made with my name on it, and my family took photos of me on the sideline with my name on my jersey. It was a great feeling to get that kind of support from those who loved me most. I also had the opportunity to travel to the Liberty Bowl game where we played against Boston College and Doug Flutie, but I did not get to dress for that game.

Being accepted into an academic institution like Notre Dame and walking on the football team is quite an accomplishment, but staying there requires continued work and determination. There are academic and athletic challenges, but there are often financial challenges as well.

During my summers I worked for a gentleman named Frank O'Brien (ND '57), an engineer out of Notre Dame who owned an insurance and surety bond company in Albany, NY. Mr. & Mrs. O'Brien had six children, five daughters and one son, all of whom went to Notre Dame. I worked for a sub-

contractor that Mr. O'Brien had as a client, and my responsibility was to run a jack hammer on a large suspension bridge and road construction in upstate New York. It was great money at the time, and the expectation was that it would be used to put toward school. Frank and Mary Beth O'Brien's son Frank Jr. (ND '88), was a varsity lacrosse and hockey player at Notre Dame. Frank Jr. passed away at the age of 39 of a brain tumor. If you catch a hockey game at the Compton Family Ice Area, visit the 3rd level that oversees the ice hockey arena, aptly name O'Brien's, where you will see Frankie's jersey proudly displayed.

I didn't know how I was going to pay the remainder of my tuition bill.

As I headed back to school for my sophomore year, how to finance another year of college tuition was a primary concern for my family. I had student loans and I was confident that paying the remainder of my tuition bill was going to be challenge. I went to the financial aid office that summer going into my sophomore year and explained to them my situation, and asked them if there was anything that they could do to help me. Joe Russo, the head of the Financial Aid department, knew who I was because he used to come out and watch our practices. Somehow he managed to find a $1,500 scholarship from a Notre Dame Alumni Club in New York and that allowed me to be able to come back to school that fall. I never forgot that. Throughout all of the years that I've gone back to visit campus, I always go to visit Joe Russo first, even before I go to the football office.

For the past nine years I have proudly served both as a board member and advisor on the Notre Dame Monogram Club Board. During my tenure I have met and worked with some of the most accomplished student-athletes in Notre Dame history. There is a process in the Monogram Club to nominate an individual who in addition to representing the values of Notre Dame in all things they do, has contributed to Notre Dame Athletics in a significant way. I felt that Joe Russo was most deserving of this honor, as he is considered the "dean" of the financial aid department and many of us knew him well. All grants, all scholarship monies, including athletic scholarships, went through Joe's department. When I nominated Joe and put him up to the Board of Directors and the Awards Committee, Joe's nomination was approved unanimously. Tradition has it that if an honorary Monogram is approved we try to make the presentation special. The Monogram Club asked me if I would like to present the monogram jacket to Joe at his retirement luncheon as a surprise to him. The luncheon was terrific and the presentation went off without a hitch. Joe Russo helped so many athletes with the opportunity to be at Notre Dame that we will never forget his generosity.

As a walk-on at Notre Dame, you are absolutely, one hundred percent thrilled to even be there. But being a walk-on at any Division I school comes with its fair share of hurdles to overcome. There is a unique dynamic between you and your coaches, as well as between you and your teammates.

- *Are you treated differently? Somewhat.*

- *Did they mean to? Did they do it on purpose? No.*

But I was not the most athletic guy on the field! Some other walk-ons though were, like John Carney, they were extremely athletic. John went on to play almost 20 years in the NFL. That just wasn't who I was or was going to become and I knew that. The coaches are hired to teach us how to win, and when the team wasn't winning their jobs were on the line. It is a results driven profession, and performance meant winning. Did they mean to treat us differently as walk-ons? No, but when you understood that they had to win, it made it easier to understand the pressure they were under, and what they had to do to put the best players on the field.

I played 11 actual plays in my first three years at Notre Dame. As a junior, I made the travel squad for a few games, but I did not make the travel team when Notre Dame traveled to Miami - which was Coach Faust's last game, over Thanksgiving break, and then Coach Faust resigned following that game. Then Coach Holtz came in and everything changed.

I can't believe that God put us on this earth to be ordinary. ~ Lou Holtz

When Coach Holtz first came in we had to fill out a questionnaire, and one of the things that was in there was to list:

1. *What do we do good?*

2. *What don't we do good?*

3. *What can we do better?*

Coach Holtz interviewed every player, one-on-one. At the conclusion of the interviews we gathered back in the auditorium for a team meeting.

"Fellas, we have some things we need to work on, and team unity is number one. If this is going to work, we are going to have to rely on each other. You rely on me, and I will rely on you. That is the only way this football team is going to win." And that was the start of a new beginning. By the end of the season, our team was so close. Especially the senior class, we were a very tight knit group. Even to this day we are so close. Coach Holtz put a stake in the ground and said, "we've got to address some fundamental issues and we're going to face them head on."

If you think one person can't come into your life and turn it upside down, you clearly haven't met Coach Holtz.

> *The first day that we met Coach Holtz in December 1985, Tom Riley, Tom Rehder, Byron Spruell and the rest of big offensive and defensive linemen were sitting in the front row of the meeting room. Coach Holtz walks in and tells us, "When I walk in the room you will sit up straight and all eyes will be on me. I am the new Notre Dame head football coach. Here's what we're going to do: starting on January 6th, we'll be at the ACC at 6 am for practice. And also, set your watches to my watch, also known as LLH Time. I set my watch 10 minutes early. If you are on time, you're late. If you're late, it means you miss a meeting. You miss a meeting that means you don't care about your teammate. If you don't care about your teammate that means you don't care about the team. And if you don't care about the team that means you don't want to play."*
>
> *Coach Holtz sure knew how to make an entrance.*

Coach Holtz's first year was Galloway's senior year and the only thing in the world that he wanted was to earn a varsity letter jacket.

I knew right then and there that Coach Holtz and his staff were for real.

> *We had 6:00 am morning practices under Coach Holtz and I viewed them as one last opportunity to prove to a new set of coaches that I could play at Notre Dame. At those early morning sessions, I was determined to be the first in line for the drills, and to go as fast as I could go. At the spring game the coaches gave out several awards, referred to as Herring Awards. The recipients were not informed of who the coaches had chosen, but at half time they asked me to stay out on the field and they gave out four or five awards, and the Most Enthusiastic Player award was given to me! I knew right then and there that Coach Holtz and his staff were for real and that there might actually be a place for me to contribute to this team. My brother, John, and my girlfriend, Colleen, were in the stands and watched the whole thing!*

As a non-scholarship athlete at Notre Dame the financial burden to stay in school is great. But the Notre Dame Value Stream instills the courage and drive to persevere.

> *I went home (the summer before my senior year) and worked construction again for a subcontractor of Mr. O'Brien. About a week prior to returning to school for my senior year, Coach Holtz called me at home and said, "It's not so much for your talent but for your example that we're going to award you a full Notre Dame football scholarship for your senior year!" Hardly able to*

contain my enthusiasm, I thanked Coach, said my family thanks him, and arrived on campus a week later ready to go. After having played in only about 11 plays in my first three years on the team, I dressed for every home game, made the travel squad to every away game, played in every game on special teams and accomplished my goal of earning my varsity letter jacket!

There are milestone moments in a college football career that you expect to remember forever. But sometimes the unexpected moments outshine the expected ones and live on in lore for eternity.

Coach Paterno thinks there isn't anything special about coming onto this campus.

Before the Penn State game my senior year, Mike Kovaleski, our team captain, came up to me after our Friday practice and said, "Tom, I'd like you to speak at the pep rally this afternoon." I'd never spoken at a pep rally and I'd never dreamed of speaking at a pep rally. Back then the pep rallies were held at the Stepan Center, there was only one speaker, and it was going to be me. So here I am, an hour before the pep rally, back in my room with my roommate Mike Seasly, preparing what we knew had to be a brief pep rally speech. That day in The Observer there had been an article on how Coach Paterno didn't believe there was really "any mystique" at Notre Dame. And that was it – we would build the speech around that. We went to the stadium and grabbed my helmet, put it inside a brown paper bag, and I wrote my speech. "Everyone has been reading in the Observer how Coach Paterno thinks there isn't anything special about coming onto this campus. Let me tell you something about the guys standing behind me. Coach Paterno, I've got one message for you. If you think there's no mystique at Notre Dame, I have this for you…" and I took my helmet out of the paper bag, held it up in front of the crowd, and well, the rest is history!

Four or five years at Notre Dame are filled with memories too numerous to count, both on and off the field. But when asked to pick the one thing that best illustrates his time at Notre Dame, the answer came quite easily for Galloway.

As I look back at my time at Notre Dame, I really remember the guys I played football with; they were my family. During my years under Coach Faust I became close with Mark Bavaro. I remember being on the prep team and Mark was the tight end that I lined up against. I was very serious about doing my job on the prep team. One day at practice I got into a fight with Mark on the field, and, well, he won! We walked to the training table afterwards together and he thanked me for working so hard. As far as on the field memories go, I recovered an onside kick against Ole Miss. I did what I was supposed to do, I fell on the ball and I didn't fumble it. As a walk-on, when you actually participate in a play and were successful at it, it was a big deal.

Professional Career

After finishing his Notre Dame football career as a scholarship athlete, Galloway was ready to set out into the world and make his mark.

Following my graduation from Notre Dame I accepted a position with one of the major accounting firms, Price Waterhouse. Colleen and I were married in 1988 and started our family in 1991 when our first child, Ben (ND '13) was born. Colleen saw what was happening in the business world and strongly suggested that I begin to pursue a Master's Degree, so I went back to school at Johns Hopkins University and earned a Masters in Financial Management. My wife Colleen earned her undergraduate degree in marketing from Siena College and then went on to get a certificate in mediation. It was in graduate school where I met some folks who then helped me begin a 20 year career on Wall Street, working at brokerage firms Alex. Brown & Sons, Wells Fargo, and Stifel Nicolaus. In 2014, I joined Legg Mason Global Asset Management in Baltimore as a Vice President on the National Accounts team covering the independent broker dealers as a relationship manager.

You can leave Notre Dame and set out into the world to create a life, but the Notre Dame Value Stream never lets ND completely leave you.

When Colleen and I were first married and starting our family, I was in graduate school at Johns Hopkins, and we didn't make it back to Notre Dame for too many games. We'd always try to see Notre Dame when they were playing on the east coast. As we began to get established in our careers we were able to start going back to more home games on campus. We were at the Monogram Tent at a Notre Dame home game when I ran into one of my former teammates, the All American from Texas, Van Pearcy. Van was a phenomenal athlete in college (a track star from Texas who was also a wide receiver at Notre Dame). He asked me what I was up to and I told him about my family and where my career had taken me up to that point.

We understood the importance of giving back of your time, talent and treasure.

Van said that he was on the Monogram Club Board of Directors, and that they were looking for board members. Van suggested that I send him and the board a letter documenting what I had been up to after graduation. Colleen and I were very involved with the Notre Dame Club of Baltimore and were running the Summer Service Program in conjunction with the Center for

Social Concerns. Colleen was the assistant director of development for a local hospital at that time and we understood the importance of giving back of your time, talent and treasure. So I sent the letter expressing my desire to join the board and shortly thereafter I received a note congratulating me on my new position on the Monogram Club Board of Directors. I served for three years on the board. The incoming President, Joe Restic, then asked me to come back as an advisor for his two year term. Dick Nussbaum asked me to come back as an advisor to him during his Presidency. And then Haley DeMaria asked me to be an advisor during her term as President. It's been a terrific run.

I am very active with the Monogram Club's "Student Welfare and Development" committee which helps current student athletes find jobs through the creation of the Monogram Club Network (MCN). It's fantastic to be able to help these kids make the transition into the next phase of their lives.

I also sit on the board for the Lou's Lads Foundation. Coach Holtz did so much for us that we feel so very blessed to be able to give something back to him. His "do the right thing" philosophy: Do the right thing, do the best you can, and always show people you care; I try to live by this philosophy and remind myself every day of these three basic rules. Coach just had a way about him that made us respect him first and like him second. The statue of Lou Holtz over by the stadium became a reality after many of his players made contributions to help to pay for it, along with many other benefactors. We wanted to show him how much we appreciate what he did for us.

College life challenges student-athletes at Notre Dame both on and off the field. But it is these challenges that prepare you for the ups and downs that you will face the rest of your life.

Being a student-athlete at Notre Dame was very hard. I think it's more difficult today, though, to be a student-athlete than it was back then. We had to lift, watch films, go to practice, keep up with our class work ... we knew it was difficult, but we also knew what the expectations were. I was in the business school and studied accounting because I noticed as a freshman that all of the accounting majors had jobs in the fall of their senior year. Mike Seasly, my roommate, was a philosophy major, Mike Visovatti and Byron Spruell were engineering majors. We had a very diverse and talented group of guys.

Holtz who leveraged his coaching staff but still had command of every single detail. Holtz fully utilized his coaches but was completely involved. Coach Faust appeared to be more of a delegator and was not so much into all the details. As a result, Coach Holtz really spent a lot of time not only with his coaches but with his players, too. He helped us grow and develop into men - and this carried off the football field as well. I still remember going into his office for career advice as I was deciding between several employment offers. He advised me to focus on "What's Important Now" (WIN) and to secure a good foundation with a company that cared about my continued growth and development; a place that promoted excellence with people I could trust. Those words have always been in my mind throughout my career and the organizations I have been associated with.

I follow three rules:
- **Do the right thing**
- **Do the best you can, and**
- **Always show people you care**

You've got to make a sincere attempt to have the right goals to begin with, then go after them with appropriate effort and remember that you can't really achieve anything great without the help of others. ~ Lou Holtz

Coach Holtz made sure you understood three things. One, he cared about his players. Two, he made sure you were ready for what you were going to face on the football field. Three, he was your coach for life, and made sure you were ready for your future both on and off of the field. He prepared you with the details that would make you a good football player, but also prepared you for the post-football journey in the business world or wherever life would take you. One of the most important factors that led me to choose to attend Notre Dame was how well they combined academics and athletics. Coach Faust helped me make the transition to college while Coach Holtz was a big part of why the proposition worked so well. Coach Holtz prepared you for the details that would make you a good football player, but this same attention to detail was also what was going to make you a good man and successful at whatever you pursued after football. He also lives up to the concept of "4 for 40"; i.e., you give me four good years at Notre Dame and I will support you for the next forty.

Being a member of Coach Holtz's first team at Notre Dame provided Byron with many memorable moments at Notre Dame, but the one that most sticks out in his mind is the game against USC in 1986.

Out in Los Angeles the whole environment - the Coliseum, the Trojan horse, down by 22 points ... we rallied together as a team that day to pull out the win. It was Coach Holtz's first year at Notre Dame. We lost five games that year by a total of six points. It was crazy how close we were but just couldn't pull out the wins. It was the final game of the season and we were down 37-15 at halftime. Sure, we were down 22 points out in Los Angeles, but we rallied under Coach Holtz's leadership and came back to win the game on a last-second field goal by John Carney. We had started to build some real camaraderie that season and that win over USC gave us great momentum to carry us into the next year. On the flight back Chuck Lanza and I got the indication that we would be co-captains next year. To have that type of victory in a hostile environment and then to know the team felt that I was a leader moving forward is something I will never forget.

Being a student-athlete at a school like Notre Dame is never easy, but the Notre Dame Value Stream is always there to guide its student-athletes and instill a work ethic in them that prepares them for anything that lies ahead. But it is still a challenge to balance school and athletics.

For the most part it was all about balance, work ethic, and discipline. I like to be busy anyway, but you need to cut through the clutter and be organized to succeed as a student-athlete at a place like Notre Dame. I really liked the environment at Notre Dame. It was a good fit for me. At Notre Dame you are truly a student-athlete. There are no athletics dorms. You are a student first and an athlete second — you carry yourself that way. You are given certain opportunities but you are not separated and you are not made to feel special or privileged compared to your fellow students. With the exception of Wednesday training table and game day (when we had steak), we ate dining hall food just like everybody else, only a few hours later.

At Notre Dame you are truly a student-athlete. There are no athletics dorms. You are a student first and an athlete second.

You have class, film, study, practice, training table, and then you go back to your dorm and study some more. You are tired and don't feel like studying, but you still have to get it done. I definitely spent some late nights with David Letterman on in the background getting my work done. It took hard work and discipline to play football and get my engineering degree and my MBA from Notre Dame.

My wife lived in Badin Hall. I met her at a school sponsored dance freshman year, which was our first date. We dated all four years at Notre Dame, studied together as undergraduate engineering students, and got engaged between our fifth year and the final year of graduate school. She got her graduate degree in Aerospace Engineering and I got my MBA. She has also been a spe-

level. For a young man whose eyes were longingly directed at Notre Dame because his grandfather and three uncles all went there, the wonder and wait would eventually pay off. Freeman would go on to follow Gerry Faust's calling and play football for the University of Notre Dame and finish his career under legendary head coach Lou Holtz. How does a young man who thinks that he was merely an un-athletic kid from Kansas City end up playing football for Notre Dame? This is Tom Freeman's story.

Putting clients first makes all the difference.

I always loved playing football. I grew up with three brothers and it's what we always did: go out and play football. It was something I enjoyed and loved. My grandfather and three of my uncles graduated from ND, but I felt that Notre Dame football was something great athletes did, not something un-athletic kids from Kansas City did. My high school coach had a rule that colleges couldn't talk to you until after the last game your senior year. I went through my entire senior season not knowing if I had any chance to play college football. We went to the state championship game, and the Monday after the game my coach called me into his office at 3:30 in the afternoon and asked me if I had any interest in playing football in college. To which I replied, "Of course I do!" He asked me once more, "Are you sure?" "Of course I'm sure, who wouldn't want to play football in college?" I replied. He went on to tell me that Nebraska's head coach Tom Osborne was waiting outside to speak with me, Oklahoma's head coach Barry Switzer wanted to come to my house that week for dinner, and Jim Johnson, Notre Dame's Defensive Coordinator, is going to stop by tomorrow. Then he pulled out a big box of letters from all of the colleges who were interested in me playing college football for them. Notre Dame was always my dream, but I never thought I'd actually have an opportunity to play football there. When they offered me a scholarship I jumped at the chance and it set my path on the right trajectory.

I couldn't help thinking that I wasn't good enough to back up the great Mike Golic.

The Notre Dame Years

I played both offense and defense in high school. I played offensive tackle and defensive end, and I was recruited by Notre Dame to play defensive end. I was an All-American and All-State in high school. I had plenty of accolades, but Notre Dame recruited me to play defensive end and wanted me to come in and back up Mike Golic. I accepted this challenge, but I couldn't help thinking that I wasn't good enough to back up the great Mike Golic. I knew I was good, but I didn't know if I could compete or not. Once I got to Notre

Dame, got pads on and started practicing with the team I realized I COULD play with them. Three weeks into camp I tore a muscle in my leg and missed a couple of weeks.

Missing a few weeks so early in your collegiate career is devastating. Since they couldn't use me my freshman year at defensive end, they decided to put some weight on me and move me to the offensive line. I didn't want to do that because I didn't feel that playing on the offensive line was real football. Real football to me was lining up on defense and running in with reckless abandon to tackle someone. Playing offensive line was more like controlled aggression, more cerebral football. Because I told the coaches I did not want to play offensive line I played my sophomore season as a defensive lineman. During the spring workouts following my sophomore season they moved me to middle linebacker, where I ended up being the leading tackler in the Blue Gold game that spring. However, I was not good enough in the coach's opinion so they told me that if I ever want to see the field I would need to play offensive line, and so that made the decision easy… I moved to the offensive line. In the end I went from mediocre speed middle linebacker to a relatively fast offensive lineman… it was the right decision.

I took my visit to Notre Dame in January and Tony Furganic and Ron Plantz were my hosts. It's not so easy to sell Notre Dame in January when the weather is not ideal. My trip was no exception as it was freezing rain all weekend. It was a serious and somber experience for me. The guys wanted to take me out, but early on in the night I just wanted to go back to the Morris Inn. Gerry Faust had offered me a scholarship that day and I knew it was a serious decision and I just wanted to think it all through. One of the great strengths of Coach Faust was that he knew how to market the football team and how to market the University. As part of the recruiting process he showed us the video "Wake Up the Echoes." I don't know how you could watch that movie and not come out dying to play for Notre Dame. I could have gone anywhere, but I wanted to leverage my athletic ability in order to get the best education I could. You can say what you want about Coach Faust, but he loved Notre Dame, he knew what was special about ND and he marketed it well. He made you feel you just had to be a part of it and that sealed the deal for me. I have never spoken to a former player who did not feel the same way. By playing for Notre Dame you become part of something special, something great, something timeless. Those traditions are integral to what makes Notre Dame great and what makes it so attractive for young men to play there.

You can say what you want about Coach Faust, but he loved Notre Dame, he knew what was special about ND and he marketed it well.

The ability to prioritize the tasks in front of you is an important skill to be successful in life. But as a student-athlete at Notre Dame, this ability becomes even more important when your daily to-do list is a mile long and every single moment counts. The Notre Dame Value Stream does an excellent job at instructing Her students in time management and keeping their focus on which tasks are critical and which are not.

When you are a student-athlete playing college football you don't have one free minute. It did not take long for me to figure out you didn't have any free time and you didn't have any time to rest. You had to budget every minute of every day in order to get everything done. Being a student-athlete is a full time job and to be successful you have to focus on your job all of the time. That was one of the things that Coach Holtz taught so well. He had this acronym, WIN: "What's Important Now". You have to focus on what is the most important thing at that moment. That's one of the big life lessons that I learned from him and I use it almost every day. I am always asking myself if what I'm doing at any given moment is important. As Coach would say, "Is what you are doing at any given moment getting you closer to your goals or further away?" You have to be cognizant of it at every moment. He also taught us to figure out what you want and then work backwards to figure out step-by-step what it will take to get you there. Being successful as a student-athlete takes great focus and desire. You don't want to go in there and waste any reps. You have to take advantage of every minute of every day. You don't have time to do anything else but to focus on doing your job and doing it to the best of your ability, to be "committed to excellence" as Coach Holtz would put it.

After witnessing Gerry Faust's tremendous love for Notre Dame and all that Our Lady's University stands for, Freeman followed Coach Faust to ND to pursue a coveted Notre Dame degree and play football for the Fighting Irish. Three years into Freeman's time at Notre Dame, Coach Faust's time was over and Lou Holtz came in to take over the football program. While they each had their own coaching style and talents, they both used the Notre Dame Value Stream to develop Freeman and his teammates into exemplary young men ready to head out into the world and achieve success both on and off the field.

I loved Coach Faust, but my takeaway was that while there was no doubt in my mind that he knew football very well, he delegated a lot of the leadership roles to his assistant coaches. I don't think he ever got everyone to rally around him or got his players fired up and motivated. I think he was great, and he knew the game, but I think the fact that he delegated so much of his coaching responsibilities resulted in there not being one central figure, one larger-

than-life personality for the guys to look up to. I learned from Coach Holtz that if you executed what he coached you were going to win. I didn't get that feeling from Coach Faust. With Coach Holtz, however, you knew it. He established in his very first meeting that he was an expert and if you did what he told you to do you were going to win. You had zero doubt in your mind that all you had to do was execute Coach Holtz's plan to win. As a team, we were willing to work as hard as it took to win. Knowing this you did not want to be the weakest link, which motivated us to do whatever it took to win. All you had to do was what Coach told you and we would all get what we wanted: to win.

He established in his very first meeting that he was an expert and if you did what he told you to do you were going to win. You had zero doubt in your mind that all you had to do was execute Coach Holtz's plan to win.

Coach Holtz came in and established strong discipline, but what really struck me was how he communicated that he was committed to excellence, and if we did what he said we would win. During his first meeting he stood up in the front of the team and on the black board he went through what seemed like a bunch of plays against several different defenses. He knew what every position's responsibility was for every play, and I sat back and thought, this guy is a genius and knows this game inside and out. All we have to do is follow his direction. He makes it clear from the very beginning that he is an expert and knows how to win and if you are not willing to do things his way you better leave right then because there is no room on the team for anyone who is not as committed to excellence as Coach Holtz. We walked out of that meeting knowing we were going to win with him because he knew what he was doing.

Coach Holtz taught us using the following mantra: Trust, Love and Commitment. He asked the team three questions:

- Can I trust you?

- Do you care about me?

- Are you committed to excellence?

His commitment to excellence was established right out of the gate, and he demanded excellence from us. You couldn't be lax in anything. He always made sure we were prepared for anything. If you're in a big pressure situation and you're not used to living that level of excellence, you let doubt slip into your mind. We never had any doubts, and we were never nervous as a result. We had complete confidence in our abilities because of the preparation Coach

Holtz demanded of us. I rarely noticed the crowds; I was so focused on the game. This is what preparation does for you. I took these lessons of preparation with me into my career. I work with high-powered billionaires and I am never nervous when I walk into a presentation, because I am prepared. As Coach Holtz said, "If you are prepared you will never be nervous"…one of the greatest lessons of my life.

Coach Holtz said, "If you are prepared you will never be nervous"… one of the greatest lessons of my life.

He showed you exactly how to achieve any goal. You walked out of school the year you graduated with the secret to success. Figure out what's important, figure out the steps that it takes to get there, do as many reps as it takes to achieve excellence and you can achieve whatever you want. I never shy away from any challenge because I know if I execute the lessons Coach Holtz taught me I will be successful.

Coach Holtz arrived at Notre Dame and set the world on fire. Freeman explains why he thought Lou Holtz was so successful at Notre Dame and in life.

He was such a great football mind, however I think he was so successful because his primary focus was building character in young men, and winning football games was a byproduct of his efforts to develop young men. You didn't recognize it when you were there, when it was going on, but after living the ups and downs of life, you see what he did for you. He told us, "You have to go through fire to make steel." He made it as tough as possible for us in practice so that game day was a piece of cake. It allowed you to overcome any adversity placed in front of you and to become successful. That carried over from the football world into the rest of your life. I think there are still some coaches like Coach Holtz, it seems most coaches were like him 40 or 50 years ago; but my sense is that it's no longer like that anymore. So much money is involved in college football and winning at any cost is so important. As Coach says, young people today are more concerned with their rights and privileges rather than their responsibilities and obligations and the college administrations perpetuate this. They are no longer using football as a vehicle to develop young men. When used properly, the collegiate football experience can be a great way to teach the lessons of life; it seems that is not even a consideration anymore.

When used properly, the collegiate football experience can be a great way to teach the lessons of life; it seems that is not even a consideration anymore.

Coach Holtz had a great love for Notre Dame and he understood that a lot of kids also had the same great love and wanted to be a part of something larger than themselves, to be a part of that incredible Notre Dame tradition. You may not be able to compete with the Alabama's of the world when it comes to weather or social life, but you sure can when it comes to tradition and values. As Coach Holtz says, "Notre Dame is a 40-year decision, not just a four year decision." If you take that approach, you'll get the good talent. Coach Kelly is doing that today. I think there are still coaches out there like Coach Holtz, but today they are not as easy to find. Our 1987 team has a group email, and it's always refreshing to see some of the great stars, some of the most successful guys, still come back to campus and remind us all that the most important thing when you're back at Notre Dame is to uphold the traditions and values which Notre Dame gave to us. To remember that we are different, that Notre Dame is a special place and that it is so much more than football. When you play for Notre Dame you must understand you carry the mantle for the school and you need to represent Notre Dame in the best possible light.

Notre Dame is a 40-year decision, not just a four-year decision.
~ Coach Holtz

College football brings its players, students and fans an endless amount of memorable moments. Moments that will be retold over and over at reunions for years to come. The one that Freeman reminisces about with his teammates and will tell his grandchildren happened in 1986 when unranked Notre Dame played #17 USC at the Los Angeles Coliseum.

We were down 17 points in the fourth quarter and came back to beat them on a last second field goal (by kicker John Carney). It was Coach Holtz's first year and we only went 5-6 that year, but the games we lost, we lost by very small margins. We came back from the low point of Coach Faust and here was Coach Holtz turning it around and we felt like we were winners. It wasn't showing up on the score board yet, but we knew we could do it. In the fourth quarter we were down by 17 points and came back to win the game. We felt like we had finally broken through and we had accomplished something big. We knew we were better than what our final record showed that season and that game was the confirmation that we could do it, that we could do it and it was working. It was an exhilarating experience. I always loved playing USC. They were good competitors and they were on par with us tradition-wise.

Professional Career

After the 1986 season, because of my freshmen year injury, I had a fifth year of eligibility and so I applied and was accepted to the business school which allowed me to play a fifth year for ND. Five years at a place like Notre Dame seems to fly by in the blink of an eye, and then it is time to head out into the world and put to good use everything you've been taught.

With the lessons learned and skills taught to him by the Notre Dame Value Stream, Freeman set out to see if he had what it takes to play in the NFL.

I like to say I had a cup of coffee with the Chiefs. (Freeman laughs) I signed with the Kansas City Chiefs and made it all the way through to the last round of cuts. They invited me to be on their development squad but I had one more year to complete my MBA, plus I also had gotten married over the summer and was really too small to play in the NFL. I was playing offensive guard at 280 pounds, and the guy I was playing behind was 330 pounds. I was just too small and I knew that. I would have gotten paid $60K a year, which was a pretty good salary coming out of graduate school, but I knew that wasn't where my future was headed. From the experience that I had with the Chiefs, playing football in the pros was the most fun I'd had since grade school. Nobody cared if you made it or not. They were professionals, but it was just a bunch of guys out there playing. It was just fun to play. There was no pressure. At ND you're in a fishbowl and people are always watching you. In the pros, no pressure, no one was watching, AND you got PAID to play. But by the time I got cut from the main squad and was invited to play on the development squad, I just felt that wasn't my future. Plus I came out of my football career with no serious injuries and I felt very blessed for that.

Today

At that point Freeman knew it was time to set out on his next adventure and put to work the degree he received from ND.

I left Notre Dame with my MBA and was hired by Merrill Lynch as a financial advisor/stock broker. My concentration in MBA school was security analysis but I knew I wanted to come back to Kansas City, which wasn't exactly a big financial Mecca. It was fortuitous, but it was a very good fit for me. Coming out of college I was used to working 16 hours a day every day, focused on achieving my goals. When I got out into the real world, that's exactly what I did. When you're starting out, that's what it takes. It set me apart from everyone else and I've had great success in my career as a result. I don't have to work like that anymore, but at the time it set me up to reach my goals and achieve great success. At Notre Dame, I learned how to focus, how to overcome adversity, how to set goals, focus on them, execute and never give up. There's no doubt in my mind that's why I've had such a successful career.

***At Notre Dame, I learned how to focus, how to overcome adversity, how to
set goals, focus on them, execute and never give up.***

*Today, I'm a managing director with UBS Private Wealth Management.
I am ranked in the top 50 in the country and I am number one in my
region which includes the state of Texas. When you do business in Kansas
City, you're competing against and winning over your peers in big cities
like Dallas and Houston; I take quiet pride in that. My philosophy is be
honest, work hard and do right for your clients and you will do well.
Coach Holtz used to tell us, "Whenever you fail, there are only two ways
to react: either with enthusiasm or self-pity." Whenever I fail, I go back
and attack it with enthusiasm. You can either feel sorry for yourself or get
fired up and get after it. As a result of that mindset, I'm never afraid to
fail because I know how to overcome adversity. After we failed at something, Coach Holtz would ask us, "What are you going to do now? You
can sit there and dwell on it, or you can pick yourself up and move forward." He had simple lines that said it so perfectly. He had a great
teacher's heart.*

Coach Holtz left an indelible mark on every single one of his players. Freeman
talks about what Coach Holtz left with him that he carries with him each and
every day.

He had a great teacher's heart.

*What I loved most about Coach Holtz was how he motivated people, and
in particular, how he motivated me. He knew how to get you to play better than you ever thought you could play. When we played Air Force, I was
an offensive guard and lined up across from Chad Hennings, who was a
defensive tackle, an Outland Trophy winner and who went on to have an
outstanding NFL career for the Dallas Cowboys. The day after the game,
at 8 pm at night, I received a call from Coach Holtz's secretary Jan. Jan
said, "Coach Holtz would like to see you at 8 am tomorrow morning." Of
course I said I would be there. I spent all night wondering what that was
about; wondering if I was getting moved. I didn't think I had played
poorly against Hennings, but when you get a call like that, you begin to
wonder.*

*So I go into Coach Holtz's office the next morning and Coach says, "Tom,
how do you think you played on Saturday?" And I replied, "Well Coach,
I graded out pretty well." Coach Holtz cut me off in mid-sentence, "Hell
no, Tom. You played terrible. And if you play like that again you'll never
be playing for the University of Notre Dame ever again." "Okay Coach,"*

*I replied. "I'll take it up a notch." And Coach Holtz said, "You better."
On Mondays we practiced in shorts and shoulder pads and it was usually
a pretty easy practice, because we were putting our game plan into place.
At that point I was a pretty accomplished linesman and I felt I knew what
I was doing pretty well. However, when we came up and ran the first play,
and I heard, "Hell no, Tom Freeman, that's not right." We ran the play
again and I hear, "Tom Freeman, I told you if you don't get it done, you're
done here. You go down and get the freshman and send the freshman
guard up here." So I trot down and spend the rest of the practice with the
scout team. To this day I am confident I ran the play correctly, but Coach
wanted to get my attention... and he did!*

*Back then the starting 11 players wore black jerseys and everyone else got
a gold or white jersey. On Tuesday before practice I went up to the cage to
get my black jersey to wear during practice and I was handed a gold jersey. I asked the equipment manager where my black jersey was and he
said, "Coach Holtz said you don't get a black jersey." So I took the gold jersey and in practice I lined up with the starters that I've been practicing
with all season and I hear, "Hell no, Tom Freeman. I told you I'm done
with you." So I practiced with the second team all week. I couldn't sleep
all week thinking about what I am going to tell my friends and family. I
felt humiliated being demoted. The following Saturday the game was getting ready to start and I was with the second team. I was sitting on the
bench in the back and having a pity party when as the first team runs out
Coach Holtz yells, "Where's Freeman? Get out there and show me what
you can do." I shot out there and was so fired up I had the best game of my
life.*

*As it turns out I was playing against All-American lineman and Outland
Trophy finalist, Jerry Ball (SMU) that game. Coach Holtz knew if I was
going to be able to handle this guy I needed to have the game of my life.
(Jerry Ball went on to be a three time pro bowler in the NFL.) Coach
Holtz's tactic of having me play with the scout team and demote me was
to get me so fired up that when I had the opportunity to go out there I'd
play out of my mind. For me, that strategy worked great. He knew exactly
how to coach each and every one of us. He broke you down and built you
back up again. He knew what it was going to take to get me to play at my
absolute best. He was such a phenomenal motivator and knew how to get
the best out of you. He knew how to get people fired up and it worked
great for him. He told me once that I wasn't a very good athlete, and as a
result I spent the rest of my time at ND working as hard as I could to*

Tom Freeman

prove him wrong ... that just exhibited his motivational genius. He used to tell us, "I'll never treat any of you equally but you'll always be treated fairly," and he was so good at that and I'll always have a great deal of respect for him as a result.

When I came out of Notre Dame I was so naïve, but with the preparation he gave me for life I credit Coach Holtz for all of the successes I've had over the years, whether in the business world or in my family life. He has such a tight family. He's always been supportive of his wife in everything that she does. He's so genuine. What you see is exactly how he is. He is incredibly unselfish, a man who lives for others.

Freeman currently resides in Kansas City with his wife; they have two sons and two daughters.

Tom Freeman's Lessons from the Notre Dame Value Stream:

- For the student-athlete: The biggest thing your student-athlete career does for you is act as a means to an end. You need to leverage your athleticism in order to get the best education you can and to put yourself in the best position to succeed in life.

- Once you're done playing sports your athleticism is worthless, but your diploma is priceless. It's what can open doors and get you places.

- 99% of people who play sports in college do not play professionally post graduation. You've been given a great gift in receiving a great education, recognize that.

- I didn't think I was going to play football in the pros. You've got to use your athletic ability to get the best education you can get. It's not a four year decision, it's a 40-year decision; make the most of it.

Notre Dame vs. Southern California (USC), 1988. Notre Dame football player
Wes Pritchett (#34) about to make a tackle. Photo by Mari Okuda.
(Photo courtesy of Notre Dame Archives.)

CHAPTER SEVEN

The Legacy Planner

Wes Pritchett

Over the years there have been many colorful descriptions of Notre Dame squads. One of the most memorable was written in 1924 by sportswriter Grantland Rice as he described Notre Dame's offensive backfield. "Outlined against a blue-gray October sky," Rice wrote, "the Four Horsemen rode again. In dramatic lore they are known as Famine, Pestilence, Destruction and Death. These are only aliases. Their real names are Stuhldreher, Miller, Crowley and Layden."[2] In 1988, a trio of Notre Dame defensive players, Frank Stams, Wesley Pritchett and Michael Stonebreaker, who referred to themselves as knuckleheads, became "The Three Amigos." How does Wes Pritchett, a National Merit Scholarship winner who excelled at high school football and hailed from a Southern

Baptist upbringing end up at the University of Notre Dame, stir a little excitement and life into his team, and become a leader of a group of young men that would go on to win a national title? This is Wesley Pritchett's story.

The road to Notre Dame is often a straight path, but not always. Sometimes the journey to Notre Dame is filled with ups and downs, twists and turns; but Our Lady is always shining Her light at the end of the long road.

I grew up in Atlanta, Georgia, as a Southern Baptist. My dad, despite not having the Catholic background, loved Notre Dame and had grown up listening to Notre Dame football games on the radio in the 40s and 50s. Notre Dame was romanticized as "the place" where all of the great college football players went to play. My family always went to see ND play when they would come to Atlanta to play Georgia Tech. When I was being recruited to play college football Herschel Walker was in the midst of his glory days at the University of Georgia, and so the top two schools on my list as a Georgia kid were the University of Georgia and Notre Dame. I took official visits to Florida State, Georgia, Vanderbilt, Duke and Notre Dame. I really thought I was headed to Georgia until Georgia pulled my scholarship and then Notre Dame was it. Georgia ended up being placed on probation during my freshman year in college, so everything worked out for me just fine. I attended Westminster High School in Atlanta, which was one of the top private high schools. A large percentage of their students go on to Ivy League schools. It is known for its academic prowess. I graduated from high school at the age of 17. I was a National Merit semi-finalist winner and my parents and I had talked about me going to an Ivy League School. At the end of the day, though, I not only wanted to get a good education, but I also wanted to play Division I football, and so Notre Dame brought the best of both worlds to the table.

Coach Mal Moore was the person from Notre Dame who recruited me. He was a fellow southern boy. He played football at Alabama and had coached there as well. The year he recruited me was his first year coaching at Notre Dame. He was a big part of why I ended up attending Notre Dame. He made the whole process very comfortable for me and was a big reason why I was even considering Notre Dame at that stage in the recruiting process. Coach Moore ended up eventually going back to Alabama and became their athletic director. When I made my official visit to Notre Dame they took us into this theater and showed us a movie about the history of Notre Dame

Excerpt from the New York Herald Tribune, October 18, 1924. Read more: http://archives.nd.edu/research/texts/rice.htm

football that had Knute Rockne in it (Wake Up the Echoes). That movie made quite an impression on me. When Coach Faust and Coach (George) Kelly came to visit my parents and me at our house, I made Coach Faust bring the movie and a movie projector so that my dad could see it, too.

Before Coach Faust came to visit my parents and me in Atlanta, he asked Coach Moore what kind of kid I was, because the majority of my correspondence up to that point had been with Coach Moore. He told Coach Faust that I was a southern kid from a Southern Baptist family and after hearing that, Coach Faust didn't think they even had a chance with me. When my father opened the door with a cigar in his mouth and a drink in his hand Coach Faust said, "I think we've got a chance!" Coach Faust was such a wonderful person. He recruited me to go to Notre Dame. What makes my recruiting process even more remarkable is this: I only played seven quarters of football during my senior year of high school. In the first game of my senior year I got hurt at the end of the third quarter, and didn't play again until the last game of the season; and only one of the games that I played in was filmed. And even with only seven quarters of play I still was invited to play in the Georgia All Star game and caught a touchdown playing tight end. I was still recruited by Georgia, Florida State and Notre Dame, and I still made the list of the top players in Georgia.

The Notre Dame Years

Success at Notre Dame isn't always a given. It is something that can be elusive, must always be earned, and requires a great deal of effort and determination. Even though success isn't always readily at your fingertips, the Notre Dame Value Stream prepares you with the tools needed to fight the hard fight and bring success within your reach.

I was redshirted my freshman year. I had just turned 18 and I injured my knee, which slowed me down. I was basically "Rudy" for the first year. I played on the scout squad and worked my butt off trying to prove that I deserved to get a chance. The next year I got the opportunity to play on special teams and also started playing in the linebacker position. I did so well that year on special teams that my stats ended up being the best amongst the special team players, but that got lost in the shuffle once I started playing more. The following year I played linebacker 50% of the time, splitting playing time with Ron Weisenhoffer and continued my role on special teams. After two years of playing for Coach Faust, Coach Holtz came in and turned our world upside down.

Turmoil in the head coaching position can divide a team and tear it apart. It can also unify it and lift the team to levels they never thought attainable. The latter was Pritchett's experience during his time at Notre Dame.

> Coach Faust always tried his hardest, but he wasn't as refined as Coach Holtz. Coach Holtz came in from day one and had a plan. He told us, "These are your priorities in life: God, family, school, football, social life," and in that order. When he came in that first day we were all sitting in the meeting room slouched in our chairs and feet propped up. He told us he was going to walk out of the room and when he came back in we were going to be sitting up in our chairs with both feet on the floor; and we were. He told us, "We're going to be the best and then we're going to be first," … and we were! After that first meeting Coach Holtz began his 6 am workouts. I think at least half of the team threw up that first day. It was awful. I lived in Holy Cross hall. I had to get up at 5 am and walk across the frozen lake to get to practice at 6 am. The transition from Coach Faust to Coach Holtz was a bit of a wakeup call for us, to say the very least.

Motivation is simple. You eliminate those who are not motivated.
~ head coach Lou Holtz

> I loved Coach Faust, but Gerry always seemed as though he was trying to find his way. He didn't have much of a program or platform to plug into as far as dealing with the players and their mentalities or attitudes. Coach Holtz was a motivator, which was very different from Coach Faust's approach. Lou expected us to win. He said, "first we will be the best, then we will be first." He set the bar high and he expected a lot from us. You just knew you had to do what he said and that if you screwed up you were gone.

Being a successful head coach at Notre Dame is no easy accomplishment. You've got to balance managing your players and maintaining the support of your administration, along with keeping your fan base happy. Decisions that are ultimately necessary and good for the development of the team are not always easy to make and are not always supported by the masses. The Notre Dame Value Stream guides its student-athletes along their journey, and also guides the coaching staff to do their best to shape these young men into exemplary representatives of the University of Notre Dame. A prime example of this came in the 1988 ND vs. USC game.

> Fast forward to the Notre Dame vs. USC game in 1988. You had the number one and number two teams in the nation facing each other in the last game of the season. It was Thanksgiving weekend. Tony Brooks and Ricky Watters had shown up late to a meeting and Coach Holtz had to decide what

the consequences would be for their tardiness. They already had a few strikes against them, but I don't think Lou really intended to send them home. He had the seniors on the team sit down in a room to discuss the situation. They were our leading rusher and leading wide receiver and Lou followed our decision to send them home. The whole thing ended up being a huge rallying cry for us. A bunch of guys got up and gave "Braveheart" speeches and the team went out there the next day and just smoked USC. Stan Smagala had an interception for a touchdown. Our defense was so good that day against USC's very prolific offense. We were a six point underdog and we very handily took care of business.

Physical ability is an important factor in achieving athletic success, but mental toughness is equally as important. Head Coach Lou Holtz did a great job at not only preparing his team for the physical aspects of the game but for the mental aspects as well. The 1988 season was the result of a well-coached and extremely well prepared group of young men.

We started out the year beating a very tough Michigan team. We beat Michigan State, who is always tough, and then we beat Purdue, Stanford and Pittsburgh which all lead up to that famous Notre Dame vs. Miami game on October 15th. I was old enough to remember the last Miami game that had been played at the Orange Bowl where they had beaten us 58-7. In that game, following every single catch that Michael Irvin made, he would take off his helmet and run over to the sidelines to celebrate. They were the king of the block. They had not lost a game in two years. They were the bad boys for sure. I had never felt that much electricity around campus in my entire time at Notre Dame, and I never felt it again afterwards either. The students were crazed, we were crazed; it was such a weird sensation. There was a huge buzz surrounding that game.

You save Jimmy Johnson's ass for me!

Both teams were highly ranked (Miami #1 and ND #4). There had been some heated exchanges in the newspaper. We came into the stadium like always for our warm-ups and when the Miami players finished their warm-ups they didn't run around us as they were supposed to; they ran straight through our drill. I was standing next to Ned Bolcar and saw the Miami squad running towards us and the next thing I knew there were 150 people on the field in a fist fight. All of the ushers and security personnel were rushing onto the field to get us separated. It was a full-blown brawl. That cranked up the tone of the game even higher. We got into the locker room and everyone was punching walls and throwing helmets. I think someone broke the chalkboard. And then there was the infamous Coach Holtz speech culminating with, "You save Jimmy Johnson's ass for me!" I was so incredibly jacked up for that game. And although the Miami players were the nation's "bad boys," we weren't exactly choirboys ourselves. We were nasty, or at least we thought we were nasty, and who you are really is 90% what you think of yourself.

I was so jacked up when we took the field. Then, towards the end of the first quarter I got hit extremely hard and broke my hand when I landed on the ground after a big tackle. My hand immediately began to swell, I knew it was broken. (Pritchett had broken the fourth metacarpal, the bone that connects the wrist to the ring finger.) I had so much adrenaline at the moment, though, that I couldn't really feel it. During a TV timeout I ran off the field to get defensive play direction from Coach Alvarez and told the medical staff, "tape my two fingers together, I just broke my hand." Everyone looked at me like I was crazy, but the trainer did just that. I played the rest of the first half with a broken hand. By the end of the half my hand had swollen up like a balloon and as the adrenaline was starting to wear off I realized how much it hurt and started to panic. They quickly got a compress on my hand to reduce some of the swelling and I went back out and played the entire second half. I finished the game with 15 tackles. I never once considered coming out of the game.

I can't over emphasize the whole feeling of electricity that surrounded that game and filled the stadium that day. All of the students had mannequins hanging out of their windows dressed as Miami football players. The pep rally the night before the game was absolutely insane. Coach Holtz had predicted an Irish victory at the pep rally, confident that anything he said that night would not make it into the morning paper, which ended up being an incorrect assumption. Coach Holtz later claimed "you should never be held responsible for what you say at a pep rally." Everything surrounding that game was truly unforgettable.

Three Amigos

When you think of "Three Amigos" an image comes to mind of three men donning sombreros and equipped with guitars, or it may remind you of a comical moment in a Steve Martin movie. The three amigos that Pritchett was a part of were equally slapstick and definitely more fierce. Who were Notre Dame's "Three Amigos" you ask?

Frank Stams and I were in the same class. He came to Notre Dame highly touted, the Ohio player of the year. We were friends from the start. He broke his ankle in the spring practice before our junior year (this was his redshirt year) and got moved onto defense. We met (Michael) Stonebreaker when I was his host during his official visit to campus from New Orleans. We ended up having a phenomenal weekend with Stoney. During the weekend I kept saying, "Get a load of this kid, he's so arrogant." But what I didn't realize was that he wasn't ignoring us or blowing us off, he was deaf in one ear! When he ended up coming to Notre Dame, he fit in perfectly with Frank and me. We played our fair share of practical jokes and pranks on people, but we played pretty darn well on the field, too. It's all fun and games when you're winning and excelling on the field. Stoney was the silent one, Frank and I were the vocal ones. Coach Alvarez leaned on Frank and me to set a good example for the younger guys. To show them how hard we worked in order to be successful and what it took to be prepared. When the lights were on we played harder than anyone else, and we learned that from the older guys who came before us.

In order to win you have to have a little bit of luck, but you have to also have passion and chemistry. That team had great chemistry, especially the guys on defense. The players had an amazing chemistry between each other, and the coaches had a great chemistry with the team. We all really liked Coach Alvarez; he was really special. And Coach Holtz was smart enough to give Alvarez the reigns and let him do his thing.

The luck, passion and chemistry that the Notre Dame 1988 team shared created the perfect storm and led them to the pot of gold at the end of the rainbow.

The Fiesta Bowl was an exclamation point on a long journey.

The 88 Miami game has to be up there, but the national championship Fiesta Bowl game was a pretty big experience as well. My father had a stroke the summer before my senior year at ND and was in a coma and never regained consciousness; I dedicated the season to him. I showed up to the Fiesta Bowl in tears, which then turned into me being so fired up before that game. That game was icing on the cake, after a year of hard work. We knew that winning that game would be the attainment of everything we had worked for our entire lives. Winning that game was bigger for me than playing pro football in the NFL. When you play college football you're so much closer to your teammates. It's a brotherhood. In the pros, everyone is moving around and no one really cares much about their teammates. It's not the same at all. The Fiesta Bowl was an exclamation point on a long journey. There were only three 5th year seniors on that 88 championship team, and we had been through some tough times, that is for sure. We went from being in the outhouse to being in the penthouse. We went from getting booed off the field to winning the national title. We realized exactly where we had come from and appreciated every moment of our success.

The transition from high school to college is bigger than any kid can imagine. You can tell them over and over how important time management and a good work ethic is, but until they actually experience it for themselves, it's practically impossible for students to know exactly what they're walking into. The rigors of Notre Dame are intense, to say the very least, but one thing Her student-athletes have in their corner is the Notre Dame Value Stream to lift them up when they falter and to teach them how to succeed.

Kids should be going to Notre Dame for all the right reasons. I chose Notre Dame for the combination of academics and Division One football that they offered me. I came from a very advanced academic background so I was very prepared for Notre Dame. Even with the preparation that I had, being a student-athlete was quite a challenge. Managing your time was taken to a whole new level at ND. There were no free passes in college. The time requirement of football alone was a full time job and then you had to figure out how to fit in classes and studying.

You had 6 am workouts, class until 1:30 pm, film at 2 pm, rehab and ice and medical treatment, then practice, dinner. You wouldn't get back to your room until 8 or 9 pm and then you had to study in order to keep up with your work. It definitely was a challenge. In order to succeed as a student-athlete you have to be both mentally and physically tough. I think everything I went through at Notre Dame as a student-athlete made me extremely prepared for life. It created a work ethic in me that is now a habit. I take the same attitude that I had with football and athletics and use it in my business today; and that has a great deal to do with why I am successful. I work well as part of a team, I can talk to people, I work hard, and I am consistent. As a student athlete, you didn't have any free time. You didn't even think about having free time, you were always trying to be productive. This is a great attribute to carry into the business world. The quality of people coming out of Notre Dame is consistently outstanding ... smart, hard working, spiritual; exactly what businesses are looking for, then and today.

Professional Career

The intense daily life of a collegiate student-athlete may seem overwhelming at times, but when all is said and done you are happy to have gone through it as it's made you into the man or woman that you are meant to be.

I got drafted by the Miami Dolphins in the 6th round of the NFL draft. That was the first year the NFL introduced the practice squads. They would cut rookies and place them on their practice squads to use when they needed them later in the season. I got cut by the Dolphins that year and was placed on their practice squad and was then picked up by the Buffalo Bills. I played for the Bills for two years and then signed with the Falcons. After my year with the Falcons, my agent talked me into playing in the World Football League for the New York/New Jersey Knights (which was a lot of fun, by the way). After that year my agent was ready to push me back in to the NFL but I decided at that point the NFL wasn't all it was cracked up to be and it was time for me to move on; it was time to retire from football and get a job. I had earned an economics degree from Notre Dame, and I had sacrificed those 4 years at Notre Dame to give myself a 40-year career, and it was time to cash in on that. I made more money in the second year of my financial career than I ever made in the NFL.

Life is all about the journey, but sometimes the path isn't clear. This is when the Notre Dame Value Stream appears to guide you and point you in the right direction. Head Coach Lou Holtz often was the vehicle the Notre Dame Value Stream used to point Her student-athletes toward the correct path.

When I decided I was ready to retire, I called Coach Holtz and asked him to write a letter of recommendation for me. I also called Dick Rosenthal because I knew he had been working on Wall Street, and used his connections as well. I wanted to be an institutional bond salesman. One of my buddies from high school had gotten his MBA after college and was an institutional bond salesman at First Boston and that was exactly what I wanted to do. It was "the" job to have on Wall Street. It is what everyone wanted to do at that time. I literally walked up and down Wall Street and knocked on every single door. I used Dick's contacts, my Atlanta connections and any other connection I could think of. I had job offers from Morgan Stanley, Salomon Brothers and Kidder, Peabody. I chose Kidder because they were one of the top investment banks and they wanted me to move back to Atlanta after a couple of years in New York. There were 37 people hired into their training program. 35 of the 37 trainees had Ivy League MBA's, two of us did not. I had a Notre Dame undergraduate degree and the other guy had an undergraduate degree from Princeton and had just finished 4th in the discus in the Olympics. That was the start of my Wall Street career in 1993.

Three years after that training program, I was Senior Vice President and in the top five percent in the company in production globally. I hit the ground running and never looked back. It was a great business for me. It was competitive. I got to entertain clients, form working relationships and work and think outside of the box. It was kind of like a locker room environment in that we were all on teams. I thrived in the competition. Playing football at a school like Notre Dame, managing my time and understanding how to work with others was an integral part of my success as an institutional bond salesman. I understood the lingo and it was a very comfortable business model and culture for me.

For 20 years I've helped institutions manage their credit and interest rate risk. We work with them to maximize their returns within the framework of their investment parameters. I have learned a great deal about markets actions and reactions over multiple business cycles. I am an Executive Director at J.P. Morgan. I have partnered with my brother who has also been in the business for 22 years. Together we manage the assets of high net worth individuals. Relying on the experience in fixed income, we help customers construct portfolios and provide tactical allocation guidance to clients on their investible assets, reflecting either changing market conditions or their personal situation. Our 20+ years of industry experience spans periods of extreme volatility from which we have developed a disciplined process to help assess clients' risk parameters and position their portfolios to navigate inevitable market fluctuations. We differentiate ourselves by providing personalized experience and investment philosophy. We focus on Goal Based Planning and Legacy planning within a Comprehensive Wealth Management platform. It is important for successful people to plan the best way to pass wealth to their heirs and fulfill all their philanthropic desires. We design a plan within a timeline to help them accomplish that. We want to start having these discussions with people sooner rather than later. The more you can save and take advantage of compounding interest, the better your future and your children's futures will be. It's not just hearsay, it's real and it's relevant.

With so many Notre Dame graduates heading to work in jobs on Wall Street, the University's Monogram Club has established a relationship with many of these companies to help pave pathways for its student-athletes.

The Monogram Club does a Wall Street dinner in New York City. They are working towards creating internships and forming gateways for students to guide them from school to internships to full-time jobs. I am working to start a similar program in Atlanta. Now that Notre Dame is in the ACC, more and more kids want to move back to the south.

It may take a lot of hard work and determination to be successful at a school like Notre Dame, but it does not have to be all work and no play. Pritchett was a prime example of this. Following the 1988 national championship game victory, the team had the opportunity to travel to the White House and be recognized for their accomplishments. Pritchett decided to have a little fun while they were there.

I joked that I was going to try and take the Gipper's sweater. Frank (Stams) and I were literally holding the Gipper's sweater when they gave it to President Reagan. That was an unbelievable day. We had won the national championship and now were meeting President Reagan. We got our photos taken with President Bush and Vice President Quayle. And then Frank and I were in the Rose Garden handing Reagan the Gipper's sweater with Monk Malloy. Unbelievable.

Pressure is when you have to do something you aren't prepared to do.
~ Lou Holtz

The young men who played football for Coach Holtz, who now have families and careers of their own, would without a doubt drop everything if Coach Holtz needed them. But back in the day, Coach may not have been their favorite person in the world.

The relationship we have with Lou now is fun. When we played for him, he was not fun to be around. Typically, if you were in front of him, you were in trouble. The first day he walked in, Coach Faust was saying goodbye to us, and Holtz and Faust crossed paths in the hallway by the meeting room. (Player) Chuck Lanza had his foot propped up on the stage and Lou kicked it off when he walked in. "When I get up here to speak you will sit up straight and you will look me in the eye," he said. From that very moment, when he began to speak, he had taken control of the team. Lou had an aura of, "I know what I'm doing, follow me, believe in me and we will win." He could teach you an entire life lesson in 10 minutes.

The thing about Lou is, he would say these things over and over again and you'd think he was crazy. As you grew up and got older you began to realize that the things he told us over and over again were in reality life lessons; and that he lives what he preaches. He is the prime example.

When he first came to Notre Dame, we would have these relaxation sessions the night before a game. We'd go to the pep rally and then he'd take us over to the Loftus Center, turn all of the lights out, and there you'd have 100 players lying quietly on the floor. He would walk us through what was going to happen in the game the next day. He would say, "When you wake up tomorrow, thank God for the day and realize how blessed you are to have this day.

Wes Pritchett

Picture yourself in the stadium. See your teammates. See yourself in the huddle. See yourself making successful plays." We thought he was nuts! But after about the second week I woke up on game day and said exactly what he had told us to say and I thought that was so weird. Coach always said, "What the mind perceives, the body can achieve. You're either growing or you're dying."

Wes Pritchett's Lessons from the Notre Dame Value Stream:

- Give it 100%. Don't take your college years for granted. Appreciate what you're doing, appreciate the camaraderie, and appreciate that you'll have a job when it's all said and done.

- Don't waste your time focusing on things that are not important. Maximize your grades and excel in whatever sport you're involved in.

- Give it your all and know you've been given a unique opportunity to excel and be respected for the rest of your life. If you've given 100% you'll never look back, but if you don't you'll always wonder, "what if?"

Portrait of Notre Dame football player Pat Fallon, 1988. Notre Dame University Photographer. (Photo courtesy of Notre Dame Archives.)

CHAPTER EIGHT

The World Marathon Runner

Pat Fallon

*E*very life is full of ups and downs, successes and failures, triumphs and tragedies. It's how you react to each success and failure you face that will determine the course your life will take. Do you see life as a glass half-full experience, or do you always see life as a glass half-empty? Have you built a village to support you and cheer you on? Former Notre Dame wide receiver Pat Fallon has done just that. After being mentored at Notre Dame by head football coach Lou Holtz, Fallon has held on to some key Holtz-isms that have helped guide him through the rough waters of life, eliminate the naysayers, and have turned his failures into glowing successes. Now a successful business owner, a member of the Texas House of Representatives, and World Marathon Challenge survivor,

Fallon has not only never turned down a challenge, but also faces each and every one with a fearlessness and positive attitude that we can all learn from. How does a kid from Pittsfield, Massachusetts, play on a national championship winning football team at Notre Dame while simultaneously completing Air Force ROTC, and then continue to serve his country in political office? This is Pat Fallon's story.

You're going to fail, you're going to have challenges; it's how you overcome them, circumvent them, and climb over them that matters.

I grew up in Pittsfield, Mass. in the western part of the state, and my father is a 1957 graduate of Notre Dame. So much like a lot of other ND children, the Fighting Irish of Notre Dame played the perpetual role as the good guys and teams like USC and Alabama (back in the 70s) were the bad guys. It was always a dream of mine from an early age to play football at Notre Dame. When we would toss the ball around, I would project myself playing football for the Irish; never a professional team. Always Notre Dame. Then you start to take your dreams more seriously and begin to develop as a player. Gerry Faust was the head coach at Notre Dame when I was in high school but he did not recruit me to play football at ND. Two of my high school football coaches played at the University of Massachusetts, which was a Div I-AA school at the time, so I took their advice and guidance and went to U Mass. From the very first day I arrived at U Mass the only thing I wanted to do was get good grades and go to Notre Dame. You see I didn't even get accepted into ND my senior year in high school. It was a good lesson to learn as a high school student: you're going to fail, you're going to have challenges; it's how you overcome them, circumvent them, and climb them that matters. As I was crying, sitting on my front porch on April 7, 1986, with a very thin white envelope in my hand from ND, I began to formulate my plan. I am going to U Mass, I'm going to spend a year there, study very hard and then transfer to Notre Dame. I would tell people at U Mass when I met them, "Oh I'm not going to be here more than a year; I am going to transfer to Notre Dame." Everyone would say back to me, "Yeah whatever." No one really took me seriously. My friends were rather indifferent. I didn't study all that much in high school. As a result, I was just a B student. Not bad but not exactly ND material either! But my first semester at U Mass I got a 3.77 grade point average (GPA), and my second semester I got a 3.5 GPA. That first year at U Mass I didn't play football, I didn't do any extracurricular activities. I was very focused and all I did was study. It was a large state school, a world of difference from ND. I applied to transfer to ND after my freshman year at U Mass, and I got a thick manila envelope in the mail on June 20, 1987. Not that I remember the exact date or anything!

Not every path to Notre Dame is straightforward, but the Notre Dame Value Stream guided Fallon from the very beginning, and showed him that anything worth having was also worth fighting for. And so his journey began.

The Notre Dame Years

Getting into Notre Dame is an accomplishment to be celebrated, but being a transfer student at Notre Dame came with challenges.

I learned a lot at 19 years old as a transfer student at Notre Dame. Getting into Notre Dame was all well and good except for the fact that they didn't have housing available for transfer students. They sent you a list of apartments and rooms you could rent in South Bend. My parents were teachers making modest salaries and so I took the cheapest room available, which was a little over two miles from campus. It was a house in downtown South Bend, down the street from Tippecanoe Place, owned by two sisters in their 80s. I had access to my room, a bathroom, but had no access to the rest of the house. I could not have guests over. I had to get up extra early to catch the bus to school, and had to leave campus earlier than I would have liked in order to make the final bus downtown. Had I studied harder in high school, I probably wouldn't have had this problem, but instead I had to pay my dues. The two sisters may have seemed a bit senile to me, but when rent was due, they were as sharp as tacks!

During my first year at Notre Dame, in the back of my mind, I kept wondering if my football career was over or if I should try and revive it. At first I was just so happy to be at Notre Dame. But with that accomplishment in hand, there were the beginnings of what became an unremitting undercurrent that just wouldn't go away: revive your football career.

I was dating a girl that first year at ND who lived in Breen-Phillips Hall. I was quite fond of her. Beautiful girl. Well one day I was walking over to see her and saw her a bit too cozy with another fella on the quad. I was furious. I didn't confront her, and obviously didn't see her after that either-not that she was all that concerned of course! What I did was channel that anger. I asked myself why I wasn't pursuing my dreams. Why not try out for the football team and let the chips fall where they may?! Right then and there I marched straight over to the football office and shared my intentions with Coach (George) Kelly. I wanted to participate in winter conditioning and try out for the football team in the spring. He instructed me to come back tomorrow and they would get me started.

Winter conditioning was fascinating, but when you are hungry, you do have somewhat of an advantage. I was not as fast as Pat Terrell, or as strong as

Ricky Watters, but my desire was white-hot. You have to get over the doubts as to whether or not you belong. You have to say yes, yes I can do this. I was extremely active at winter conditioning. One of the graduate assistants called me, "The Worker." I had carpet burns all over my legs from the artificial surface. The pain actually felt good to me because it showed I was putting in the extra effort. Some of the other reserve players, however, didn't like it. Mark Green and Steve Belles helped me out and took me under their wings. Pete Graham, Antwon Lark, James Dillard and many other guys began to see that I wasn't just going through the motions but that I really wanted to contribute and compete. The guys started to see that I had something and I began to fit in.

The Notre Dame Value Stream shows Her students which path they should be following, but also shows them how to put in the hard work to be successful and not get lost on that chosen path.

After winter conditioning I was invited to play spring ball and that was an awesome experience. But you go from being thrilled about the invite, to being worried about the fall season. Pete Cordelli was the receivers' coach at the time. Two of top receivers (Pierre Martin and Bobby Carpenter) left ND and so opportunities began to open up. Tony Rice was absolutely wonderful in every regard. He was always so positive. He didn't care if you were Heisman Trophy winner Tim Brown or someone coming off the bench, he always had a smile for you, a helpful suggestion, a tight spiral, and a pat on the back. Even if you did something wrong, he encouraged you.

Senior Brad Alge was another guy who mentored me. He had a knee injury but he was one of Coach Holtz's favorites because he was one of those guys who could never be outworked. There was something special about that 1988 Notre Dame football team when you saw it unfold. Ned Bolcar, Mark Green, Corny Southall, George Streeter, Tony Rice, Andy Heck, Wes Pritchett, Frank Stams, they were players first but they were also leaders who coached their fellow teammates. Especially Pritchett and Stams who were fifth year seniors. If they went in early to practice, you went in early to practice. They set a good example for all of us. If we hadn't had their leadership on that 1988 team there's no way we go on that 12-0 run.

At the end of spring ball they let you know whether or not you made the team for the fall season. My parents had limited resources, similar to many of my peers who were also from middle class families, and when I went home for breaks I would take the train back to Massachusetts; a 15 hour overnight train from South Bend to Pittsfield. On my trip home at semester's end, my parents picked me up in the morning, and at that point I hadn't even told them I was participating in winter conditioning and spring practice, let alone that I had made the team for the fall. Well, I had mentioned it to my mom in somewhat vague terms, but she was supposed to have kept it a secret from my dad (which she did not). When I got off the train I joyfully told them I had made the team. Having that opportunity was such a tremendous experience for me. To see the pride and joy well up in my dad's ND Alum eyes was a special moment!

Playing football at Notre Dame was like being in a different kind of classroom. There was so much that I was trying to soak up that I started taking copious notes about the whole experience. A lot of it is unprintable (Fallon laughs), but funny. Coach Holtz said it over and over again, "I look at myself not as a football coach but as a teacher. It's my job to teach you to not only excel on the football field but also to excel in life." At the time we may not have appreciated it as much as we should have and even been a bit skeptical of those words. My teammates and I had our fair share of "too cool for school" moments on the campus way back then. But in hindsight, with the wisdom of a few decades now under our belts, we see with perfect clarity what Coach was doing and what he meant.

If not for the experiences that I had with the guys on that 1988 squad and that group of coaches, I would not have tried to do a lot of things I've done and experienced in my life. I wouldn't have been as eager to leave my comfort zone - you know what feels safe. I don't know if I would have become an entrepreneur, started my own business, or ever even run for public office. A lot of the time we are taught that success, or notable success, is for other people. You are just supposed to get a job and be employed. But if you have a calling for something more, you have to scratch that itch or you are never going to be happy with yourself. When I saw Todd Lyght get drafted in the first round of the 1991 NFL draft, witnessed one of my teammates and friends being that successful on the big stage, I begin to realize that success doesn't only happen to strangers, it can happen to guys like us. Even, maybe, to me! And though I wasn't drafted into the NFL, that didn't mean that I couldn't achieve my dreams. You're not going to succeed at everything you try, but that's okay. When I did cold call sales in my 20s I would welcome the no's. I figured that for every seven no's I got, there would be three yes's. So the quicker I got the no's out of the way the quicker I could rack up the yes's.

The Notre Dame Value Stream did a great job of teaching Fallon and his teammates success is 100% attainable. It also taught them that naysayers will always be there, and that adversity is often the catalyst needed to propel you towards your dreams.

Running for political office was interesting. We've all had people in our lives that encourage us, and people in our lives that are negative. Many motivational speakers tell their audiences, "take the toxic people who point out every obstacle to you and eliminate them from your life, and keep the positive ones." Just by having that one person in your life who believes in you, you can often go much further than you ever thought you could. The positive people in your life are there to believe in you until you can believe in yourself. You're going to be down sometimes, especially after you fail and throw yourself that pity party, but then you need to find someone to help you get back up, who can help expedite the process. You make these lifelong friends in college, friends who shared experiences with you, such as Notre Dame football, they become your brothers.

It is not the critic who counts; not the man who points out how the strong man stumbles, or where the doer of deeds could have done them better. The credit belongs to the man who is actually in the arena, whose face is marred by dust and sweat and blood; who strives valiantly; who errs, who comes short again and again, because there is no effort without error and shortcoming; but who does actually strive to do the deeds; who knows great enthusiasms, the great devotions; who spends himself in a worthy cause; who at the best knows in the end the triumph of high achievement, and who at the worst, if he fails, at least fails while daring greatly, so that his place shall never be with those cold and timid souls who neither know victory nor defeat. ~ Theodore Roosevelt

Being a student at Notre Dame is challenging. Add to that being a student-athlete and in the Air Force ROTC and you've got quite the workload. Fallon's challenges of being a student-athlete at Notre Dame and the habits he learned from the Notre Dame Value Stream have helped him throughout all of his endeavors in his life.

As a student-athlete at Notre Dame you have to be extremely disciplined with your time. Then I was also in Air Force ROTC so I was juggling class, football, and my ROTC obligations. For a while I was working, too, but I had to give that up to do ROTC. I did sell t-shirts door-to-door to help pay for school and expenses. Time management was a huge component of being successful as a student-athlete; being able to expand your comfort zone and do things that felt uncomfortable, even though difficult, was crucial to cultivating your character and a critical ingredient to your growth as a person. Having the belief that you can do more than you think you can was, and is, important to being successful as well. It was neat to be that young and have people say, "You are on the ND football team?! Wow." That really did make your heart glow.

Professional Career

What is even tougher for most student-athletes is the transition from life as an athlete to life post athletics.

It's challenging for a lot of people when competitive team sports are no longer a part of your life. When that's gone so many people feel that loss and go through a transformation period from athletics into regular life. You have to start this next chapter of your life with new goals and interests to fill that void. For me that new goal was becoming an entrepreneur. I wanted to start my own business and work for myself. Coach Holtz taught us to write down our goals and make a plan on how you're going to get there. You can't hit a target you can't see, so create the target. And that's just what I did.

After I graduated from Notre Dame, I served in the Air Force until I was 26 years old. After I was honorably discharged, I wanted to start a business. So I set my target and worked backwards from there.

- *How do I start a business?*

- *How do I create a successful business, take care of my employees and my customers and become independently successful?*

- *And long term, how do I get into politics so that I can once again serve and give back to this amazing country that's already given me so much?*

I started my company out of my living room in a rented house in Wichita Falls, Texas. I had a total net worth of about $80. No kidding! But with drive, perseverance, a bit of good fortune and a growing team of dedicated employees, Virtus Apparel and our sister companies now employ nearly 100 people, we have 12 locations and have been blessed with an ever growing bottom line for nearly two decades. This success enabled me, in 2009 at 41 years old, to seek public office for the first time as I ran for a city council seat in Frisco, Texas. Frisco, at the time, was the fastest growing city in the country. In 1990 there were approximately 6,000 people living in Frisco. In 2000 that number jumped to 30,000 and in 2009 it tripled to 100,000 people. Today there are approximately 160,000 people living in Frisco. In the next 10 years it is predicted it will reach 300,000 people.

When I decided to run for city council, of course there were the naysayers. They were the same people who told me that I couldn't transfer to Notre Dame. That I should just stay at the University of Massachusetts and make the best of it. Now they were telling me, "You've only lived in Frisco for two years, no one knows you. You haven't been here long enough. You don't know how to run for city council. You have a pregnant wife who is going to give birth right around Election Day. You also have a young son and a business to run." But I did not let this stop me. I told them thank you, but that I didn't think the announced candidates would be as passionate about the job as I would be. And furthermore I don't think all of the new people who have moved into Frisco care that I've only been here a couple of years.

I don't think we would have had the outcome we had if I had not been a part of the Notre Dame football team.

There were four of us in the race, and if one candidate didn't win outright (receive more than 50% of the vote), the top two candidates would have gone into a runoff election. The convention wisdom had myself and the clear favorite in the race heading to a runoff. But if you can get 50% of the votes you can win outright. I decided we were going to go for broke. If I didn't win the election with 50% or more in the first round, the runoff would have occurred right around the time my wife was due, and that wasn't an inviting scenario. I personally knocked on hundreds of doors and campaigned for 100 straight days. On Election night, May 9th, 2009, we received 57% of the vote. The candidate who was the clear favorite only got 29%. I don't think we would have had that kind of outcome had I not been a part of the Notre Dame football team. That experience taught me to surround myself with people who believed in me, and to get rid of the toxic people in my life. Like Coach Holtz said, write down a goal, then a plan to achieve. Well, we hit the bull's eye!

I was on the city council for three years and during my third year on council my colleagues unanimously elected me as Mayor Pro Tem (vice mayor). Just about that same time, a seat in the Texas House of Representatives came open, a position which represents 170,000 people. After getting the "OK" from my bride, I decided to run for the State House. And then, yup, here are those darn naysayers again! "How are you going to win this seat? You think you can go from city council to state representative? There is a clear favorite running for this seat. You can't beat her! Why don't you just wait a few years and run for something else."

My response? Thank you for your advice but I'm going to try this. It's not up to me or my opponent, it's up to the thousands of people that will be voting. Once again I reached back to those words from Coach Holtz, "Set your target, write down all of the things you have to do to hit that target in the center and then do it."

I didn't hire a campaign consultant. I would run the campaign myself. I did hire a couple of support staff and we ran an all-positive campaign to coun-

teract my opponents highly negative approach. We ignored her and told the voters why they should vote for us, not why that should vote against the opposition. The election ended up being delayed from early March to late May due to a redistricting lawsuit. And while this delay did increase expenses, it was also a blessing. It provided us an opportunity of three more months to knock on a thousand more doors!

Across the state of Texas there were 35 seats that had no incumbents in the 2012 primary election cycle, and of those 35 seats, we won by the widest margin in the entire state. We received almost 73% of the vote and my competitor got just 27%. Sometimes "they" don't know all that much!

For the general election, which occurred in November of 2012, I still campaigned even though everyone told me I didn't have to. We are in a very Republican district, but I still wanted the voters to know that I am acutely aware of who I work for - them! Not the special interest and certainly not anyone in Austin! In the election cycles where people are voting for the president, there is something that occurs called "under voting;" which is where people only vote for the big races on the ballot, and leave the rest of the contests blank. I was curious as to how many more votes Mitt Romney got in our district, compared to how many votes I got. I started to do the math, and to my shock, it turned out that I had actually received more votes than Romney did in our House District. To not have any under voting in the year of a presidential election was quite an accomplishment. In fact, it's pretty much unheard of to have a down ballot candidate like state representative receive more votes than the party's presidential candidate. All of the hard work of our campaign team really had a pretty wonderful, if not entirely unexpected, effect!

Fallon's time at Notre Dame developed him as a person and established a solid work ethic that still serves him well today. The values taught to him by the Notre Dame Value Stream, and the words from Coach Holtz that he faithfully holds so dear, continue to guide him in his everyday life. It is no surprise that one of his favorite Notre Dame football memories involves his beloved coach, Lou Holtz.

I was one of the two people who had the opportunity to carry Coach Holtz off the field after we won the national championship in 1988. I positioned myself behind him and figured unless someone pushed me out of the way, I'm going to do this. The plan was when we won, not if we won, we were going to carry the seniors off the field. There was no doubt in our minds, there was no chance that we were going to lose. We knew, hands down, that we were going to win that game. Underclassmen were assigned in groups of two's and three's to carry a senior off the field, but I hadn't been assigned to anyone. So my plan was to carry Coach Holtz off the field. And I executed that plan to perfection! The very next morning after the championship game, The Arizona Republic newspaper ran a big photo on their front page of Coach Holtz getting carried off the field. You can see Coach with his hand up in the air, index finger raised to the heavens, and in the corner of that photo there's a ten thousand watt smile on the face of yours truly. Man, do I love that picture! Years later Coach came to speak in Austin, Texas to the Republican House Caucus and I had the honor of introducing him. They had that photo printed out and Coach Holtz signed it for me.

When you look at all that Fallon has accomplished in his life and the challenges he has overcome, you can clearly see a man who is not afraid of failure and who doesn't take no for an answer. Fallon's most recent life adventure, attempting the World Marathon Challenge (WMC), is more remarkable than any other target he has tried to hit - so far. The Challenge entails completing 7 Marathons on all 7 Continents in just 7 days. As of this printing, August 2016, there are just 26 people in the world that have successfully completed the World Marathon Challenge. In comparison, 4,000 people have summited Mount Everest. Fallon was also attempting to become the first person in the world, without any previous marathon experience, to complete the WMC!

Last summer there was a story on ESPN about the World Marathon Challenge, and up to that point I was completely unaware that this event even existed. I thought to myself, man, I'd love to do that someday. But often times you have thoughts like that knowing you'll never actually do it. One of our friends – Jill McMillan, who lives in our neighborhood, has twin 5 year old boys. She had a friend Kimberly Wade who lives in Jerseyville, IL, who also has twin boys who were 7 years old. In Dec of 2014 one of the Wade twins, Jonny, was diagnosed with a rare form of brain cancer. Our friend Jill began posting about the Wade family and Jonny's journey and struggles on Facebook, but I never read the posts. I just couldn't bring myself to read them because it hurt too much. Having 9 and 6 year old boys myself, it just hit too close to home. So I'm ashamed to say, at first, I took the ostrich approach and buried my head in the sand.

One night in Oct of 2015, I was reading about the World Marathon Challenge when I saw a post about Jonny Wade in my Facebook feed. For some reason I read it. It brought me to tears. His mother asked him if he could have one wish, what would that be. Instead of answering with the obvious and expected, "To get better Mommy," Jonny responded with selfless wisdom beyond his years with, "I just wish no other kid ever has to get cancer." His words filled my soul with emotion. My God, I wanted with all my heart to do something to help this brave little boy. And then this thought popped into my head. What if I ran the World Marathon Challenge? A guy like me trying something like that could get a lot of attention. We could raise awareness and money for Jonny and pediatric cancer research! And he's a little boy, he loves adventure, he could follow the journey and it could be a good distraction for him and his twin brother Jacky while he battles this awful disease. So here I am, 47 years old, completely out of shape, weighing in at 235 pounds, and I hadn't even run a 5K in years. No one had ever attempted this, let alone completed this, without being an ultra marathon athlete. I contacted Richard Donovan, with Polar Running Adventures, to express my interest in participating in the World Marathon Challenge and he told me, "You're in luck! A spot just opened up we have one left."

Only 15 people can participate in the World Marathon Challenge each year. Now all I had to do was convince my wife to let me do this. After a 33-page PowerPoint presentation on why it would be good for our family, North Texas, cancer research and the Wade family, she said yes. She told me, "I'm going to let you do this, not because of all of these reasons, or the nice presents you promised me in the presentation. I'm saying yes because of the cause." You see, for the entire year, she had been reading Jill's posts on Facebook the whole time. She told me, "If you do this for the Wade family, I am completely on board."

The World Marathon Challenge consists of running seven marathons in seven days on seven continents, and must be completed in 168 hours: first on a mile thick glacier in Antarctica, and then Punta Arenas, Chile (South America), Miami (North America), Madrid (Europe), Marrakesh, Morocco (Africa), Dubai, United Arab Emirates (Asia) and Sydney (Australia).

And then a horrible thing happened.

So now I've got to get in shape! I weighed 195 pounds when I was at Notre Dame, I weighed 200 pounds when I was in the Air Force, and on my first day of marathon training, October 16, 2015, I weighed 235 pounds. And it sucked. And I didn't like running. But I lost 30 pounds along the way and now I feel great; I feel 20 years younger. When there is less of you to carry, you get faster by the way! You have the same muscle mass, you're just not carrying all of that fat. And then a horrible thing happened. Jonny Wade's cancer came back and he passed away on Christmas Eve, December 24, 2015. We decided to continue on with the World Marathon Challenge, to do it as a distraction for the Wade family, and especially for Jonny's twin brother, Jacky and to honor Jonny. We sent a packet to the Wade family that included a globe with stars on each of the seven locations we were going to be running and everything and anything we could get our hands on about the World Marathon Challenge and the trip around the world. The Wades were so supportive and were amazed that a perfect stranger would do this to honor their son. What they didn't realize was that by welcoming our meager gesture they were the ones giving us a wonderful gift.

I only had three months to train. I had to be very disciplined and I ran very hard six days a week. During my most grueling week I ran 102 miles. And because of the intense training I was able to get into pretty good shape, pretty quickly. But you know, there's really no way you can fully prepare to run seven marathons, in seven days, on seven continents. I remembered how awful those two-a-day practices were at Notre Dame, and I wondered if this would be that bad. Because up until then, those two-a-day practices were the hardest thing I had ever physically experienced.

Jacky, Jonny's twin brother, ran the last mile with me and the marathon coordinators gave him a medal just like the one that I received.

We flew from Punta Arenas, Chile (at the southern tip of South America) to Antarctica for the first marathon, which was on a glacier a mile thick. Antarctica is the highest, windiest, driest and coldest of all continents. If you don't wear polarized goggles you will be blind in an hour. There are deep crevasses and the course had to be checked with sonar and marked with flags for the safety of the runners. Let's just say that you don't cut corners when you're running a marathon in Antarctica!

Running in temperatures of -12 degrees on a barren landscape devoid of life isn't easy. In fact when I completed the marathon in 5 hours and 47 minutes, I was told that I became the first person in the world to do their first marathon on the continent of Antarctica. And now I can tell you why…because it's an exceedingly BAD idea to do your first marathon on the continent of Antarctica!!

Of all of the participants of the World Marathon Challenge, I was the only novice long distance runner. So I was pleasantly surprised to not have finished dead last during the first marathon (I came in 11th). During the second race, we returned to Punta Areas and I was 12th with a time of 4 hours and 52 minutes. Next we flew to Miami where I finished in 13th place (out of 15), and again in 13th place in Madrid Spain, the next day. But I was finishing, and that was my goal. Finish each marathon and raise money for pediatric cancer research.

I had never actually met the Wade family before, I'd only communicated with them on Facebook or through our friend Jill. So I was thrilled when they flew to meet us in Florida for the Marathon #3 in Miami. Jacky, Jonny's twin brother, ran the last mile with me and the marathon coordinators gave him a medal just like the one that I received. This is a really big deal because the race officials only give out medals to participants who finish. Jacky is the only one who has a medal that hasn't completed an entire marathon. And up to that point there had only been 11 people who had successfully completed the World Marathon Challenge.

Marathon #4, Madrid (Spain) and Marathon #5, Marrakesh (Morocco) were only five hours apart, and those were very tough. Heck the entire week I only got 18 hours sleep and only 6 of those hours were in a bed! My fitbit watch was set to Miami time and grouped the Madrid and Morocco Marathons in the same calendar day. I had over 96,000 steps that "day". Now at this point I had hit my physical limit. Finishing two marathons in a 24 hour period after having already completed three marathons in the prior three days brought my body to utter exhaustion and near total physical collapse. I was thinking to myself, "how am I going to be able to fly to Dubai and do another race tomorrow?" I wasn't worried so much about finishing, I was more worried about even starting!!!

When we got to Dubai, we had a little time and I managed to get three hours of sleep in an actual bed before the race, and then something magical happened. Something I can't really explain even now. I don't know how or why it happened, but it did. You see up until this point I was averaging five and a half hours per marathon, which I thought wasn't all that bad for a 48-year-old man who has never run a marathon before in his life and only trained for 3 months. But right before the race in Dubai I got a text from my wife that said when Kimberly Wade, Jonny's mom, had gotten back to Jerseyville, IL, from Miami, she'd had the worst day since Jonny's passing. She went to visit his grave site and couldn't even leave. Her sister had to come and pick her up. It had only been three weeks since the funeral, and it was just their family in the house. The realities of losing a child were settling in. A family of four was now only a family of three. My heart bled for her. I suddenly felt this white hot flame within my chest. I was bound and determined to do something for Kimberly. I couldn't give her what I wanted but I could give her what I had. And today I could run. And today I was going to run all out for her.

Of the 15 competitors, there were four that I just flat out couldn't compete with: two of them were 27 year old US Marines, Dan Cartica and Cal Ramm, and Cal was on the Marine Corps Marathon team! When not running seven marathons in a row both were capable of running 26.2 miles in two and a half hours! No shot to compete with them. Another was an Australian named James Alderson. He'd competed in over 150 Ultra Marathons (at least 50 Kilometers-32 miles) and is a world class distance runner. The fourth was Becca Pizzi, a 36-year woman who has been running long distances since she was a little girl, has completed over 50 marathons and is also a highly competitive cross fit athlete. And even though all of the other runners are far more experienced than myself, better trained, more talented and most of them have been smoking me during this adventure, I figured I got an outside shot, a long shot, of competing with them. In short, the best I can do is 5th place. And that is NOT a probability, just a remote possibility. So that was my goal for the day. That was the gift I wanted to give Kimberly. Fifth place.

As soon as the gun went off in Dubai, I came out like a bat out of hell and the other runners are all thinking that I started out too fast. All of the marathon books say that if you start out too fast you will hit a wall somewhere around mile 18, 20 or 22. But at the halfway mark, I'm in fourth place and I'm miles ahead of my normal pace. Well, that dreaded and feared wall never came, for the first time all week I ran the entire race (never walking once) and I also never stopped for a bathroom break. I ended up finishing in fifth place, with a time of 4 hours and 19 minutes. An hour and a half faster than the marathon I'd run the day before, when I could barely walk onto the plane! It was a miracle. How on earth was I able to shave that much off my time? No one could believe it. The organizers couldn't believe it. The other participants couldn't believe it. I knew why I did it, but I didn't know how I was able to do it. I was and still am absolutely convinced that Jonny Wade was the wind at my back and I had a guardian angel with me for those four hours in Dubai. I can't explain it any other way. And together we gave his mom some warmth and solace. It was proof for her that Jonny was on this journey with us.

As amazing as Marathon #6 turned out, what happened the next day eclipsed even that. We flew to Sydney, Australia, for the seventh and final race. It was hazy, hot and humid; and it was an out and back marathon, which meant you ran the same out and back course for 13 roundtrips. It turned out to be as monotonous as it was painful! As we were getting ready to start the wind was at our back, which meant that when we turned around the wind was going to be in our face, making any time we had gained on the way out turn into a net loss. I was trying to figure out how to stay hydrated without over hydrating, how to limit my pit stops, how much water to drink to combat this heat, how many goo packs to take; so many calculations to make. One of the participants, James Alderson-Ultra Marathon man, was from Sydney, Australia, and lived just five miles from the course. Before the race, James was explaining to me, "You're going to like the outbound leg 'cause the winds with us, but you're going to hate the return!" Then James asked me, "Are you going to thrive today Pat or just survive?!" I told him that I wanted to break the 4-hour mark today. I wanted to do that for the Wade family. Only four of the competitors had been able to do that this entire week: James, the two US Marines, Cal Ramm and Dan Cartica, and Becca Pizzi. James was a bit taken aback to say the least. He explained that while he was truly amazed and impressed with my performance in Dubai, that running a 4-hour marathon is much different than running a 4-hour 20-minute marathon; it's a different animal. It's nearly one minute faster per mile. He told me he was going to try and do a 4-hour marathon today, but he wasn't even sure he could do it. And hell, he had beaten the Marines in Dubai and had actually won that leg. It was the only time the Marines didn't finish 1-2. So four hours was a tall order for anyone. Even James. For me, he feared it was simply out of reach. And if I pushed too hard I was risking an injury that could end my challenge and I'd be unable to finish

By this point, after running 157 miles in 6 days on 6 different continents our bodies had had it! We were all pretty seriously banged up. Everything hurt. We were using icy hot, Advil, pain patches, five-hour energy drinks, we had shin splints, aching IT bands, sore hamstrings…the works! James then told me, "OK, if you want to try and run a 4-hour marathon, stay with me, and I'll pace ya!"

The first lap out I stayed right with him, the wind was at our back which was helpful and then we approached the cone to turn around and I hear James say, "As soon as we hit the cone and turn 'round the wind will be in our face," but it wasn't. A small miracle occurred and just as I hit the cone to turn around the wind changed! It was at our back the entire return leg as well. I looked up at the stars and whispered, "Thanks Jonny!" James said he'd never seen that happen before on Manly Beach. In fact, for the rest of the race the wind was never a factor.

The humidity lifted on lap three. The temperatures dropped on lap five. And then James was suddenly way out in front of me and I became very frustrated that I could not keep up with him. I shouted at him when we would pass each other in opposite directions that I needed help with pacing because I hadn't bothered to bring my phone along for time because *he'd promised to pace me. So being from Sydney he had plenty of friends that had come out to cheer him on. He deployed his friend Peter to run with me. Peter was a trooper and stayed with me the whole rest of the way. Then on lap ten he told me I was doing very well, but the time keepers wouldn't tell me my time (which later on I found out was because they didn't want to jinx me). Meanwhile, the race organizers told everyone what I was trying to do and how fast I was going so everyone in the crowd started to cheer for me. On the last lap, lap 13, Peter tells me, "When you get to the half mile marker, I want you to sprint home as fast as you can." I did as instructed and took off. Close to the end, there was a woman 100 meters from the finish who was holding a United States flag and a Texas flag for me and I grabbed them from her and sprinted home as fast as I could. I get to the finish line and they tell me, "We've got good news for you, you broke four hours. You finished in 3 hours and 53 minutes, you came in third place, and you beat James (he had to stop at the aid station). The only two people who were faster than you were the two marines, and they only beat you by a few minutes-which was remarkable considering that in Antarctica they had bested me by two and a half hours! I went from running the first five marathons and just surviving, to actually competing in the last two marathons. After hearing the stories from my last two races, Kimberly was 100% convinced that her son, Jonny, was with me; that it was his sign to us that he is still with us. Just beautiful.*

That night, Jan 29, 2016 Pat Fallon became only the 14th person in the world to complete The World Marathon Challenge and even more impressively he became the first person in the world, without previous marathon experience, to run 7 marathons in 7 days on 7 continents. Also:

Total Notre Dame Graduates to have completed the
World Marathon Challenge: 1

Total Southern Cal Graduates to have completed the
World Marathon Challenge: 0

Fallon did not have a lucky number before running and completing the World Marathon Challenge, but now he sure does.

I will never look at the number 7 the same ever again.

I ran 7 marathons in 7 days on 7 continents for little Jonny, who was 7 years old when he was diagnosed with this rare form of brain cancer. I flew to my first race on a 777, and I also flew home from my last race on a 777. My bib

number was No. 7 for all 7 races. On race number 7, I broke the 4-hour mark by 7 minutes. On February 7th, we reached our donation target of $77,777.77 on a church donation of $7,000. I will never look at the number 7 the same ever again.

If you'd like to donate to help find a cure for pediatric cancer, please visit:

www.KidsShouldntHaveCancer.org

Pat Fallon and his family.

Pat Fallon's Lessons from the Notre Dame Value Stream:

- For the student-athlete: Know that what you're doing is unique and it's going to pass you by very quickly. Enjoy every second.

- Take full advantage of the opportunities placed in front of you. You'll never have these exact experiences ever again.

- Treat everybody with kindness.

- Appreciate the people who are cheering for you, because we all need people cheering for us in life.

- When you're humble, you set a wonderful example for others.

Portrait of Notre Dame football player Darrell "Flash" Gordon, c1987-1988. Notre Dame University Photographer. (Photo courtesy of Notre Dame Archives.)

CHAPTER NINE

The Youth Developer

Darrell "Flash" Gordon

*W*ith a nickname like "Flash Gordon" you might make the obvious assumption that Darrell "Flash" Gordon was a superhero busy saving the planet earth. While today Darrell Gordon is very much a superhero in the eyes of the many young men whose lives he touches on a daily basis, his beginnings were not as "flashy" as the town he hails from. Raised in Hillside, New Jersey, a community incorporated shortly after the appearance of Hailey's Comet in 1910, Darrell's path towards Notre Dame did not begin with a comet-like flash. Although he was a diligent student and high performing athlete in high school, his college bound path was somewhat diverted due to some typical teenage distractions. After a slight but firm nudge from the Notre Dame recruiters, Gordon promptly corrected his path, was a high school All-American in football, graduated in the top of his class and landed a scholarship to play football at the University of Notre Dame. After a tremendously successful career at Notre Dame which culminated with the fairy tale ending of a national championship in 1988, the successes that Flash has had post football far outshine the spectacular plays that he delighted fans with during his tenure at Notre Dame. How did Flash Gordon end up a superhero in Richmond, Indiana, as a champion for neglected and abused young men? This is Flash Gordon's story.

But when Notre Dame came, they didn't even meet with me

I was born in Jersey City, New Jersey, and when I was five years old we moved to Hillside, New Jersey. During the recruiting process hundreds of colleges were coming to visit my high school and they all had a great pitch as to why I should attend their institution. But when Notre Dame came, they didn't even meet with me; they just went straight to the guidance office and looked at my academic records. Coach Paterno, the head coach from Penn State University came and talked to me at school, but not Notre Dame. They weren't just recruiting athletes, but "student-athletes," and that interested me highly. At the end of my sophomore year / beginning of my junior year, Notre Dame started to lose interest in me. I guess I wasn't performing up to their standards. I wasn't taking high school seriously enough and they indicated that if I didn't start focusing on academics they would no longer pursue me. At that point I really dug in and I ended up graduating near the top of my class. I was also a high school All-American in football.

And just like that, the Notre Dame Value Stream had already found a place in Flash Gordon's life.

I made official visits to Boston College, Pitt, Notre Dame and Penn State; and then I narrowed it down to Penn State and Notre Dame. I really liked what Notre Dame was offering. The thing they said that really caught my eye was this, "we will guarantee your scholarship for four years. Whether you break your leg or it just doesn't work out, we will still guarantee your scholarship for all four years." That was amazing. I wanted to make sure that wherever I went to school there was going to be some sort of security, and in addition to the scholarship guarantee Notre Dame had a really high graduation rate, which was very appealing to me. Some of the schools that I had either looked at or that had expressed interest in me had graduation rates as low as 40%. Notre Dame's graduation rate was right around 99% at the time and that was a big deciding factor for me.

When I visited Notre Dame my host was Allen Pinkett. I made my trip to Notre Dame in the middle of January and it was extremely cold. Allen took me to visit different dorms and in the basement of the dorms they had these parties. When you're visiting schools you need to see which institutions you can bond with both academically and athletically; but being able to have a good time without even leaving the dorm was pretty appealing to me as an 18-year-old kid. The funniest thing is that in between my visit to Notre Dame and actually arriving on campus in the fall they changed the University policy and no longer allowed basement parties in the dorms. Apparently someone had left a party and gotten into an accident and the campus had since become a dry campus. So much for having fun without leaving the dorm! (laughs) Allen Pinkett did a great job of being my host that weekend and convincing me that Notre Dame was where I wanted to be.

Notre Dame's objective was to create relationships.

Coach Faust was really special to me and I still keep in touch with him to this day. When the various coaches came to visit you in high school, they would come to your school and you would get called over the loud speaker to go visit with them in the school library. "Darrell Gordon, please come to the library to see Coach Paterno." Coach Faust was the only head coach who didn't visit me at school. I came home from school one day to find Coach Faust sitting in my living room with my mother having a spaghetti dinner. He also visited my dad at his job, too. Notre Dame's objective was to create relationships. After that visit, all I heard from my parents was how great Notre Dame was and that I needed to go there. They became immediate fans of the University based on that personal touch they were given. Notre Dame felt that if you didn't have a strong family it would cause problems later when the child was off at college and unsupervised. They want to recruit a child who comes from a solid family unit with a strong foundation and good morals.

God would never give you anything you can't handle.
Whether you do handle it is another question. ~ Gerry Faust

The Notre Dame Years

Every student who arrives at the University of Notre Dame for that first year of studies shows up with a desire to create change in the world and an optimism that seems would be unwavering, but then that first bump in the road occurs and your faith is tested. This is where the Notre Dame Value Stream steps in to keep the light shining in Her student's eyes.

Unequivocally my first year at Notre Dame was the most challenging. So much was required of me academically and athletically. I was stepping out onto the field with some of the greatest athletes in the world and it was very intimidating to me. I thought I should start as a freshman, even though I was too small and needed more development. I had to work really hard to get noticed on the field, harder than I ever had to work in high school. Then when I walked into the classroom, I was with some of the brightest minds in the world. They were all valedictorians and had SAT scores that were off the charts. I had to figure out how to manage my time in order to compete both in the classroom and on the field. Or rather to survive in the classroom and excel on the field. I didn't do that too well my first semester. It's the first time you're away from your parents, you're staying up too late, spending too much time with your friends, not really making smart decisions and it really showed up on my grades that semester. At that point I decided to focus my attention on managing my time better.

If you compare a student who only has to focus on school and has a 3.5, and an athlete who has a 3.5, the student-athlete has far surpassed the student. Athletes are often stereotyped as hard workers but in reality they are working twice as hard as they would be if they were only a student. The reason why the graduation rate is so high at Notre Dame is because ND does a great job at securing the better students and keeping them there. While many institutions have a freshman dropout rate of 30 to 40 percent, Notre Dame strives to retain 99% or more of their students from year to year. Notre Dame has a good environment and you want to stay there and graduate.

Flash Gordon and each one of his teammates who were recruited by head coach Gerry Faust to play football at Notre Dame followed him with complete trust and were inspired by his love and passion for the University. And then one day this little man named Lou Holtz came marching in as the new head coach of Notre Dame's football team. Transitions such as this are never easy, but the Notre Dame Value Stream spoke through Coach Holtz 100% and helped make the transition period as painless as it possibly could have been.

Coach Holtz made the transition extremely easy. He was an extremely focused coach. He knew exactly what he wanted to accomplish, how to play the game and what kind of athlete he needed to accomplish his style of play. During his time at Notre Dame he consistently recruited top classes. Then he would master mind the X's and O's on both offense and defense. He perfected that skill set. His greatest asset, though, was as a motivator. His ability to motivate players and to have them at the highest level of their game was off the charts. If you can't motivate your players to play you're missing out on a huge aspect of coaching. He made sure we had what we needed to succeed, both on and off the field. Excellent coaches, tutors for the classroom, and nutritional meal plans.

Speaking of meal plans:

On Fridays throughout the school year they would serve us quiche because there was no meat on Fridays. Coach Holtz went to the administration and said, "How do you expect us to compete on Saturdays when these young men are not getting the nourishment they need on Fridays?!" He took it upon himself to speak with the administration. He wanted us to have the necessary diet that we needed to be able to focus and be able to compete against the highest level of teams across the country. He also knew we would need academic support so he made sure we had tutors and study hall time, but he was still very stern with us.

When Coach Holtz got to Notre Dame, he realized that many of the starters didn't practice during the week until a day or two before the game. This was not how he ran things. On Monday we practiced in t-shirts and shorts. On Tuesday and Wednesday we came out in our entire uniforms. On Thursday we practiced in shoulder pads and shorts, and on Friday we did our walk through drills. Tuesdays and Wednesdays were the days you really executed your game plan for the next game. If you didn't practice until Thursday or Friday you missed out on the execution and strategy for that week's game. Prior to Holtz, if a first stringer was injured he would sit out until Thursday to rest. This meant that the second and third string were ready for game day but not the first string.

Holtz made himself very clear from the start. If you missed practice on Monday, you didn't get to start on Saturday, even if you were a starter. If you missed two practices you didn't get to dress on Saturday. Once everyone heard those expectations, immediate changes were made. Everyone was at practice, every day. Even if you were on crutches, you were dressed, on the field and ready to practice with the intent that if you could practice you would. Those were some of the psychological changes that Coach Holtz made. He knew exactly what he needed to do to transform the team. He knew how to take a team that was struggling and bring them to perfection. Very few coaches have that gift but it all starts with discipline and commitment.

The Notre Dame Value Stream made sure you had the focus and direction needed to be prepared and successful in the classroom. Coach Holtz was also perfectly aligned with the Notre Dame Value Stream and made sure those same values were applied on the football field; even if his delivery was at times a little unconventional.

Gentlemen, I want to tell you one thing. Next time, save Jimmy Johnson for me!

My favorite Notre Dame football memory is the pre-game warm up before the Miami game in 1988. We were warming up and preparing to play the number one team in the country, and we were ranked number two at the time. Miami came to South Bend and they already had an idea of what the Catholics vs. Convicts rivalry meant and they wanted to live up to that image. They were warming up on the far end of the field and we were warming up on the end of the field closest to the tunnel. Each team had a line of players on the 30-yard line so that the other team couldn't see what formations they were practicing. When they were done warming up, instead of going around our line to go back to their locker room they decided to go right through our line. It was very disrespectful and we were high character kids but we could only take so much. Guys started pushing back and forth and a big brawl took place in the tunnel. Finally they separated us and sent us to our respective locker rooms. Guys were bleeding, hyperventilating; it was a mess. We felt like we disappointed the University and our teammates because we didn't conduct ourselves appropriately.

We were sitting there waiting for Coach Holtz to come in and ring us a good one on how we tarnished Notre Dame and how this incident was a nationally televised game. Coach Holtz walks in and says, "Gentlemen, I want to tell you one thing. Next time, save Jimmy Johnson for me!" That was exactly what we needed from Coach Holtz, the endorsement that no one can come in and disrespect our team or our University. After Coach Holtz's speech there was such electricity in the locker room that ignited the team. Here we thought we were going to get scolded and then we were told "save daddy for me!" That really gave us the confidence that we needed to beat the number one team in the country. His words didn't tell us that fighting was okay but rather the importance of fighting for what you believe in. Even though a lot of us were not Catholic, he was showing us how to fight for our respective religions and the issues we believed in. He was teaching us to be better leaders not only on the team but also in our communities and in our country. That was a very profound moment for me, in what it did for me and how it changed my life.

Even though a lot of us were not Catholic, he was showing us how to fight for our respective religions and the issues we believed in.

That same fight that we had on the field against Miami was the same fighting spirit that I had when I wanted to become the CEO of my company and there were seven other people who also wanted to be CEO. You fight for what you believe in, for what you want, and you don't give it away. There isn't a class that teaches more practical knowledge on how to succeed in life than what we learned from Coach Holtz on the football field. What we learned that day was to fight for what we believed in. I share this with my own kids every day as they compete in the classroom, on the basketball court, or on the football field. You have to fight for what you want or someone else will take it.

The lessons that Gordon learned from the Notre Dame Value Stream during his time at ND not only helped him to achieve success both on and off the football field at Notre Dame, but in all aspects of his life through today.

Always know that you are better than the person ahead of you and fight to be recognized as such.

I have two kids; my daughter played in the AAU Basketball All-Star game the summer between 7th and 8th grade. Her team won the national championship for 7th graders and she won MVP performer. She scored approximately 25 points in the championship game. She came off the bench and absolutely excelled. We always talk about the fight. Always knowing you are better than the person ahead of you and fighting to be recognized as such; believing that you don't belong on the bench. In that aspect, it's okay to be feisty.

Following Notre Dame's national title victory in the Fiesta Bowl in January of 1989, the football team was invited to the White House to be recognized for their accomplishments. It was the culmination of everything the Notre Dame Value Stream had taught them and the proof that they had accomplished their mission. Gordon talks about the team's experience at the White House.

The team's experience at the White House

That was really unprecedented. To have the opportunity to go to the White House and be recognized by the President (Bush) and Vice President (Quayle) of the United States; it was so surreal. To be in the White House, in front of two of the most powerful people in the world and to have the opportunity to shake their hands and watch how they work. To be able to evaluate the environment in which they had to operate. To have them recognize a bunch of 18, 19, 20-year-old kids for the accomplishments that they achieved on the field that required so much of our time, effort, discipline and passion. For someone to recognize the years-long investment that we had put in to get to this point; to hear the President say that we deserved it, that was pretty amazing. He seemed like he had a discrete affinity for Notre Dame.

And then that moment of clarity arrives, when you truly see all that the Notre Dame Value Stream has taught you and how it applies to each and every facet of your life.

Until that moment, I didn't realize how valuable the Notre Dame name was, nor did I understand the value of Coach Holtz. When you go to the White House and people tell you that you are at one of the most prestigious institutions in the world, you realize that the choice you made was the right choice.

Professional Career

Following the 1988 football season,

I played in the Hula Bowl All-Star game with Deion Sanders and Troy Aik-man. As a native of New Jersey, I had interest in the New York Giants but ended up hurting my knee during the All-Star game and unfortunately never was able to play in the NFL due to my injury. At that point I decided to focus my attention on work so I finished my master's degree and started working for Frank Eck. Mr. Eck was one of my greatest mentors and taught me how to lead, how to be a CEO and how to manage a company. I worked for Frank Eck (at Advanced Drainage Systems) for about five years serving as his direc-tor of quality control for all of his plants. Then I ran one of his facilities in Ohio followed by becoming a manager of his sales force. I was able to dab into all areas of his business when I was there. Then I decided I wanted to do something different so I went to law school near Cincinnati at Northern Ken-tucky University Law School so that I could become a sports agent. I clerked for Stanley Chesley while I was in law school and ultimately got a job with IMG International Management Group who represented some of the most prolific athletes in the sports world including Joe Montana, Tiger Woods, Wayne Gretzky and Chris Webber. I worked in the football division and worked under one of the most respected sports agents in the world, Tom Con-don. I worked there for one summer but I quickly realized I wasn't interested in chasing down 21-year-old football players to convince them that I should represent them.

Then I changed my career path once more and took a job with the NCAA in Kansas City, at their corporate office, which then later moved to Indianapo-lis. I worked in member services and worked on legislative efforts, which included writing rules and regulations; and then worked in student affairs where I assisted in developing student-athlete programs including the R-I-C-H-E-R program. We did a really great job in developing those programs.

Today

At that point people were starting to take note of what I was doing and I received a phone call from a board member of the Wernle Youth & Family Treatment Center. They were looking for a new CEO and they were inter-ested in me. They had a 72-acre property in Richmond, Ind., which included dorms, an administration building and a workout facility. The organization was struggling financially and it was not well respected in the state of Indi-ana. It was going to be a huge challenge for me. Although I possessed the aca-demic prowess gained from institutions such as University of Notre Dame

(Bachelor's degree in Economics and Business -1988, Master's degree of Science and Administration -1989), Northern Kentucky Chase College of Law (Juris Doctorate – 1997), Harvard Business School (certificate in specialized strategic planning), Indiana University School of Fund Raising (Philanthropy certificate), I lacked the President / CEO experience.

ND developed their students both academically and spiritually.

12 years later we have gone from having a half million dollars in reserves to ten million dollars in total assets. Our program is one of the top three in the country in terms of the work we do educating and rehabilitating young men from 6 to 21 years of age afflicted by such problems as abuse, neglect, mental illness and/or conduct disorder. Our goal is to reunite them with their families after a year of treatment; whether that is their parents, grandparents, foster home or group home. We also have a spiritual component at the center that is affiliated with the Evangelical Lutheran Church of America and we have a pastor living on the grounds. Our program very much reminds me of my time at Notre Dame and how ND developed their students both academically and spiritually. We are investing in the futures of young men and women who have been neglected or abandoned. We are the catalyst of change.

Even when you are no longer at the University, She is never far. The Notre Dame Value Stream stays with you your entire life and is always there to help you just when you need it the most.

We have received a great deal of support from my Notre Dame family. We've had visits from Father John Jenkins, Regis Philbin, Joe Montana, Tim Brown, Tony Rice, Tyrone Willingham, Charlie Weis, Jim Caviezel, Lou Holtz, Jerome Bettis and Allen Pinkett among others. We're currently in the middle of a campaign to raise 10 million dollars for the center. I couldn't be prouder of the work we are doing here. Currently I am working on a book of my own. The title is still a work in progress. It's about change and the process of change as it relates to my job, changing this organization, changing the football program at Notre Dame, changing our families to be successful. Change is a part of life, and in order to flourish in life you must embrace it.

While Gordon was working for the NCAA he became inspired to find a way to reach troubled youth before they got into trouble, and he used the values he learned from the Notre Dame Value Stream to create a character development program for our youth and their families.

I acquired the R-I-C-H-E-R principles when I was working for the NCAA. It was developed for our youth and their families. The NCAA was seeing many former players who were having questionable character issues, so the

NCAA established the Stay in Bounds character development program. With help from Lilly Endowment, Inc., the Stay in Bounds program was a collaborative effort developed by the NCAA, Indianapolis Colts, and Indianapolis Pacers, and was piloted in the Indianapolis schools before it was launched across the country. It was developed because the NFL, NBA, NHL, the Olympic Committee and High School associations came together to deal with these character issues. The NCAA decided to take the lead and create a program they would later pass on to all of these organizations to practice better sportsmanship. The mission of the Stay in Bounds program is to "build good character, foster responsible behavior and encourage enjoyment of healthy competition and cooperation." After three years of hard work we developed one of the greatest character development programs out there.

The R-I-C-H-E-R principles are:

- *Respect*
- *Integrity*
- *Caring*
- *Harmony*
- *Excellence*
- *Responsibility*

Darrell "Flash" Gordon

These six principles are what I live by and I use these principles to make all decisions in my life. Respect: Respect not only those around me but myself as well. Integrity: I have integrity in everything I do. Caring: I care about myself and other people. Harmony: People should want to be around me, and I try to instill harmony in others. Excellence: Everything I do, I do with excellence. If I can't do it with excellence, I don't do it. I expect excellence from others as well. Responsibility: Be responsible. That is so important in my life. If I'm supposed to be somewhere at 6 pm, I show up at 5:55 pm. I may not be perfect at all of these principles, but I work on them and use them every day.

Darrell "Flash" Gordon's Lessons from the Notre Dame Value Stream:

- College is not only a place where student-athletes can develop their athletic abilities but also their academic prowess and spiritual growth. If you commit to those three components then Notre Dame, or a school like Notre Dame, is going to be the place for you.

- When you are a student-athlete in college, school is not about being entertained and partying but developing your inner self, becoming a better person and being able to better contribute to society. You have to make sure that's your purpose if you are going to attend a school like Notre Dame, because if it is not you will find yourself in constant conflict.

Notre Dame vs. Michigan State (MSU), 1988. Kicker Reggie Ho (#2) attempting a field goal or point after attempt. Photo by Chuck Ray. (Photo courtesy of Notre Dame Archives.)

CHAPTER TEN

The Heart Doctor

Reggie Ho

*G*rowing up in Kaneohe on the Hawaiian island of Oahu, Reggie Ho had aspirations in high school of going to college and becoming a doctor. Becoming a legendary kicker on Notre Dame's football team was never on his radar. But as he completed his freshman year at Notre Dame he felt a void in his life and decided to try out for something, and that something was the Notre Dame football team. What happened next was magical. Reggie's journey from the warm tropical breezes of Oahu to blustery South Bend, Indiana, brought him on an adventure he never expected. It brought him the challenge of studying with some of the brightest minds and the challenge of playing football with some of the elite college football players in the land. It gave him the opportunity to receive a pre-med degree from Notre Dame and the opportunity to be an integral part of the Notre Dame football team's national title winning season in 1988. How does a gifted student-athlete from Oahu, Hawaii, help his team win a national title and go on to become a top cardiologist in Philadelphia, Pennsylvania? This is Reggie Ho's story.

Life is about our choices. Wherever you are, good or bad, it's because of the choices you make. ~ Lou Holtz

> *When I was in high school trying to decide where I was going to go to college, I wanted to go to a Catholic school. My older brother and two of my cousins were studying at Notre Dame at the time, and I also had an uncle who had previously attended Notre Dame. Notre Dame was an excellent school, and as a kid who aspired to be a doctor, Notre Dame was a great option and I am glad I got accepted. Football never really entered into my decision. Yes, I had played football in high school, but I never had any intention of continuing that at the collegiate level. Getting a good education and pursing my dreams of becoming a doctor were my primary objectives. What happened once I got to Notre Dame was something I never expected.*

> *When you are at a school like Notre Dame, you are constantly concerned about your grades and whether or not you are succeeding academically. During my freshman year I spent a tremendous amount of time in the library studying. At the end of my freshman year I did pretty well (Reggie had all A's and one A- studying pre-med his freshman year), but I had spent so much time in the library that year and looking back I realized I was missing out on the rest of college. There was more to college than just studying, and I decided that I needed to adjust the balance in my life. I knew I wanted to get involved in something besides my academics, but I wasn't sure exactly what that was. I was a kicker on my high school football team and I had never really thought I'd pursue football at the collegiate level, but after my freshman year, I thought I would give it a try. I was pretty naïve in thinking that a kid from Hawaii could just walk into the football office and try out for the football team, but that's exactly what I did.*

The Notre Dame Years

Even from the very beginning the Notre Dame Value Stream does a great job at keeping Her students' focus strong, and keeping their lives balanced.

> *In the fall of my sophomore year, when we got back to school, I went to the coach's office and asked the secretary if I could try out for the football team. The secretary told me that the coaches were busy and asked me to come back the next day. The next day I came back and she told me the same thing. This*

happened three days in a row. On the fourth day I brought my books and asked her if I could just sit in the lounge and study while waiting for one of the coaches to have time to speak with me. She agreed, and so I sat and waited. A couple of hours went by, people came and went, the secretary left for the day, the cleaning crew came in, and finally one of the coaches (Scott Raridon, the weight training coach) passed by and asked if he could help me. I explained to him that I was waiting to see one of the coaches to talk about trying out for the football team. Then Coach Pete Cordelli came out (the quarterback coach) and told me that I should come back in the spring and attend tryouts. But in the meantime he recommended that I try out for my interhall football team. I was the only kicker on Cavanaugh Hall's interhall football squad and I only had one kick and I made it. Unfortunately, we weren't that good.

During that next year, Ho would take breaks from his evening studying to practice his kicking game. At that time of night, the only place that was bright enough for him to practice that was still open was the D parking lot. In the spring of his sophomore year, Ho went back once more to try out for the football team.

So I came back in the spring to see when the tryouts were and eventually I got to meet with Vinny Cerrato, who was the special teams coach, and he explained to me when tryouts were and how they worked. I arrived at Cartier field and eight people were trying out for the kicking position. I had no idea that many people would be trying out for kicker. John Carney was graduating that year and Ted Gradel, who was the kicker behind John Carney, had decided to stay on for a fifth year, hoping to finally become the starter after playing behind Carney for four years.

I was more scared of being yelled at by Coach Holtz than I was of getting booed at by fifty-nine thousand people in the stadium.

First we did kickoffs, and then we did 10 field goals each. Some straight on, some from the right and left hash, and then from varying distances ... 30 yards, 40 yards and 50 yards. There were 10 kicks in total that we had to attempt. I made 9 out of 10, missing the 50-yard kick. Ted (Gradel) and Jim (Sacco) made 8 out of 10. Everyone else made less than eight. They kept Ted, Jim and me on the squad, and I started practicing with the team in my junior year. I was so surprised and excited! When I went to the locker room for the first practice, I was completely shocked to find out that I was tentatively number one on the posted depth chart. And then Coach Holtz arrived at the practice field in his golf cart. Before Coach Holtz arrived, I was okay; but when he came over and asked who I was, I was very nervous. During what was my first kick in front of him, I kicked the ball into our lineman. That's how I started my time on the Notre Dame football team in front of Coach Holtz. His style of coaching by intimidation was very important. I was more scared of being yelled at by Coach Holtz than I was of getting booed at by fifty-nine thousand people in the stadium.

For a kid who went from no one to a pretty important someone in Notre Dame football, Ho approached the game with a great determination and took in every single moment with equally great appreciation. The Notre Dame Value Stream teaches Her students and student-athletes to not only work hard for what they want but to appreciate the journey as well.

I think the Michigan game (September 10, 1988) would be my best memory. The first home game of my senior year (1988) was against Michigan, and it was the first time I ever got to start. I had a feeling I was going to start because I was on the first team and then, the night before the game, Coach Stewart confirmed my hunch and told me I was going to start. When I ran out onto the field, knowing that I was Notre Dame's starting kicker, that truly was my most memorable moment at ND. Another huge highlight for me was kicking an extra point against Navy the year before. That was my first play in a game, and I could have died and gone to heaven at that point. I literally could have never played another play at Notre Dame and would have been totally okay with that. It was amazing to just have any part in Notre Dame football!

Getting on the field before a high school size crowd is one thing, but getting on the field in front of 59,000 screaming fans is an entirely different experience all together. The Notre Dame Value Stream does its best to make sure you are prepared, but then you have to take it from there. Reggie talks about the transition from high school to the big stage at Notre Dame and how he dealt with the nervous butterflies.

The very first kick of a game is always somewhat anxiety provoking. Back during the Michigan game, the first kick I had was a field goal. I was nervous in the sense that it was the first game where I was the starter and it really mattered, as opposed to the kick I made in the Navy game, which wasn't crucial to the outcome of the game (Notre Dame was winning handily over Navy). The Michigan game was surreal. I was nervous but at the same time had a sense of calm and confidence. We were not going to let any team come into our stadium and beat us. We were ready to hit the field, to start the game, and just ready to get out there, play and give it your very best. It was an unknown kind of situation and I was going to give it my best and get the ball through the upright. Whether the game was on the line or not, Coach Holtz expected perfection. You absolutely did not want to miss and get yelled at by Coach Holtz. Even when we were beating Rice that year, you didn't want to do anything that would cause Coach Holtz to yell at you!

Anyone who watched Reggie Ho kick in the 1980s remembers his unique kicking style. It may not have looked like any other kicker out there at the time, but it worked for Ho, and at the end of the day that's all that matters.

My style looked pretty unorthodox.

I am a small individual and don't have the greatest of leg strength compared to someone who is bigger than me. My thought process was if I could "pull" the ball that I would be able to kick the ball farther. But the problem is if you pull the ball like that you tend to lose accuracy. So the more I practiced my kicking style of pulling the ball in order to kick it farther, the more accurate I would become, and so that's what I did. In order the pull the ball the way I did, I had to kick it at more of an angle than most other kickers, so my style looked pretty unorthodox.

Reggie kept a notebook in which he detailed the physics of kicking. His "pull theory" was that as a kicker with a smaller stature he should "pull the ball consistently each time," like pulling a ball during a bat or golf swing. And then there is "the voodoo," as it was called. Reggie Ho used to hold his arms to one side and wiggle his fingers before he would kick the ball.

That was just my way of being able to relax, to focus on the ball and not worry about anything else. It made me feel more comfortable about how I "pulled" the ball when I kicked it and helped me to concentrate. You don't want anything to distract you when you're trying to make that kick. There is so much going on around you, this was just my way of focusing on the ball and how I was going to pull it just right so that it made it through the uprights. Rituals were a way to help you concentrate and do things over and over the same way despite stress-provoking situations.

No matter who you were on the team, from the starting quarterback on down to the guys on the bench, you were completely terrified of Coach Holtz, and you did everything within your power to stay off his radar at all costs. Reggie Ho was no different.

As a kicker, one of the things I tried to do was avoid Coach Holtz! If he's not stuck to you like glue, that's a good thing. The whole role of the kicker is to kick the ball and get it through the uprights, and, if you do that, he's not going to bother you. If I could avoid being in his office then I was doing my job right. Fortunately, I didn't have too many interactions with Coach Holtz. One nice memory I have of Coach Holtz is after we won the Michigan game my senior year, he asked me to come stand up on a stool and he recognized me in front of the entire team. Very seldom did we highlight an individual because football is a team effort and games are not won by the actions of one person but by the actions of the whole team. Being recognized like that by Coach Holtz was very nice on his part. One of the not so nice memories came a few weeks after the Michigan game, when I wasn't kicking the ball too well. He had me line up and kick field goals in practice. He told me if I missed one kick he would make the entire team run. On one of my kicks, which I was sure had made it through the uprights, did not according to Coach Holtz and the whole team had to run. Letting your team down is the worst feeling in the world. Coach Holtz put so much pressure on us in practice to make sure we would be 100% prepared on Saturday. I respect him so much for how he pre-pared us for life.

Perhaps the nicest memory I have of Coach Holtz is from the Fiesta Bowl in Tempe, Arizona when we beat West Virginia to win the national champi-onship. After the game, and right before we broke off to see our families, we had Mass together. Coach Holtz got up and spoke to us during Mass. Here he is, standing in front of this group of young 18-21 year old men who had just won the national title, and he told us that, as important as this day was for us, this was not the most important thing in life. He told us, family and God, now those things were really the important things. I always respected him for that. Yes, what we had done was a big thing, but there is so much in life that is bigger than that. He really knew how to put things into perspective. He told us, you go out there and hug the people who got you here: your parents, your brothers and sisters, the fans. It's the whole Notre Dame family who is involved here. As you get older in life, you realize how true that really is.

Notre Dame was so much more to us than just academics and athletics. It taught us about service to others and how to live a good life. ~ Reggie Ho

Just as head coach Lou Holtz prepared his players for the game of football, the Notre Dame Value Stream prepares students of Our Lady's University for the game of life. And regardless of where you go in life, with that Notre Dame degree in your back pocket you'll always have the Notre Dame Value Stream and the Notre Dame fam-ily there to support you. That support begins when you're a student.

Being a student-athlete at Notre Dame required a lot of juggling and bal-ancing of time. Your time was limited by everything you had to get done. First and foremost you are a student and you want to do your best to keep your grades up. I wanted to get into medical school, so school was very important to me but it was very challenging because football took up so much of my time. It's not just during the fall or on Saturdays, it's year round. Winter workouts, spring ball, summer workouts, fall camp, daily practices, the games themselves which require a great deal of preparation, traveling, team meetings; and in the meantime you also have to keep up with the academic side of things.

When we actually had time away from the football field I would try to get in as much studying as I could. For example, when we played Michigan State we would take a bus there so I would study on the bus on the way there as well as on the way home. Yes, on the way home you'd be exhausted, but you still needed to at least try and get some studying done. Then when we'd get back to campus, I would go to the library for a few more hours instead of celebrating or even just relaxing in my room. I would always try to find my quiet place so that I could keep myself on track and maintain my class work. I wanted to accomplish something while I was at Notre Dame. I wanted to find balance in studying and football and be successful in both. I definitely learned time management skills and how to multi-task. When I got to medical school I already had discipline. Notre Dame taught me how to be successful.

Your parents and teachers do their best to prepare you for college, but I really didn't know all that it took to be successful both academically and athletically until I was there. On my own, away from family and friends, it's up to you to succeed and to find your way. As student-athletes, we all shared a similar bond. We were there to study and learn academically, athletically and spiritually. You make lifelong friends when you're at a school like Notre Dame. My teammates, they are like family. When you're in the trenches with someone, you see who they really are and that bond becomes unbreakable. You know so much about them, like brothers. We can go years without seeing each other and then, when we reconnect, we pick right up where we left off.

Professional Career

Following a tremendously successful career at Notre Dame, both on and off the field, Ho took his coveted Notre Dame degree and pursued his dreams of practicing medicine.

After I graduated from Notre Dame I attended medical school at the University of Pennsylvania in Philadelphia. I began medical school and learned the different disciplines of medicine and was very interested in the diagnosis of diseases. Internal medicine was the first thing I was truly interested in, largely because I had been exposed to it growing up as my dad was in internal medicine/oncology. Cardiology was also interesting to me. It involved a lot of physics, electronics and the practical applications of those principles in how the heart works, and I found this very intellectually stimulating. I ended up gravitating towards cardiovascular medicine and decided it would be a great calling for me. It was somewhere I could truly make a difference and help others. I specialize in the electrotherapy of the heart, for my field there are a lot of things that I can do from a surgical standpoint; from pacemakers to defibrillator implantations. It is also very intellectually gratifying for me.

Today

Ho currently lives in Philadelphia with his wife and two children (2nd grade and 6th grade), and is a cardiologist at Thomas Jefferson University Hospital.

Overachievement is a stereotype that is often used to describe successful Notre Dame Alumni. As a national championship kicker and cardiologist, Ho may seem to fit this label, but that is not how he sees himself.

Dream big and live your life to its greatest potential.

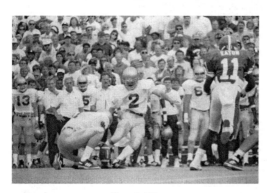

Reggie Ho

I never really thought of being an overachiever. I have always wanted to do all that I could do in my life. My first goal was to get into medical school, but then I realized that there was more to life than academics and that's when I decided to try out for the football team. I worked very hard to be successful at Notre Dame, but there was also a certain amount of luck and being in the right place at the right time. It wasn't just me; it was the support of my family, friends and teammates that helped me to be successful at Notre Dame. It was the whole team who won the national championship, not one individual. I've never seen myself as an overachiever, I see myself as doing my best, and I still hopefully have a lot to do in my life including raising a family and helping my patients.

Reggie Ho's Lessons from the Notre Dame Value Stream:

- Do your best, try hard, trust yourself and be confident.

- Take the time to thank those around you who are helping you and always have a strong belief in yourself.

- Everything you do, do it to the best of your ability.

- Make sure you go through the details of everything, be wise in how you spend your time and work hard. In the end, I think it all works out for everyone.

- Whether you are successful or not, going through tough times is just as important as achieving great things. Even if I had not made the football team at Notre Dame, the process of trying out would have been just as important.

- Dream big and live your life to its greatest potential.

Portrait of Notre Dame football player Pat Eilers, c1988-1989. Notre Dame University Photographer. (Photo courtesy of Notre Dame Archives.)

CHAPTER ELEVEN

The Equity Grower

Pat Eilers

*A*t Notre Dame the improbable occurs on a daily basis. You have students at Notre Dame, and you have student-athletes at Notre Dame and then you have individuals like Pat Eilers. When Pat Eilers was looking at colleges Notre Dame did not offer a bio-medical engineering program, but that didn't deter Pat from pursuing his dream to attend Notre Dame. Instead, he graduated with degrees in both Biology (pre-med) ('89) and Mechanical Engineering ('90). In addition, he played both football (a member of the 1988 national championship team) and baseball. Pat went on to play in the NFL for the Minnesota Vikings, Washington Redskins, and Chicago Bears. He then embarked upon a successful career in the private equity industry. Pat currently lives in Chicago with his wife and four children: Elizabeth (ND '15), Katherine (ND '17), Clare (ND '20), and Patrick. How does a kid who initially enrolled at Yale to receive an Ivy League education and play football for the Yale Bulldogs end up on a national championship team at Notre Dame? This is Pat Eilers' story.

The dream to play football at Notre Dame is shared by many high school athletes around the country. But more often than not, that dream of running out of that tunnel at Notre Dame never becomes a reality. Pat Eilers thought he was going to be one of those kids.

> *I broke my collarbone halfway through the football season of my senior year in high school at St. Thomas Academy in Minnesota. We went undefeated during the regular season but I played in only five of the nine games, given the injury. In the first game of the playoffs we lost in overtime to our rival, Cretin High School. I was a skilled, well... semi-skilled, position player from Minnesota. Given the injury, I wasn't heavily recruited by the major Division I schools, but rather by several Ivy League schools. Ultimately, I did not receive a scholarship offer from any of the major Division I schools and decided to attend Yale to play football and baseball, thinking it would be a really good fit for me.*

> *During my first year of college, I played on the freshmen football team at Yale (freshmen weren't allowed to play varsity). Our last game of the season was against Harvard, known as "The Game." My dad had come to New Haven to see me play and to go to the varsity game as well. As we sat watching the varsity play in the Yale Bowl, which was approximately half full, it simply could not compare to the times my dad had taken me to see a Notre Dame football game where the stadium was always sold out. Sitting there watching the Yale-Harvard varsity game, I told my dad while Yale was a great school, I had great friends and was committed to finish my freshman year, I would consider transferring to Notre Dame in the spring.*

Once again, the Notre Dame Value Stream began its magical pull.

I'd rather go to Notre Dame and never play than stay at Yale and never find out if I could have made it.

> *Before I left New Haven in the spring, I went to the football coach's office to see my coach, Coach Kelly. I told him I was going to my sister's graduation at Notre Dame and had also set up a meeting with Coach Holtz. I explained to him that I intended to transfer to Notre Dame. Coach Kelly told me that he didn't think it would be a good decision; he thought I had a good football career ahead of me at Yale and I would most likely go to Notre Dame and not play at all. I replied while that may be true, I'd rather go to Notre Dame and*

never play than stay at Yale and always wonder what would have happened, if I did transfer. So as I drove home to Minnesota, I stopped by Notre Dame for my sister's graduation and had my meeting with Coach Holtz.

The Notre Dame Years

A sit-down with Coach Holtz is never an easy thing, especially when you aren't even on coach's radar and are trying to explain to him why he should take a chance on you. But quite quickly, Coach Holtz could see the Notre Dame Value Stream was already firmly planted within Pat Eilers.

> *I explained to Coach Holtz that I had been accepted as a transfer student and asked him if he would allow me to try out for the team in the fall as a walk-on. He told me I could walk on and further, if I proved I could contribute to the team by vying for a starting position, there would be an opportunity for me to earn a scholarship. I practiced that fall with the scout team as a tail-back (I was ineligible to play that fall due to the transfer rules). In the spring, I was switched to strong safety. Coming out of spring ball, George Streeter and I were competing for the starting job and Coach Holtz, true to his word, awarded me a scholarship.*

We all know what a tremendously successful head coach Lou Holtz is, but one of his greatest strengths was his ability to place players in the correct positions for their particular strengths and talents.

> *Coach Holtz did a great job of identifying where each player's attributes could most benefit the team. I went from a running back as a transfer sophomore, to a strong safety in the spring and following fall, to a flanker/split end for the remaining part of my career at Notre Dame. Coach Holtz and his staff should be complimented for finding the roles where each player could best utilize his God-given ability. He developed an attitude amongst the team where everyone was respected, regardless of his role. Players put the team first. To have that many personalities and egos put their own personal goals and ambitions behind that of the team and University-oriented goals, that's a pretty unique accomplishment for a coach and his staff.*
>
> *Coach Holtz also never let complacency enter the equation. I'll use the '88 team as an example. We were 12-0 on Saturday, but we were 0-12 on Sunday. What I mean is that after each win we would go to watch film on Sunday, and despite there being plenty of positive reinforcement, the staff always identified numerous ways we could improve. Each Monday, Coach Holtz would tell us that it was going to be really, really difficult to beat whoever we were playing the following Saturday. On Tuesday, Coach would tell us if we*

bought into the game plan that we might actually have a chance. By Wednesday, he would tell us that he could see the light at the end of the tunnel. On Thursday, he was feeling really good about our chances, and on Friday it was almost a foregone conclusion that we would prevail on Saturday with another victory.

Coach Holtz excelled at making absolutely sure his team was prepared for the game, not only physically, but mentally as well.

Practices under Coach Holtz were incredibly more difficult than game day ever was.

Each Friday night we'd have a "relaxation session" with Coach Holtz. He'd have us lay on the floor at Loftus (Sports Center) and have us visualize doing our jobs, making big plays and the team winning the game. By Saturday pregame, he'd tell us there was no way we could lose, and sure enough we won. Then on Sunday, we'd start the whole process all over again. As a college freshman or sophomore you didn't realize what was happening to you each week, but you eventually understood as a junior and senior that striving for excellence requires the team to be frightened of becoming complacent. Practices under Coach Holtz were incredibly more difficult than game day ever was. If you could survive practice, then chances were you'd be very successful during the game.

There are definitely times when you think the Notre Dame Value Stream is trying to drown you, but in the end you realize that the challenges it brought to you were only there to strengthen you and to ensure your success in the end.

Four years at Notre Dame fly by all too fast and are filled with memories, choosing one or two favorites is never easy to do. But Pat has two that definitely stand out for him, one from his first spring practice, and one from a Saturday afternoon in 1988.

We were in spring practice during my sophomore year, I was playing strong-safety and my good friend Andy Heck (currently the Offensive Line Coach for the Kansas City Chiefs) was playing tight end. I was lined up against Andy and he held me on a running play where the running back broke contain and ran for fifteen yards. I heard Coach Holtz holler,

"Eilers, I'm trying to find you a position, son. Maybe you should have kept your ass at Yale."

I responded, "Coach, I didn't transfer from Yale not to play."

Coach Holtz replied, "Run the play again."

I lined up across from Andy again— mind you I was 200 pounds and he weighed 300 — I held contain this time, stopping the running back at the line of scrimmage.

Coach Holtz came up and tapped me on the helmet and said, "I think you're going to be okay son."

That was a seminal moment for me that spring. I was either going to be written off by Coach or be a part of his plans. At that moment I felt as though I was going to get a shot to contribute and play. Andy Heck ultimately switched from tight end to tackle – where he went on to become a first round draft pick for the Seattle Seahawks. Andy was probably the highest paid guy coming out of Notre Dame, I was a free agent.

That Notre Dame Value Stream always knows when you need a life vest to keep you afloat.

My other favorite moment occurred during the 1988 Notre Dame-Miami game. Miami's quarterback was Steve Walsh, who also was the quarterback of my high school rival, Cretin. In my senior year of high school we beat Cretin during the regular season where I had intercepted Steve twice, but they went on to beat us in the first playoff game. Walsh and I also played together when we were both with the Chicago Bears. Now we were playing against each other on a much bigger stage. A lot of people from St. Paul came to see both of us play. Steve played really well that day, but thankfully we won. Coach Holtz called my number close to the Miami goal-line and I scored the first touchdown of my career. It was a thrill to score a touchdown in the south end zone and look up and see Touchdown Jesus over the top of the north-end of the stadium. Beating Miami is something I will never forget; they came into the game ranked number one and hadn't lost in a couple of years. Our 1988 Notre Dame team went on to an undefeated season and won the national championship. Truly an unforgettable year.

RoboCop

One of Pat's teammates told me a story about a nickname - RoboCop - that they had given Pat at Notre Dame, and so I asked Pat to explain how the nickname came to be. (Pat laughs.)

Well, for starters, the only All-American award/recognition I attained in college was being named an All-American in strength and conditioning. I wasn't nearly as fast as Rocket or Ricky Watters but I was fast enough, and I had the strength of a lineman. There was a character named RoboCop in the Terminator movies and they thought I looked/moved like him. I was less fluid and more robotic than other skilled position players and that is how I believe I got the nickname Robocop, from Tony (Rice) and my receivers' coach, Pete Cordelli.

The Notre Dame Value Stream plays an important role in a student-athlete's time at Notre Dame by preparing them not only for the opportunity to potentially play sports at the next level, but ultimately to prepare them to be successful in life, no matter where life may take them. For Pat, this was definitely the case.

For me, one of the most important benefits of attending Notre Dame was learning to balance both work in the classroom and on the field. The Notre Dame faculty and coaches taught us how to be successful at both academics and athletics. There was a time at Yale in the 80s and before, when its football teams were competing for the national title, but the Ivy League made a decision to not continue investing at a level so its football programs could compete for national titles. In my mind, they sacrificed their football programs' ability to compete for national titles. Some SEC schools, on the other hand, would appear to sacrifice their academic focus, witnessed by their anemic graduation rates. Stanford has done an excellent job in all their athletic endeavors, witnessed by their perennial first place finishes in the Sears Director's Cup while excelling academically. I feel at Notre Dame we strive for excellence in both academics and athletics, but also in the student-athletes' spiritual development.

Father John Jenkins says it very eloquently, "We strive to be the pre-eminent Catholic, faith-based research institution in the world," and that means a lot to me. Not only have some schools sacrificed their football programs along the way, but they also lost their religious focus. Being a student-athlete at Notre Dame meant I didn't have to sacrifice my pursuit of excellence in academics, athletics, or developing myself spiritually. That was the big appeal to me.

And this is where the Notre Dame Value Stream truly took hold of Pat.

Pursue the Improbable ~ Professor Pierce

Like everyone in college, you definitely had to sacrifice. In particular I sacrificed a lot of sleep. There is an American Studies professor at Notre Dame, Professor Pierce, who spoke at my freshman daughter's athletic orientation (at Notre Dame). He gave what I call his "improbable speech." His speech went something like this: "you are told in today's society that you can't strive to be excellent in both academics and athletics. If your pursuit is academics, then you certainly can't excel in athletics and if your pursuit is athletics, then you certainly can't excel in academics. But at Notre Dame we pursue excellence in both, so we pursue the improbable." Professor Pierce then states, "when you get hurt and you have to play, press on. When you are in the classroom and get an unsatisfactory grade, press on. When you get home from training table and you still have a 10-page paper to write that evening, press on." I played both baseball and football at ND, and as long as we didn't have a baseball game, I'd be at spring football practice. It was grueling balancing the rigorous academics while playing two sports, but it is a big reason why I am who I am today.

While everyone who ends up at Notre Dame would love to stay there forever, eventually you have to move on and chart your next path. With two quite impressive Notre Dame degrees in hand, Pat's next path would be a trip to the NFL.

Professional Career

Notre Dame didn't have a bio-medical engineering program when I was a student there, so I pursued degrees in mechanical engineering and biology (pre-med). I graduated after my fourth year of college with a biology degree and given my transfer I had a fifth year of eligibility to play football. I stayed and used up my athletic eligibility and finished my mechanical engineering degree. I contemplated going to medical school, but I was given the opportunity to play in the NFL and was also able to work in the private equity industry during the offseason. I decided against going back to medical school after I finished my football career given my age and the number of year's medical school and specialization would have taken.

I received several phone calls in the later rounds of the NFL draft but was not selected. After the draft was over, I received offers from four NFL teams. The Bears and Saints were looking at me as a receiver while the Giants and Vikings were interested in me as a safety. I felt safety was my more natural position. At Notre Dame, we ran more of a run/option-style offense, which is why I was able to play flanker. However, I wasn't an NFL-style receiver so I knew my chances to make a team were much better at the safety position. And seeing that I was from Minnesota, and my wife (whom I met between my junior and senior years in college) was already living in the Twin Cities, it made sense to take the offer from the Vikings. And so that's what I did.

During my rookie year in the NFL in 1990, only two free agents made it (with the Vikings), me and John Randall. Signing with Minnesota and making the team my rookie season was a real thrill; I was playing for my hometown team, in effect a dream come true. I played predominantly special teams, and at safety on third down, short yardage, and goal-line situations. During the last game of my first preseason just before final cuts, I was told by our head coach, Jerry Burns, "Pat, in order to make the team you need to

116 | LISA KELLY

make every tackle on kick-off." On the first kickoff you're thinking to yourself, not only are you competing against the other team but now you're competing with your own teammates, too. I made the first tackle and came off the field and Coach Burns told me, "One down, but you need to make a few more!" I made the team, and ended up playing in the NFL for 6 years.

My car got shipped from Minnesota to Arizona on Saturday, and I was cut on Monday.

And just when Pat thought he had his path figured out, his course changed ever so abruptly.

After two years with the Vikings, I was a free agent and Coach Green came in as the new head coach. The Vikings did not choose to protect me and I received three other free agent offers. In addition to an offer from the Vikings, they came from the Arizona Cardinals, the Buffalo Bills, and the Washington Redskins. The Cardinals offered me the best contract with the largest signing bonus, so that's where I decided to go. Unfortunately, it didn't work out. My wife moved to Arizona on a Friday, my car got shipped from Minnesota to Arizona on Saturday, and I was cut on Monday, it was extremely disappointing. Ironically, another Notre Dame player, Dave Duerson, ended up being the last safety to make the team. That was the low point of my professional football career. We drove back to Minnesota and I resumed my full-time off-season job as a venture capitalist. As I worked, I flew around working out for the NFL teams who were interested in signing me.

Charley Casserly, the general manager of the Washington Redskins, and head coach Joe Gibbs showed a particular interest in me. Charley kept telling me that they were going to sign me. Finally, I flew out to DC and went in to see Mr. Casserly. I introduced myself to the receptionist, BJ, and said "I'm here to see Mr. Casserly." Casserly came out and said, "Pat, what is this all about?" I replied, "You've talked to me repeatedly about bringing me in to sign me and I decided it was time to figure out whether you are going to get this done or not. I either need to do this or put this behind me." He asked me if I could wait and went back into his meeting. After three hours, he came back and asked me if I could stay overnight and workout the following day. After my workout the next day, the Redskins signed me. Playing for Joe Gibbs was a tremendous experience; Coach Gibbs stays in contact with all his former players to this day. That was a real high point in my NFL career. I ended up playing for the Redskins for three years. My last NFL stop was with the Chicago Bears under Dave Wanstedt in 1995.

Failures are expected by losers, ignored by winners. ~ Coach Joe Gibbs

The Notre Dame Value Stream has a remarkable way of not only preparing you for the unexpected, but also making sure that there is always another door opening just around the corner.

> *What I learned from the whole Cardinals/Redskins experience was this: I chose to play with the Cardinals because they had offered me the largest signing bonus and biggest contract, and I ignored where my heart was, given the organizational fit and my comfort with the coaches and teammates in Washington, DC. This ended up being a great learning experience. When the Redskins, an organization and group of people that I believed in (I really admired and respected what Coach Gibbs stood for) decided to sign me, things ended up working out for the best. I learned an important life lesson that I've never forgotten, which is making decisions based solely for monetary reasons should not be the sole factor in making the best decisions.*

Today

Unlike so many players who are lost when their NFL careers are over, Pat took steps to make sure that his transition from the NFL to post football life was a seamless one.

> *During my six NFL off-seasons, I initially worked at IAI Venture Capital for Steven Rothmeier in Minneapolis and then at Jordan Industries for Jay Jordan and Tom Quinn. After I was done playing in the NFL, I continued to work at Jordan Industries. Then, I decided to go back to business school and get a MBA at the Northwestern's Kellogg School of Business. After receiving my MBA in 1999, I was hired by Madison Dearborn Partners ("MDP"), a private equity firm in Chicago managing $18 billion. In 2016, I joined BlackRock, Inc., a $4.65 trillion (as of December 31, 2015) asset management firm catering to institutional, intermediary, and individual clients worldwide.*

Pat's journey on the Notre Dame Value Stream had its ups and downs, but his journey was always redirected in a positive course when the waters got rough. As he looks back on his time at Notre Dame and what he learned beyond the academics and X's and 0's, he appreciates the man he has become.

Say you used football and that football didn't use you. ~ Chuck Forman

> *If you are a student-athlete at Notre Dame, remember that college is about developing yourself academically, athletically, and spiritually. You can't let any one of these endeavors jeopardize your development in any of the others. You have to try and develop all three and to do this, you will likely end up*

Pat Eilers

sacrificing sleep and some social activities in college. Just like Professor Pierce at Notre Dame said, you try to accomplish the improbable on a daily basis. You need to ignore the conventional wisdom that you cannot pursue excellence in both academics as well as athletics. Chuck Forman, the all-pro running back from Minnesota told me, "Pat, make sure when you look back on your football career you can say you used football and that football didn't use you." He told me there were a lot of people who wanted to be around him while he was playing football, but disappeared when he was done. It took him two years to realize that he had to get up and start another career post-football (selling copiers). He said, "You should work during the offseason to develop a second career." The average dura-tion of a career in the NFL is 2.8 years, that's why they say NFL stands for "Not For Long" — 2.8 years is hardly what you would call a career.

Pat Eilers' Lessons from the Notre Dame Value Stream:

- Remember a successful college career is when you develop yourself academically, athletically and spiritually. You shouldn't let any one of these endeavors jeopardize your development in the other areas.

- You need to ignore the conventional wisdom that you cannot pursue excellence in both academics and athletics.

- Every person's contribution to the team is equally important... *often times teammates are respected simply because they are able to produce on the field, but everyone who contributes to the team, including the team managers and those sitting on the bench, as examples, are just as impor-tant as the superstar on the team.*

- Always stay humble. *Remember to remain humble — that is para-mount, because one day you are drinking the wine while the next day you may be crushing the grapes.*

- The person you deem successful is only successful because they have failed more than anyone else, but they never gave up.

Success breeds complacency. One time I was at an event with Coach Holtz and he said, "Pat, you look around the room and there are a lot of successful people here, but if you are not careful, success breeds complacency."

Portrait of Notre Dame football player Martin Scruggs, 1988.
Photo by Bradley Photographers. (Photo courtesy of Notre Dame Archives.)

CHAPTER TWELVE

The Data Protector

Martin Scruggs

"*F*riday night lights" at a high school in Texas is like nothing else you've ever seen. From parades and pep rallies to marching bands: the whole town is there and everything is larger than life. And if you play football in Texas and show any kind of promise, the colleges will inevitably come knocking; regardless of whether or not you want to play football at the college level. Martin Scruggs was a late entry to the high school football scene in Texas, but he loved it and excelled at it, which made the mailbox fill up and the phone start to ring. When he received a letter from Notre Dame his short list took a northern turn. The opportunity at Notre Dame was unique because Martin could both play football and participate in ROTC. So this military brat headed north to South

Bend, Indiana, to see what Notre Dame was all about. The journey ended up being more than Martin could have ever imagined: a national championship, an outstanding education, and a career in the military. How does a student balance playing football at Notre Dame and the regimens of Air Force ROTC and then soar off to a military career? This is Martin Scruggs' story.

I grew up in a military family and lived in several states before I landed in Abilene, Texas, which is where I went to high school. High school football is huge in Texas and I was sort of a late bloomer when it came to football. I played football at Cooper High School and I was just playing to play. I wasn't trying to land a scholarship to play college football; that is until my coach started taking a bit more interest in what I was doing. And then the college letters started coming. The first letter I received was from Notre Dame. I had no idea where Notre Dame was; I had to look at the return address to see that it was in Indiana. When it came time to seriously look at schools my short list was: Texas A&M, TCU, Notre Dame and the Air Force Academy. I made visits to all of these schools as well as the University of Houston. The Air Force Academy was my first choice as I grew up in a military family and I was in Air Force Junior ROTC in high school; that is until I realized that I could do Air Force ROTC at Notre Dame and skip some of the drills by playing football. I visited Notre Dame in December and ended up being on the same flight as Tim Brown. He was flying back to South Bend from New York City (they routed my flight to South Bend through NYC) after being presented with the Heisman Trophy Award the night before. There was a ton of excitement on campus. My host for my visit was Cornelius "Corny" Southall who ended up being my big brother through Notre Dame football's big brother program.

As a military kid, Scruggs was used to the rigors of academics, sports and ROTC in high school, but when you bump that up to the college level it can be quite daunting. Most students would find juggling academics and ROTC in college to be strenuous, let alone add playing Division I football. But the Notre Dame Value Stream always knows how much we can handle and helps us maneuver through our to-do list, showing us that success is within our reach.

The Notre Dame Years

My biggest challenge at Notre Dame was learning how to balance the rigorous demands of academics and football simultaneously, especially freshman year. Keeping up with 15 to 18 credit hours, ROTC and football took quite a balancing act. Figuring out how much time you needed to spend studying and working that study time around football practice, travel and games came with a little trial and error that first year. I started out as an aerospace engineering major and ended up switching to government/political science. Trying to keep up with physics and calculus my freshman year while playing football caused me to decide that I needed to find a major that was slightly less demanding. I originally thought I was going to be a pilot and/or design planes but in hindsight it is difficult to decide at 18-years-old what you want to do for the rest of your life.

In hindsight it is difficult to decide at 18-years-old what you want to do for the rest of your life.

Head football coach at Notre Dame is an arduous job, but coach Lou Holtz is in a very special group of Notre Dame head coaches. He seemed to accept the challenges in front of him effortlessly, and developed the young men who played for him, mind, body and spirit using the Notre Dame Value Stream.

One of the things that made Coach Holtz so unique was that he really cared for his players and for their development into young men. He was one of the few college coaches who stressed academics during the recruiting process as opposed to only selling me on the accolades of the football program. He emphasized the importance of academics and that Notre Dame football players are expected to be professional in everything they do, both on and off the field. Many of the other universities that I visited had academic standards but it was not stressed. One school even told me that although I had to meet with the academic folks, that academics weren't really stressed there. Coach Holtz will always have a unique place at Notre Dame. While other coaches may come along and win national titles, Coach Holtz did it with standards that will always give him a place all his own.

Did I mention that you're never late to a Coach Holtz meeting? Never.

One thing about Coach Holtz that really stands out in my memory was his sense of discipline and how he held the upperclassmen responsible for molding and shaping those young men below them. Did I mention that you're never late to a Coach Holtz meeting? Never. I remember rushing over to go to a meeting when I was running late and when I got there the door was closed. Once the door was closed you couldn't go in, you had to stand there and wait because you knew exactly what was going to happen when the door opened. I was a freshman, and Dean Brown was also late that day, so we're both standing there waiting, waiting, waiting. And finally Coach Holtz comes out and gives us this intense look. He starts yelling at Dean, "How can I expect to have the underclassmen here on time when you can't even get here on time? How can I teach them when you're not doing what you're supposed to be doing!"

He taught us how to do it correctly on the field and then how to translate that into successful careers off the field. Jerome Bettis and Tim Brown are prime examples; successful NFL careers and then successful post-NFL careers. And then there are guys like Rocket (Raghib "Rocket" Ismail), who give back to current student-athletes. Coach Holtz taught us to give back to the community both during and after football. He made sure the older guys set a good example for the younger guys. And he made sure that we knew that even though we all weren't going to play in the NFL, there is plenty of life to live after football. Another great thing about Coach Holtz is that he encouraged each and every one of us to follow our dreams. He never once told me I couldn't do football and ROTC. I did Air Force ROTC all four years at Notre Dame. The ROTC program was excited about having a football player on board and vice versa; and it was a natural fit for me after doing football and ROTC in high school. I still had to go to drills and the ROTC classes but as I moved up the ranks into senior leadership I was able to manage the two schedules better. They knew that my being a football player meant that I was in good shape, so that got me out of some of the early morning runs, which meant I only had to do the mandatory ones. The football program also made allowances for me when I had ROTC activities to attend. Both the football team and the ROTC program leveraged each other to show how diverse they were by having a student who did football and ROTC.

I did Air Force ROTC all four years at Notre Dame.

Freshmen assume when they come to Notre Dame to play football that they are going to win a national championship. That usually is not the case, but for Scruggs it was his reality.

It was pretty amazing. We all came in with a great deal of talent as freshmen. My class was one of the most talented freshmen classes at Notre Dame in quite some time; Rocket, Rodney Culver, Devon McDonald, Rod Smith, and Derek Brown to name a few. We could all run well. In fact, some of us were faster than a lot of the upper classmen, but we were wild and undisciplined. It was Coach Holtz's third year at Notre Dame and he had a lot of systems in place. He had a disciplined program and there was an expectation that we were going to be better than the team before us. Coach Holtz got us in line as the new guys. We weren't disciplined when it came to running routes and we didn't completely understand what was expected of us to be successful players at the collegiate level. Coach Holtz took care of that.

During two-a-day practices in camp that first August, D'Juan Francisco and I ended up being hospitalized for dehydration. Even coming from Texas high school football, it was brutal. Each week everything came more and more together; and each week that you won another game made the next week's game just that much more important. And then we found ourselves in Arizona playing West Virginia for the national title. It was truly amazing. I went home for Christmas before the national championship game and the local news station interviewed me and had me predict the final score of the game. I predicted it within two points! And then after the game the stations were at the airport welcoming me when I flew home. It was pretty overwhelming for someone who wasn't a major player on the team.

I grew up in a single parent household with my mom who was in the military. She went in as an enlisted soldier and got her first degree from the University of Minnesota and her second degree from the University of Wisconsin. She wasn't very much into sports and she didn't really have an attachment to the traditions at either of the schools she attended; what she most wanted was for me to go to school and get a good education. After I visited Notre Dame my mom told me, "That's where you're going." She took care of all of the paperwork from there on out. She definitely understood the value of a Notre Dame education and the opportunities that playing football would give to me.

As Scruggs reminisces about his time at Notre Dame, his college football career was filled with moments that he won't forget. Two memories, however, stand out from the rest.

I didn't get a lot of playing time. I was redshirted my freshman year, and right before the kickoff classic my sophomore year I dislocated my shoulder and sat out most of that season. I came back late in the season and was playing mostly on special teams. I was thrilled just to be back and playing again. In the Orange Bowl (Notre Dame vs. Colorado, 1991) that year I was on the field on special teams when they called the clipping penalty on Greg Davis. This controversial penalty ended up causing Rocket's 91 yard punt return for a touchdown (with 1:05 left on the clock) to be called back. I was right behind him and we were all cheering because we thought we had won the game and then I looked back and saw the flag. What a crushing disappointment. I just couldn't believe it. Even though the ball came back and they were going to kick it to us again, we still believed at that moment that we could do it all over again and win the game. But, of course, we all know how the game ended (Colorado 10 – Notre Dame 9). That right there is one of my favorite Notre Dame memories. How we all pulled together and believed that even though the odds were against us that we could win the game; that we could pull off an amazing comeback. It's easy to come together when everything is going well, but the way we came together amidst adversity and hard times, that is the definition of teamwork.

On a more positive note, another one of my favorite Notre Dame memories was the Sugar Bowl (Notre Dame vs. Florida, 1992). Even through all of the negative press we were receiving - that Cheerios belonged in the bowl more than Notre Dame did - Coach Holtz kept us together and kept us positive the whole time. We couldn't practice on the field because of all the rain New Orleans was getting, so we had to practice in our socks on the cement floor in the convention hall. As always, Coach had us prepared for Florida and we went out there and showed the world that we did indeed belong in the bowl game. The Mass before that game was quite memorable as well. They knew exactly how to center us and ready us for our big moment.

When you play football at Notre Dame, Our Lady's University becomes your home away from home, and your fellow students, teammates, coaches and professors become your family. Saying goodbye is never easy. But with a wide open future stretched out in front of you, the Notre Dame Value Stream redirects your focus and you set off to make your mark on the world.

Professional Career

When I graduated from Notre Dame I received my commission as a Second Lieutenant in the Air Force and began my training as an air traffic controller and air field manager. One of the lessons I learned from Coach Holtz was how to deal with great amounts of stress and how to motivate people who are under pressure. The stress of being an air traffic controller didn't bother me at all because of everything I had gone through under Coach Holtz. To be able to concentrate through Coach's yelling in the midst of a high pressure situation prepared me for just about anything that life could place in front of me. Coach Holtz taught us how to maintain great attention to detail and the importance of memorization, all of which came to bear in my Air Force career. I had 52 air traffic controllers working for me. I was the fifth youngest person in my group, trying to deal with work issues as well as people issues. At 23 years of age I was in charge of people who were 48-years- old and dealing with family and marital issues. Being able to lean back on the experiences I had at Notre Dame was a huge benefit to me. To know how to treat people and how to be fair and honest; those were very important traits as a manager.

In September of that year 9/11 happened which pulled me back into active duty.

I did that for a while and then I was cross-trained to become a special agent in the Air Force Office of Special Investigations (AFOSI); there I had the fortune of meeting another mentor, Colonel Francis Taylor, who also was a Notre Dame graduate. He was the one who thought I would be a good special agent, and under his guidance I specialized in counter intelligence and ended up working in that role for the rest of my Air Force career. I left the Air Force in March of 2001 and went into the reserves and then in September of that year 9/11 happened which pulled me back into active duty. I was deployed to Afghanistan in 2002, as a special agent for AFOSI and was one of the first agents to deploy in support of the post 9/11 missions. It was a really interesting experience. I had endless amounts of training, but this was the first time I got to put my training to use in a real world situation. Six months after I came home from Afghanistan I was deployed again to Iraq and was in Bagdad supporting combat operations, another exciting opportunity in which I learned a great deal.

Initially, when I joined the reserves in 2001, I had decided that my next career move would be in medical sales, selling instruments used for plastic surgery and cardiovascular surgery. Following my second deployment in Iraq, in 2004, I was recruited into my next career move which was to work for the CIA, which was another tremendous experience. In that role I was able to travel and see the world. I had trips to Afghanistan, Iraq, the Middle East, and Asia. I did that for four years, and in 2008 I made my next career move which was working in IT. I joined a small firm doing IT Operations and IT Support and Development. It was a very good fit to me until one day I found myself being "downsized," at which point I realized I had enough life experiences in running other businesses that it was time for me to start a business of my own.

Today

Since that initial move my company has had a couple of iterations, but since 2012 I've been running Hybrid Data Security. We do IT support. We support other business's IT needs such as security development, cyber security, cloud security, and cloud data security. We do a lot of SharePoint development and partnership with SharePoint in the sharing of data. We provide companies with the necessary security to be able to share data safely both within their company and outside of their company. We make sure that the intended person is not only receiving the data safely, but using the data properly. In addition to working with companies in the private sector we work with the federal government.

The Notre Dame Value Stream imparts on Her students during their time at Notre Dame the importance of giving back. The service opportunities at Notre Dame are around every corner and once you've experienced the joy of helping another, it becomes an integral part of your life.

As I've gotten older I've had the opportunity to be able to give back to the University. I began as the Monogram Representative on the Black Alumni board, and now I'm the Region 13 Director for Diversity. I cover the states of Texas and Oklahoma and deal with diversity issues in the alumni clubs. Mainly I look for students with diverse backgrounds who might be interested in attending Notre Dame. I also help the clubs with their diversity programs in order to help provide a more diverse environment at Notre Dame, and promote diversity in sports such as golf, tennis and hockey.

Part of being a student at Notre Dame was having the opportunity to meet people from other parts of the country and even the world.

Martin Scruggs

We had some diversity issues when I was at Notre Dame. There was a sit-in on campus in response to some diversity issues resulting from the actions of some professors, but the diversity issues I encountered on campus did not overwhelm student life. Part of being a student at Notre Dame was having the opportunity to meet people from other parts of the country and even the world. This helped me a great deal in my military career. To be understanding of other cultures and religions and to have respect for all people was a great asset for me. One of the other great things about Notre Dame was that you were truly a student-athlete. You didn't live in a football dorm like you would at many other universities; you lived in a regular dorm mixed with athletes and non-athletes alike. For my last three years at Notre Dame I lived with non-athletes. It was nice to experience living with people outside of athletics.

Martin Scruggs' Lessons from the Notre Dame Value Stream:

- Make the most out of every opportunity across the entire university spectrum. Remember there is more to the college experience than going to class and playing sports. You can learn important lessons not only inside the classroom but outside the classroom as well.

- Take advantage of student services and career development. Your four years of college are preparing you for the next 40 years of your life so use every resource available to you to prepare you for the next phase of your life.

- Get to know all of your classmates, not just your teammates. There is more to college than just spending time with your teammates. Those are your special brothers for sure, but don't forget about the rest of the student body that you're at school with. When football is over, whether it's next week or years from now, it's those classmates who are going to have opportunities for you. If you don't get to know them now, what makes you think they'll be there for you down the line when you need them?

Notre Dame vs. Air Force, 1988. Notre Dame football player Derek Brown (#86) trying to make a catch. Photo by Allan Lim. (Photo courtesy of Notre Dame Archives.)

CHAPTER THIRTEEN

The Energy Supplier

Derek Brown

*D*erek Vernon Brown, one of the legendary tight ends from Notre Dame's 1988 national title team, spent most of his childhood on the move. His father worked for IBM and relocated often, with Brown following in tow. Brown is a man of many firsts, two of which include being a first team All-American at Notre Dame and a first round NFL draft pick. Brown took his Notre Dame triumphs with him to the NFL where he had a successful nine-year career with the New York Giants, Jacksonville Jaguars, Oakland Raiders and Arizona Cardinals. Brown now lives in Clifton Park, New York, with his wife, Kristin, and their two children, Sydney and Reece; where he supplies commercial and industrial businesses with their energy needs. How does a young man who is used to changing scenery and ZIP codes end up in small town USA to play football for the legendary Fighting Irish? This is Derek Brown's story.

My dad worked for IBM and before I was eight years old we had already lived in Virginia, California, Texas, England (the country), Washington, DC and Atlanta. I'm not exactly sure how Notre Dame crept into my decision pool, but smooth-talking Irish recruiting coordinator Vinny Cerrato most definitely had something to do with it. I didn't know much about Notre Dame football or its history, and I didn't really have a favorite football team either. If I had to pick one, I probably would have picked the Pittsburgh Steelers because I was a big fan of Terry Bradshaw, but that was obviously a professional team. I was very athletic growing up and played whatever sport was in season: football, basketball, baseball, soccer and track and field, surfed and skateboarded. In high school I narrowed it down to basketball, football and track. The baseball team wanted me to pitch, but it interfered with spring football. My senior year in high school I narrowed my choices down to the University of Miami, University of Florida and Notre Dame. Where I lived in Florida during my high school years, the area was split in thirds: Gator country, Hurricane country and Seminole country. Four or five guys from my high school went to Miami and were playing for the Hurricanes when we (Notre Dame) played them in 1988.

I got off the plane wearing my Ray Bans, Miami Vice sport coat, t-shirt, slacks, loafers and no socks.

What it basically came down to was me being tired of people telling me where I was going to school. Everyone kept telling me, "Oh, you know you're going to be a Gator." My junior year I dreamt I was going to go to UF, but then everyone tried to push it on me and it got really annoying. Because of that I started to take a real hard look at Miami. I started going down there quite a bit. I loved Miami. So then it was down to Miami and Notre Dame. Ultimately, what I was looking for was a football team like Miami had with an academic program like Notre Dame had, but I had to make a decision. Back in the 1980s Miami was mostly known for being "Thug U," but I loved Miami — those were my guys. Perception isn't always reality, and the "thug" reputation was not ALL that Miami was (it is a private university with excellent Business, Medical and Law Schools). I took my official visit to Notre Dame in the middle of December. I got off the plane wearing my Ray Bans, Miami Vice linen sport coat, turquoise t-shirt, slacks, loafers and no socks; greeted by one and a half feet of snow. Welcome to South Bend. My host that weekend was Andre Jones. One Saturday morning during the winter of my senior year of high school I popped in this videotape I had called, "Wake up the Echoes." No one was home and I started watching it and the video gave me goose bumps and at that moment I thought, "Screw it. I'm going to Notre Dame."

Screw it. I'm going to Notre Dame.

And just like that, a kid who never imagined giving up his Ray Ban sunglasses, the white sandy beaches of Miami, and his Florida lifestyle, did just that. Brown traded them for rigorous Notre Dame academics, trudging to class though blizzard conditions and drifting snow, and a football career with the Fighting Irish. Swept away by the Notre Dame Value Stream, his life was altered forever.

> *It was tough saying no to Jimmy Johnson not just once, but twice in my living room, but I did and I am glad I made the decision to attend Notre Dame.*

The Notre Dame Years

Brown's decision to attend the University of Notre Dame ended up being one that brought him great fortune. He was part of the 1988 national championship team, First Team All-American in 1991, and chosen by the New York Giants as the 14th pick in the first round of the NFL Draft. Brown explains what being a part of the 1988 national championship team meant to him.

> *When you are in the middle of the kind of successes that we were in, you don't really think about it. But looking back at everything, it is truly amazing. No disrespect to the recent Notre Dame teams, but when I played college ball you couldn't compare our team to any other ND team; we were that much better. There were 63 combined guys from the Fighting Irish and Hurricane teams that went pro from that (1988) game. The most amazing thing about that 1988 Notre Dame team was how deep our team was. My backup was Irv Smith. His backup was Oscar McBride and this was just the tight end position, a position that wasn't a big deal back then. And it was like that at every position, not just tight end. Coach Lou Holtz and his recruiting staff did an amazing job of keeping the talent rolling in.*

When you experience a magical season such as Brown did in 1988, you may get the feeling that you've used up all of your luck in one fell swoop. But Brown's time at Notre Dame was filled with numerous moments of good fortune including appearing on the cover of Sports Illustrated during the 1991 football season.

One Wacky Season

> *I was on the cover of Sports Illustrated during the 1990 football season and I didn't believe it until I heard about it. Chris Zorich was walking by and said to me, "You're on the cover of Sports Illustrated," and when I said he was*

crazy he went and got it, and there I was! The issue was called, "One Wacky Season," and the featured article was about how many times the number one spot had changed hands during the football season. I was stunned that I was the one they picked for the cover.

The role of the tight end in college and in the NFL has greatly changed since Brown played the game in the late 80s and early 90s.

Man, I wish I could have played tight end in college and the pros today. I would have had a field day with these offenses. I love watching the likes of Tyler Eifert. What a great kid - big time player. He is doing tremendously well in the league.

As a student-athlete on the Notre Dame football team, it doesn't matter what your role is, whether you're a show-stopping starter or a walk-on waiting for your moment to shine. Your time at Notre Dame is something that will stay with you your entire life. The people you meet and the lessons you learn during your journey on the Notre Dame Value Stream will build you into the person you are meant to be and that will be evident to everyone you encounter throughout your life. Everyone has that one or two special moments during their time at Notre Dame that stand out from the rest.

I would have to say beating Miami 31-30 in 1988 (often referred to as the "One Shining Moment" game) was probably the most memorable game of my collegiate career. It meant a lot more to me than most of the guys on that team, being from Florida, and having been told during the recruiting process that we'd never beat them. It was a great feeling to walk off the field with a victory. And beating them two out of the three times we played them. Another memory that sticks out for me was after we beat West Virginia in the Fiesta Bowl for the national title. After the game I stood there on the field with Todd Lyght and looked at him and said, "Now what do we do?" And Todd replied, "Alright, let's go out!" It was like it was no big deal to us. We had just won the national title and it was just another win to us. I guess because our coaches made us feel like there was no doubt in their minds that we would win, it was kind of anticlimactic. Coach Lou Holtz had told us, "You don't win a national championship, you wake up to it."

Every football player thinks that the team they are a part of is special, but there was something truly remarkable about Notre Dame's 1988 national title team, and they showed that to the world.

It was a good mix of old-school guys and new-school guys. We had great senior leadership: Pat Eilers, Tim Grunhard, Mark Green, Andy Heck, George Streeter, D'Juan Francisco, Frank Stams, Wes Pritchett and so on; and then we had a group of young guys who came in with a chip on our shoulders. Quite frankly, we didn't give a shit what anyone thought. We were coming in and if you didn't play up to the expectations we were taking your spot. We were there to win games and we had some serious swagger.

A team as special as the 1988 Notre Dame team is not only a product of its players, but a result of its leadership and coaching staff as well. It is crucial to have a head coach and assistant coaches who can not only motivate the players, but also make sure they are in the position where they can develop and grow into their full potential. Head coach Lou Holtz was definitely this type of leader.

My favorite Lou Holtz memory was when he was getting us ready for the 1988 "One Shining Moment" game against Miami that we won 31-30. This has to be the best Lou Holtz quote ever. In Lou's pregame pep talk he told us, "You have an afternoon to play, a lifetime to remember. But I want you to do one thing: You save Jimmy Johnson's ass for me." Of course it sounded great and we were all about delivering Johnson to Coach Holtz, but honestly, there is no way Coach Holtz could have taken Jimmy Johnson (laughs).

Professional Career

The show and fanfare of the NFL Draft today was not like that when Brown was drafted in the early 1990s. Most of the players didn't journey to New York City to be a part of the spectacle that today's draft has become. They either stayed at school and watched with their friends, or went home and watched the draft with their family.

I was in Florida on my draft day. I had a hotel suite in Cocoa Beach with a large group of my family and friends. I had been invited to come to New York City to be at the NFL Draft but I didn't want all of those cameras in my face just in case something went wrong. I was expecting to go to Cleveland in the number nine spot, but when they took Tommy Vardell I knew it would be a bit more of a wait. Then I got a call from Ray Handley, the head coach of the New York Giants saying that they were going to select me as the next pick (14) to play for the Giants. I remember walking out to the hotel balcony by myself and reflecting on everything that had just happened.

Reaching the pinnacle of your football career and playing football in the NFL is a dream come true for any collegiate football player, but the realities of life in the NFL often do not live up to expectations that many young men have going into it. What were the highs and lows of the NFL life like for Brown?

Just the exclusivity of it all — being a part of something that very few people have the opportunity to do was one of the biggest highs for me. Being in that

NFL locker room, in the huddle, being on the road and shutting up 70,000 people is unreal and is something that I'll never forget. As far as the lows go, I didn't think that my NFL career panned out the way that I thought it would. If I would have played in different systems, had different opportunities, maybe it would have turned out differently. I wanted to be a 10-year pro bowler and to play for 12 seasons. I played for nine seasons, and didn't make the pro bowl, but I am still happy with all that I accomplished during my football career.

The highlight of my NFL career would have to be getting to the AFC championship game in 1996 with the Jacksonville Jaguars. It was our second year of existence (the franchise had just started in 1995) and we had a players-only meeting and had told each other we have got to start making plays. If we were going to accomplish anything, it was up to us. We were 3-6 after nine games into the season and then from there we really came on strong and ended up beating Buffalo at Buffalo (30-27) in the Wild Card game and knocked legendary quarterback Jim Kelly out of the playoffs. Then we beat Denver (30-27) at their place in the Divisional playoff game (Denver's regular season record was 14-2), but then we lost to New England 20-6 in the AFC championship game. Even though we lost that game, we were really only a blocked punt, fumble and interception from going to the show. It was quite a run for a team that was only in its second year of existence.

Playing in the NFL not only came with success, it also came with its share of challenges for Brown. The Notre Dame Value Stream stepped into Brown's life to show him how to keep moving forward along his journey and that overcoming adversity was not only possible, but a reality.

Brown missed the entire 1995 season as the result of a hit from Denver Broncos safety Tim Hauck during a preseason game. He suffered bruised ribs, a collapsed lung and damage to his spleen and kidney. He was in the hospital for 10 days and in a wheelchair for a few weeks after that.

Steve Beuerlein was Jacksonville's quarterback in 1995 and it was the last game of the preseason. It was my coming out game; five targets, three receptions and a touchdown. This was going to be my year because in the first year of an expansion team the quarterback typically would not have much protection and I was sure as the tight end I was going to get a lot of balls thrown to me. In the second quarter the pass to me was tipped and I was making an attempt to come down with it when I got hit hard right in the back. When I came down I heard a clicking sound every time I took a breath and I knew something was not right. I was able to get up and jog off the field. They took me into the locker room to have x-rays done and I had a broken rib. I took a shower and then the first time I went to the bathroom I peed blood. One of our trainers had seen a similar accident in a baseball game and decided that I needed to go to the hospital for further examination. My girlfriend (now wife) took me to the hospital and once I was admitted my condition worsened with every passing hour.

I went from having a broken rib, to a collapsed lung, to a bruised kidney, to a cracked spleen, to having air bubbles around my heart. I was in intensive care for four days and then six more days just in a regular hospital room. In those ten days I went from 262 pounds to 247 pounds. When I was released from the hospital I was confined to a wheelchair for several weeks because I still had so much internal bleeding. After weeks of recovery I started to work out to come back for week 10 when I developed a pseudo-cyst around my pancreas. They had to put a catheter between my ribs to take care of the bleeding in my pancreas. At that point they put me on the injured reserve list and I was out for the remainder of the season. Despite all that I went through that year I played for five more seasons after that. My girlfriend (now wife) was such a huge support to me that year.

Then in the year 2000, I was with the Arizona Cardinals (my ninth season in the NFL). I was released right before the last preseason game. Vince Tobin was later fired and Dave McGinnis was hired as the new head coach. Dave brought me back to play and then four weeks later I was released again.

Today

After that season my wife's sister was diagnosed with breast cancer and we decided to move back to be near her so that we could help her out, and that is how we settled in Albany, New York. My in-laws also lived in the area and so my first business opportunity was working for my father-in-law in the food business, working for a food marketing company, Panoply. The next opportunity was with a friend who I had known since junior high school. We decided to open up several Quizno's Sub stores. It went gangbusters at first but then we quickly learned that it was not as great as we had initially thought. We ran the Quizno's stores for two years. Then I decided to get into commercial real estate just before the bubble burst from 2007 to 2010. I then took a job in the energy business, first with Blue Rock Energy, where I was for five years and then with Engie (formerly GDF Suez), which is where I am today, but I still do some real estate work on the side. Engie is an energy supply company. We supply commercial and industrial businesses with their energy needs. I have been there since the beginning of 2016 and love what I do!

In addition to working for Engie, Brown also gives back to the local community and is involved in two charitable organizations.

Derek Brown and his family.

I sit on the board of directors for two charitable foundations: Capital District YMCA (www.cdymca.org) and the Double H Ranch, a "serious fun camp." (www.doublehranch.org) The Double H Ranch, co-founded by Charles R. Wood and Paul Newman, provides specialized programs and year-round support for children and their families dealing with life-threatening illnesses. All programs are FREE of charge and capture the magic of the Adirondacks. It really is a wonderful foundation. It is amazing what they can do for these kids. In the winter, they have an adaptive skiing program where even kids who are on ventilator machines can ski down the mountain. It really is amazing stuff.

Derek Brown's Lessons from the Notre Dame Value Stream:

- I know when you are young you think you know everything, but the first bit of advice I would give is to have fun and enjoy every moment. When I was in high school I wanted a car really bad. My Mom said that if she could afford a car that she would get me one. She would not let me have a job during the school year because her philosophy was you're only a kid once, you have the rest of your life to work so you should enjoy yourself now.

- I can't imagine all of the information that these kids have to process these days between texting, the internet and social media. My best advice for young people today: work hard but play hard, too. (Not partying!) Take time for yourself. Try and have a true understanding of what really matters. People so often stress about things that just don't really matter.

Portrait of football player Adrian Jarrell in uniform, c1990. Notre Dame University photographer. (Photo courtesy of Notre Dame Archives.)

CHAPTER FOURTEEN

The Performance Analyst

Adrian Jarrell

*G*rowing up in the college town of Athens, Georgia, in the shadow of the University of Georgia, if you excel at football you are expected to become a Georgia Bulldog. But that never was in the cards for Adrian Jarrell. He had spent years watching what happened to the Georgia football players whose careers ended too soon and the struggles they faced when they were not equipped with an education that prepared them for life after football. And then the Lady on the Dome caught his attention. A school where student-athletes are not only prepared to compete at the highest level on the field, but who are also prepared to succeed in the classroom and in the rest of their lives. A University that molded its young men and women to become leaders who go on to inspire change in the world and became champions for those who needed their support. And so instead of following his high school teammates to Georgia, he chose the University of Notre Dame and played there as a wide receiver from 1989 to 1994, receiving a fifth year of eligibility after breaking his arm during his junior season. Now a senior financial analyst and active volunteer in his local Notre Dame Alumni Club, Jarrell enjoys giving back to his local community. How does a hard working young man from the land of sunshine and peaches end up playing football where the snow drifts and the winters are endless? This is Adrian Jarrell's story.

It didn't matter where I had to travel to achieve my dreams.

When I was being recruited in high school to play football at the collegiate level, I was one of the top rated quarterbacks in the country. I grew up in the shadows of the University of Georgia, but UGA really wasn't where I wanted to be. I was very familiar with many of the guys at UGA. I also saw what happened to many of these guys when their football careers ended and they did not put their education first. They did not have any skills to fall back on and many of them were lost. Notre Dame, on the other hand, was a different story. Notre Dame had just won the national title my senior year in high school. I was a kid who was really focused on getting a good education when I was in high school, so Notre Dame was a good fit. It didn't matter where I had to travel to achieve my dreams. I was going to get there. I am grateful to my family (mom, dad, grandma, and grand-dad) for instilling discipline and a solid work ethic in me. My high school coach, Billy Henderson, who was in the mold of a Lou Holtz, helped develop my talents and my mental toughness in sports. We had some great talent for the high school level, but he pushed all of us to be our best.

The list of top schools that I was looking at included Michigan, Notre Dame, Florida State, Ohio State and UCLA, which were all great schools; but Notre Dame was a perfect fit for me. Not just in the area of sports, but also academically. I also had to make a decision on whether to play quarterback or receiver. The final thing that won me over was the personalities and attitudes of the players that were at Notre Dame at the time. When I made my official visit, I discovered that many of them had the same interests that I did and I already felt like I was part of the Notre Dame family. We all knew what we wanted to do in life and we also knew that while we were at Notre Dame we were going to fulfill our dreams. One of the guys that made a big impression on me that weekend was my host, Rodney Culver. He was such a positive guy. He always saw the bright side of any situation. He was a big part of my choosing Notre Dame, and was a big part of my experience at Notre Dame.

The Notre Dame Years

Jarrell was blessed to arrive at Notre Dame in the fall of 1989 and play for a team that had just won the national championship. While it is difficult to pick one favorite memory out of a football career at Notre Dame, Jarrell talks about two that stand out in his mind.

There are two football memories that really stick out for me. The first was the game-winning touchdown catch that I made on a pass from Rick Mirer with 1:40 left on the clock in the Notre Dame vs. Michigan game my sophomore year. It was the season opener, under the lights at Notre Dame Stadium and was the first game that Mirer started in at Notre Dame. We were ranked number one in the country (and Michigan was ranked number two) and it was my first big contribution to the team. It was my first real opportunity to come into my own. Coach Holtz put me in the game, called a corner end zone pass play, and Rick Mirer made a perfect throw. Coach Holtz showed confidence in me to give me the opportunity to help win the game.

The second most memorable moment in my mind was the 1993 Notre Dame-FSU game during my fifth year. Notre Dame and FSU came into that game ranked number one and number two and the touchdown that I scored on the reverse in that game was a big moment for me. Florida State scored quickly on the opening drive, which made the home crowd a little uneasy. The touchdown that I scored tied the game up and we never looked back after that play. I was a fifth-year senior, and it was my first game back after missing the first 10 games of the season because I tore six ribs from my sternum just six days before the season started. I worked hard all season to make a comeback and be able to play in that game. It was great to be able to get out there for the Florida State game and to be able to showcase my talent once again.

Being away from home and learning how to be successful at college is an adjustment for any student, but student-athletes have an additional set of responsibilities. In addition to going to class, studying and performing well on tests and papers, they also have to keep up with practice, team meetings, weight room, training table, travel and games. Even the most well prepared student-athletes face a certain amount of turmoil when they make the leap from high school to college. This is when they become incredibly thankful to have the Notre Dame Value Stream in their back pocket to lead them and guide them in the right direction.

The biggest challenge I faced as a student-athlete at Notre Dame was getting used to the demands of playing football and keeping up with my education at the same time. I played wide receiver behind Rocket and we often rotated taking snaps during games. If anything happened to Rocket, I had to be ready to go. As a result of that, the coaches were on me pretty hard. We started practice in July, but once school started in August you have to get right into the books and keep it going. Playing football at Notre Dame during that time was very competitive, but so were our academic responsibilities.

Injuries were a big setback for me, but I always felt like I would be back out there in no time and able to contribute once again. Typically when you break your arm, you are out for six weeks and then back in the lineup again. There was never any doubt in my mind that after my six weeks of recovery and rehab that I'd be back at it. Unfortunately, I had a slow-healing break and I ended up missing a year of playing time. Mentally it was devastating to have to sit out that long. However, I always felt like I was going to get back to top form once I was healthy. My second injury was probably the most crushing to me because it occurred when I had just begun my fifth year. I was ready to finally have the opportunity to fully showcase my talent. I had put everything behind me once again, and was of the frame of mind that this is going to be the year. My parents had booked several trips to South Bend to see me play. Then, the week before the season started, I tore several ribs off my sternum in a scrimmage a mere 6 days before kickoff. After telling my family how I was going to be starting this year, I then had to call them back and say, "Maybe you might want to cancel a couple of those trips back." It's one thing if you don't get to play because you didn't earn the opportunity to play. It's another thing when you have earned it, but never get to fulfill it.

Our room at Notre Dame could not have been any bigger than 10 x 10.

(My) freshman year was a big adjustment for me overall. Dorsey Levens was my roommate freshman and sophomore year. We lived in Morrissey Hall, and were shocked when we first saw our room. We had both visited the best programs in the country when we were looking at colleges, and the dorms there had very spacious rooms. Our room at Notre Dame could not have been any bigger than 10 x 10 or maybe 10 x 12. We both walked into this room and said to each other, "Oh my. How is everything going to fit?" Then we look across, and realize that our room is right across from the rector's room. We are living next door to a Priest? We both looked at each other, how did this happen? So we go talk to the Rector to see if we can get our room changed and he kicked us out of his office. That was the beginning of many adjustments freshman year!

Any university can piece together a team filled with successful football players from around the country, but without the right head coach to lead, motivate and develop them, they'll never achieve the successes for which they are destined. With a head coach like Lou Holtz at the helm, who used the Notre Dame Value Stream to drive home his philosophy of "Do the right thing, do the best you can, and always show people you care;" anything is possible.

He's like a walking Notre Dame encyclopedia.

My strongest memories of Coach Holtz are all of the times that he stood in front of us, giving us one of his famous speeches about life. He always talked to us about sports and football, but always made it apply to life. He also did this meditation every Friday night to prepare us for Saturday's game that usually put us all to sleep! Coach Holtz is a very inspirational guy. He had a special gift at being able to bring us all together, talking about the value of the Notre Dame family. He is also one of the best sources of Notre Dame history around! He knows the dates and years of when everything happened at Notre Dame. He's like a walking Notre Dame encyclopedia.

A good coach can change a game, a great coach can change a life.
~ John Wooden

Not only was Lou Holtz a great leader for us, but during my years at Notre Dame we had great leadership amongst ourselves. We had great role models in our senior leaders. The way the guys carried themselves: Tony Rice, Bob Dahl, Tim Ryan, Dean Brown, Irv Smith, Ned Bolcar, Rocket Ismail, Chris Zorich, Ricky Watters, Anthony Johnson, Rod West, Pat Terrell, and D'Juan Francisco; they all led by example. The coaches may have set the tone, but the players continued with it on and off the field. Lou Holtz ran the program in such a way that the players were an integral part of it, and passed their leadership skills down to the younger players. His veteran players showed the younger players the way and taught them the standard of excellence by which we lived. At Notre Dame, we were like a family. When you got to Notre Dame, you knew you were talented. Then the upperclassmen like Derek Brown and Todd Lyght came along and showed you what you needed to be doing to be successful: the new level of talent that is expected now that you are a member of the Notre Dame football team.

Professional Career

When you play football at a school like the University of Notre Dame you can't help but dream of one day playing in the NFL. When you are coached by a head coach like Lou Holtz and play with the caliber of players that were at Notre Dame in the late 80s and early 90s, it wasn't a big stretch to believe that you would indeed someday be NFL bound. However, the players that make the leap from college to the NFL are few. Preparation for anything that you could face post-college is something the Notre Dame Value Stream tries to instill in each one of Her student-athletes.

I had a feeling I would not get drafted into the NFL, but I still knew in my heart that I was talented enough to play in the NFL. If only my injuries had not held me back to the extent that they did during my time at Notre Dame. Once it was confirmed that I was not going to play in the NFL, my agent called the office of the arena football team in Las Vegas, and it turned out that one of the guys responsible for finding talent for the team was Ian Welch, a Notre Dame graduate. Welch graduated from Notre Dame with his MBA in 1990, the year of my big catch during the Michigan game, and he knew exactly who I was. Even though I was excited about getting the opportunity to continue playing football in the Arena Football League, it was still tough not getting the opportunity to showcase my talent in the NFL.

My experience playing arena football was great! It allowed me to pursue my NFL dream for a few more years and get football out of my system. Especially after the NFL didn't work out immediately after college. I played in the arena league for five years. The bad thing about being the number one wide receiver on an Arena Football League team is there is not much running the football. It is all about the pass and you are catching passes almost every play. The wide receiver takes the pounding instead of the running back. So there were a lot of bumps and bruises as a result. When you are a wide receiver in the NFL, in a regular season game you might catch three, four or five catches. When you are a wide receiver for an arena football team, you are averaging 10 to 12 catches a game. You have to learn to work within the space restrictions of playing in an arena, and everything about the game works fast. Kurt Warner was playing arena ball the same time that I was, and we used to play against him before he moved on to the NFL. But those years allowed me to display my receiving skills with a 90 plus catch season and achieve the 1,000 yard season that eluded me at Notre Dame due to injury.

And then it happens. One day you wake up and just know that it's time to move on. Football was fun, it was an incredible way to receive a top education and at Notre Dame to become a member of a network that stretches across the globe. But one day the Notre Dame Value Stream gives you that nudge that it's finally time to put that tremendous education to work.

My fifth year at Notre Dame finished just six courses short of receiving my MBA. In the early years after graduation, if I would have gone back to Notre Dame I could have easily finished it. But I did not want to pass up the oppor-

tunity to keep playing ball in the Arena Football League. When I finally had the time to finish my degree somewhere, most schools wanted me to either start over, or were willing to give me nine credits towards my degree. While I was playing arena ball, football only took up four months of your year, and it did not pay enough to last you until the next season started. In 1995 I started working during the off-season in the finance industry, and every off-season I would return to my job.

Today

Adrian Jarrell

Right now I am a Senior Financial Analyst for L-3 Communications. I analyze the financial performance of the company through performance indicators and the financial statement. My degree from Notre Dame is a Bachelor of Business Administration with a concentration in MIS, but I am more of an accounting guy with a niche in information systems. The financial analysis industry is really a combination of accounting and MIS. ERP systems (SAP, Peoplesoft, JD Edwards, Orcale, etc) drive the world today. The best thing about being a Notre Dame alumnus is that any time you meet someone else who is a Notre Dame alumnus, you have an instant connection with them. I ended up joining the Notre Dame Alumni Club in Dallas to reestablish some of these connections and eventually went on to become the treasurer for the club in 2006 and 2007. There are 500 active members within the club, and it is a great way to reconnect with Notre Dame.

Adrian Jarrell's Lessons from the Notre Dame Value Stream:

- Be committed to do whatever it takes to achieve your dreams.

- Live your life with a standard of excellence and lead by example.

- Become a life-long learner and continue to grow your skill set.

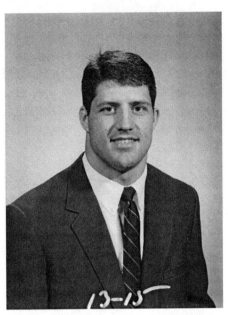

Portrait of Notre Dame football player Brian Ratigan, May 1992.
(Photo courtesy of Notre Dame Archives.)

CHAPTER FIFTEEN

The Bone Mender

Brian Ratigan

*W*hen Brian Ratigan arrived on the scene at Notre Dame in August of 1989, he suddenly felt like a tiny fish in a very big pond. Ranked as the No. 5 athlete in the country by SuperPrep and the Gatorade Player of the Year in Iowa, Ratigan found himself amidst some of the best talent that Notre Dame, and college football overall, had seen in 50 years. The 3.97 grade-point average (on a 4.0 scale) student from St. Albert's High School in Council Bluffs, who was All-State in football, basketball, baseball and track graduated with a Marketing degree from Notre Dame. After graduation with a bright professional football career on the horizon, Ratigan knew that he would not be satisfied sitting behind a desk once his football career was over. Instead of playing golf with his teammates during the NFL offseason, Ratigan decided to pick up a few science classes in order to pursue his next passion: medicine. How does a kid from Council Bluffs, Iowa, end up as the Orthopedic Surgeon for the Notre Dame football team? This is Brian Ratigan's story.

It's so different now with social media.

As I grew up in a Catholic family and attended both a Catholic grade school and high school, my family, and whole community, knew about Notre Dame. But no one from my high school had ever played Division I football until a kicker three years ahead of me, and my brother, Larry, a linebacker, two years ahead of me, both went to Iowa State University. Although I watched college football, I had never considered Notre Dame to be the place where I would go to college and play football. It's so different now with social media. You know every little detail about every school. Back then, you just played football and had fun. I knew I wanted to experience more than what I already learned from Southwest Iowa, and I worked hard, both in the classroom and on the field, to open up my options. I started getting letters from colleges my freshman year. I sent the forms back and went through the process step-by-step.

I had an offer from Notre Dame the summer before my senior year in high school.

I excelled at sports in high school. I was All-State in four sports throughout my high school career (football, basketball, baseball and track), which you could do back then, but I was not dominant in any one sport. Someone finally said to me the summer after my junior year that I should consider playing football at Notre Dame, and so I went to Notre Dame for its football camp that summer. I did all the drills and gave it my all. I ran the 40 in 4.58 and 4.56; they offered me a scholarship before I even left camp. I had an offer from Notre Dame the summer before my senior year in high school and then had the chance to watch ND go undefeated that year and play for the national title. Once I got the offer from Notre Dame, other offers just poured in. I was a straight A student, so academics were not an issue for me. Stanford also offered me a full scholarship to play football and/or baseball. I was asked to play baseball at Notre Dame as well. It was a lot of fun to watch it all develop and receive offers from Division I programs, but the process itself was overwhelming.

And just like that, without Ratigan even understanding what was happening, the Notre Dame Value Stream took hold of him and directed his course towards South Bend.

The Notre Dame Years

We don't have a scholarship for you anymore.

Funny story. I almost lost my scholarship to Notre Dame. My high school coach and I visited Notre Dame during the 1988 Penn State game, and then I went back to ND in December for the big recruiting weekend. Most of the guys who had received offers from Notre Dame officially committed during this recruiting weekend. I didn't know, however, that I should commit while I was there. Unfortunately, my parents also had no idea that I was supposed to formally announce my intent to play football for Notre Dame that weekend. My brother had only one scholarship offer to a Division I program (Iowa State) and he accepted, so his recruiting process had been much different than mine. Although I intended to accept my offer from ND, I still had several other planned visits to Division I schools (including Nebraska, USC, and Stanford), and, out of respect to those other programs, I didn't think I should commit to one while I had scheduled visits to the others. In January of 1989, Stanford still did not have a coaching staff, so I cancelled my Stanford trip and called Coach Alvarez to commit to Notre Dame. He said, "What?? We don't have a scholarship for you anymore." My heart just sank. Then he told me they thought they had a guy who was committed to both Notre Dame and Miami. He said they were going to find out that evening if that truly was the case, and if they found out that he was committed to both schools, they were going to pull his scholarship and give it to me. That was a rough night for me. At 6 am the next morning, Coach Alvarez was at my house offering me my Notre Dame scholarship. I learned that I needed to be a bit more aware of what was going on.

And just when the waters are so rough that we think our ship is about to sink, the Notre Dame Value Stream swoops in, rights the ship, and sets us on our intended course.

Notre Dame knows that the best way to sell the University to prospective football players is to place them with current players who have similar backgrounds or goals.

My hosts during my recruiting trip to ND that December were Dave Jandric and Mickey Anderson, who both played at Creighton Prep High School, in Omaha, Nebraska, which was just across the Missouri River from Council Bluffs, Iowa. Junior Bryant and I took our recruiting trip to ND together and we both were hosted by Dave and Mickey, but Junior already knew them because he played football with them at the Prep. It was an easy, comfortable visit for me; it didn't matter what I experienced during my visit, as I was already sold on Notre Dame. Notre Dame offered outstanding academics, the number one football program in the country, a beautiful campus, and the Catholic identity that I sought in my education. It was the perfect fit for me. Iowa State was probably second on my list simply because my brother was playing there.

Every week during the recruiting process, I received more full scholarship offers and more national, state and local athletic awards. Once Notre Dame started recruiting me, everyone suddenly became more interested in me, and not all of them were positive experiences. So many schools were very vocal at how much they disliked Notre Dame, but many of them could not articulate exactly why they thought I should decline my Notre Dame offer. There's no perfect place. My high school coach and I created a "pros and cons" list on what I wanted out of life and how each school could help me to achieve it. Honest to God, Notre Dame was first in every category except for "family," – Iowa State won that spot because my brother, my best friend, was there. Hands down Notre Dame was as close to perfect for me that I could possibly find.

As a four-sport athlete in high school, Ratigan was no stranger to hard work and a busy schedule. But even so, the leap from high school to the college level is much bigger than any freshman student-athlete ever expects. The expectations are higher, the time required to be successful in both academics and athletics is greater, and somehow a balance must be found. This is where the Notre Dame Value Stream emerges to teach its student-athletes how to survive in this new and challenging environment.

The biggest challenge for me as a student-athlete at Notre Dame was cultural in nature. Coming from Council Bluffs, Iowa, I was a pretty sheltered kid. Even though Notre Dame was still in the Midwest, people who enrolled at Notre Dame came from all over the country and all over the world. I learned as much from hanging out with students from all over the country as I did in the classroom. My schedule was grueling: academics were tough, and football practice and physical conditioning at the collegiate level presented a steep learning curve. I expected and looked forward to that new schedule, and it never bothered me. But recognizing the cultural differences between the students and student-athletes, and trying to fit into the mix, was a big challenge for me. There were extremely bright people sitting next to me in class, and they invented things, started up businesses I could never conceptualize, and already succeeded in subjects to which I was not yet exposed. Notre Dame students brought so much to the table. Even though I had straight As in high school and was recognizable on campus as a Notre Dame football player, I often felt inferior among my ND peers. I'd only traveled to three or four states before I went to college, and the first time I had ever flown on a plane was for my official visit to USC. The cultural diversity at Notre Dame was a challenge, but it was also the greatest part of the University for me.

At many Division I schools a football player who wants to become a doctor is unheard of, but not at Notre Dame. Notre Dame football players are encouraged to follow whatever dreams they hold in their hearts. But at the same time, they have to realize that chasing football dreams and academic dreams can be overwhelming. The Notre Dame Value Stream recognizes these struggles and helps its students find a way to achieve all of their dreams, but not always on the most traditional of paths.

I was told I had the highest GPA of any of the freshman on the football team.

When I came to Notre Dame, I wanted to be a doctor. Initially, I didn't receive any advice regarding how to sign up for pre-med classes. Notre Dame sent me a registration form, and I selected my classes. I checked Chemistry and Calculus and all pre-med classes, and then I headed off to college. When I arrived on campus on August 3rd, a full three weeks before the rest of the freshman class, Emil Hofman, the Dean of Freshman Studies, sat me down and said, "Let's talk about your schedule." He advised me to adjust my schedule to get my required classes out of the way before I jumped into a pre-med curriculum. He felt I needed to get a handle on what it really took, time-wise, to simultaneously balance academics and play collegiate football as a full scholarship player. Even without the pre-med classes, I got crushed that first semester. I graduated from high school with close to a perfect 4.0, yet I didn't even crack a 3.0 in my first semester at Notre Dame. Ironically, they congratulated me as I had the highest GPA of any of the freshman football players. Although I was disappointed, I thought, well, at least I'm doing better than the rest of my peers on the team. My roommate earned only a .67 that first semester, and he was placed on academic probation twice.

During my freshman year, we were undefeated until we lost to Miami. That fall, I met Frank Eck who said to me, "Brian, you're going to get a Business degree from Notre Dame and when you graduate you're going to work for me and run my corrugated piping division for my plant in Ohio." And I thought, "Oh my God, I'm going to have a job!" Talking to Mr. Eck, a successful ND alum, about a potential job after graduation not only motivated me, but it focused my major in business. Originally I thought I wanted to specialize in finance or accounting but was eventually drawn into marketing by Professor Murphy's passion and teaching style. I ultimately earned a Bachelor's Degree in Business Administration in Marketing.

As I look back, my academic challenges during freshman year were not surprising. I started to get a lot of playing time; Coach Alvarez really liked me; and I spent all of my time studying the playbook rather than my textbooks. My roommate was a wild man, which didn't help me much either, and I was basically just trying to keep my head above water. I learned very quickly that I needed better time-management skills to succeed. Notre Dame provided me the foundation to not only make mistakes, but to keep working and overcome those initial missteps: I lived a football dream, earned a business degree, made good friends, and established myself as a proud Notre Dame alum. In many ways, all of those trials during freshman year helped me to become the doctor I am today

When you play on a team that just won the national title the year before you arrived, it's pretty much assumed that you're going to win every week. This can create unrealistic expectations on one hand, but on the other hand it exposed Ratigan to some amazing football during the four years he played for Notre Dame.

There are a couple of great memories that stick out in my mind. Reggie Brooks making the catch in the end zone against Penn State my senior year (the 1992 "Snow Bowl") is a phenomenal one for sure (all made possible by the Ratigan fumble recovery). For me personally, as a linebacker and special teams guy, my favorite memories are on the other side of the ball. The interception I made against Michigan (picking off quarterback Elvis Grbac) to get us within field goal range to tie the game is one of my favorite memories. After I made the pick, I was running off the field and Rick Mirer was running back onto the field and told me, "Rat, we're going to have the lead after this series." They drove down and ended up having to kick the tying field goal and when he came off the field I said to Rick, "Some lead, Rick!" (laughs) To this day, I still hang that over his head.

One of my proudest moments is from the game against Boston College during my senior year. Our senior year was the first time Notre Dame had played Boston College in quite some time. It was the renewal of the "Catholic Rivalry." We beat them 54-7 that day, and my job as linebacker was to play the nickelback spot and to prevent the BC tight end from catching the ball. Their tight end was catching 10 to 12 balls a game. Rick Minter was our defensive coordinator. He had really trimmed the fat with our play-calling for that game, and we crushed the BC tight end. He didn't catch one single ball. *After the game, the team awarded me the game ball. There was noth-ing in particular in the stats to show how much I did to help Notre Dame crush BC, but I successfully took out one of the most effective offensive play-ers on BC's team. It is a lot of fun to come through for your team when they are counting on you.*

Practice isn't the thing you do once you're good. It's the thing you do that makes you good. ~ Malcolm Gladwell

The success or failure of a team has to do not only with the talent of its players, but also with the leadership and guidance of its head coach. Lou Holtz was one of the best of the best when it came to getting his guys ready for game day. And while the players may have viewed him as an extremely strict coach back in the day, they are tremendously thankful today for the lessons they learned from him. What was Ratigan's favorite memory of his beloved coach?

My answer to this question is different now than it would have been in the early 1990s. Having since been on this side of Notre Dame football (as the Head Orthopedic Surgeon for the team), I see how difficult it truly is to be the head football coach at Notre Dame. There are an unbelievable amount of people tugging at you for things they want you to do: coaching, recruiting, running camps, traveling, signing balls, talking to the media and alumni, resolving team issues. It's hard to believe you can do all of that and still be a successful head football coach. Yet, Notre Dame has a history of coaches who succeed. They are intelligent; they multi-task; and they build teams with players who support them through their focus and commitment to Notre Dame. Coach Holtz had an impeccable knack of being able to navigate the crowd, manage the University's responsibilities and coach at a high level. He kept us extremely organized. When I played football for Coach Holtz, I always knew exactly what the game plan was. John Wooden always talked about having a perfect practice, and Holtz subscribed to that style: 80 to 90 percent of what we did at practice was repetitive. Through consistent and organized practice, we became really good at what we did. And, most impor-tantly, he kept us accountable for own actions, both on and off the field.

Every Sunday at 1 pm we watched the game film as a team. We could watch the entire game in about an hour. What Coach Holtz did with every game was show us 3 to 5 plays where the game was on the line — plays where if we did not execute them correctly, the game would have been lost. We could see everything: the blocks we made, the blocks we missed and how the game was altered. He highlighted seemingly minor details: if we made that block instead of missing it, we would have scored 7 points instead of 3, and we would have won the game by 1 instead of losing by 3. I really appreciated his understanding of how critical each person's role was and that every play mattered. As players, we didn't love him. We didn't truly love him until after we graduated. There were times we felt the way he ran the team wasn't fair, but his style forced us to stick together. I think he did this by design. He motivated us to become a group of brothers who wanted to play, and win, with and for each other. Coach Holtz will always be our Coach – he cares about each of us, and I know, through my own personal experience, that he will help us in any way he can, at a moment's notice.

Even though the players didn't always understand why Coach Holtz did the things he did, the Notre Dame Value Stream helped them keep their eyes on the prize and work toward their unified goal, which was winning.

When I arrived at Notre Dame my freshman year, I had just had knee surgery three weeks prior to arriving on campus. I tried to practice right away and my knee really got swollen three or four days into training camp, and as a result they made me sit out. It was embarrassing to have to sit out. I had just met my team, and now I can't play. I was riding a stationary bike during practice, and Coach Holtz walked towards me. I didn't really know him at that point. My only real encounter with him had been during the recruiting process. He walks by me, stops, looks, and says: "That's too bad, son. You could have been a good player here," and kept walking. What did I do? I immediately got off that bike, put on my helmet and begged (trainer) Jim Russ to let me practice. That's what Coach Holtz did. He had you motivated to do your best at all times.

As a student-athlete football player at Notre Dame, you spend a great deal of your time with your teammates and coaches, and those memories become a treasured piece of your life for years to come. Many of those memories consist of the big plays and exciting wins, but many of them are the hard lessons learned that helped mold and shape them into the men they are today. This is especially true for Ratigan.

A freshman decided to take it upon himself to dictate the game.

The first game that I had the opportunity to play in my freshman year (post knee surgery recovery) was the Purdue game in 1989. I recovered a fumble and almost had an interception in that game. By the fourth quarter we were winning 40-0. With just over a minute left in the game I got called for a late hit, and as a result, Purdue got 15 yards. I came off the field and had to stand next to Coach Holtz as Purdue took that 15-yard gift, drove down the field and scored. After the game, we all went into the locker room and Coach

Holtz tells the team, "Unfortunately a freshman decided to take it upon him-self to dictate the game, got a late hit and cost the defensive guys a shutout." I was just crushed. All the while Coach Alvarez is looking at me as if to say, "Don't worry. You're fine."

That night, I had a little too much fun celebrating my first official college football game, and I overslept the next day. We had a 1 pm meeting on Sun-day, and my brother called and woke me up at 1:15 pm. I hung up on my brother, sprinted to the meeting, and tried to open the locked door. I had to sit outside of the meeting room. I missed watching the game film with my teammates, the film from the first game I played in. After the meeting was over my roommate and I had to go meet with Coach Holtz. My roommate went in first, quickly came out and said that it wasn't too bad. However, I met with Coach Holtz, and for 10 or 15 minutes, Coach explained how I not only let the University down, but I also let down the Lady on the Dome, the staff, my parents, and my grandmother. You see, my grandmother previ-ously wrote Coach Holtz a personal letter about me. Needless to say, I was crushed. In the end, I will never forget the first game I played at Notre Dame. It was the highest high and the lowest low of my ND career.

Professional Career

After four amazing years at Notre Dame, Ratigan was ready to set off on his next adventure and try his hand at the NFL.

I had no idea where I would fall in the 1993 draft. I wasn't an "every down" player. In fact, I didn't even go to the combine that year because we already had seven or eight guys going from Notre Dame. But, because of our talent level and our late bowl game, ND hosted a mini-combine on campus in which I participated. We had five different days of tryouts for the private combine. I competed well, and I was hopeful that I would get drafted or picked up as a free agent. I was a smart player with great numbers, and I came from a winning program. I wanted to play in the NFL for ten years. That's how I envisioned my future. We had 14 Notre Dame players drafted, and the Indianapolis Colts picked me up as a free agent. The Colts called me on a Sunday, the very same day that my team and I won Bookstore Basket-ball, Notre Dame's storied spring basketball tournament and one of the largest amateur five-on-five tournaments in the country. It was a good day.

My fellow NFL teammates thought I was crazy for taking pre-med classes in the NFL offseason.

Even though I had a degree from Notre Dame and a job as a linebacker with the Colts, I interviewed for business positions through the Notre Dame career center as a conservative "Plan B." I quickly realized, however, that I still wanted to be a doctor, and someday, somehow, I wanted to help the Notre Dame football team. In addition to my ND degree, I needed four science classes (Biology, Chemistry, Physics and Organic Chemistry) to take the MCAT and apply to medical school. During every offseason with the Colts, I took a science class. After working out every day from 8am-12pm in the Colts' complex, I went to class. It wasn't easy to watch my teammates go golfing or bowling after workouts, but I had a goal, and I wanted to achieve it. I knew that every NFL career was unpredictable, at best. After four years, I finished the required courses, took the MCAT and was accepted to several medical schools. My fellow NFL teammates thought I was crazy for taking science classes in the NFL offseason. That was certainly not the norm.

In my rookie season with the Colts, I ruptured a disk in my back, and I suffered a painful foot drop. I thought my football career was over. But, I had a two-year contract with the Colts, and they honored my contract, placed me on Injured Reserve, and let me workout and focus on recovering. I was healthy for the 1994 season. I played all but two games and won one of the Special Teams Player of the Year awards, which came with a salary bonus. While I was playing that year with the Colts, I enjoyed it all, but I also ended up having three surgeries in a very short time. I knew my time in the NFL would not be a lengthy one. I planned for life after football.

One of the great things about the Notre Dame Value Stream is that it's always there to right our course when we start to stray, or lose sight of the big picture.

Going into my fourth year in the NFL, my desire to play was dwindling. Because I had medical school in my sights and because my desire to be healthy was greater than my passion to play, I retired, without regret, after suffering another knee injury. Life after football, however, was more difficult than I had anticipated. For five or six years, I stopped watching football. It was hard to watch a sport that I had played for so many years. My self-esteem took a hit when I realized that I could no longer physically play the game. Over the years, as I watched my teammates retire, I called them to see how they were doing. I wanted to be there for them as they entered the difficult transition from player to fan.

The great age disparity between players in the NFL makes it difficult to bond with your teammates.

I did enjoy my time in the NFL. But, the NFL experience is significantly different from collegiate football. Not only does the NFL, at times, feel more like a business than a sport, but the age disparity between NFL players makes it difficult to bond with teammates. As a 22-year-old, I often faced a 34-year-old guy, married with kids, on the line across from me, and I was paid to hit him as hard as I could. He's looking at his watch to coordinate his kids' after-school activities, and I'm planning my night out with my younger teammates. It's just not the same as a college brotherhood with guys my own age, who are away from home for the first time and who, together, have to make quick decisions under great pressure and stress. That bond will last forever. In the NFL, however, it's no longer just about the X's and O's, and I missed the cerebral parts of the game. Much to the surprise of most people, football is a very intelligent, complicated game. The broad salary ranges on an NFL team also create challenges. Often, a team will have vocal players who express their discontent about not being paid what they feel they are worth. This creates a lot of issues in the locker room.

Ratigan made good use of the skills he learned at Notre Dame and began prepping for his next career path while he was still playing in the NFL.

As my NFL career ended, I finished my science courses, took the MCAT and applied to medical schools. I then waited several months to find out where I was accepted. During my time with the Colts, my then girlfriend (now wife) was a law student at Notre Dame Law School. We got married the same year she finished law school, and she was hired by Jones Day, in Washington, DC. In my gap year between the NFL and medical school, I worked with a business that sold performance gear and resistance training. It was a home-based business that utilized my NFL connections, sports training, and business degree. It helped to ease my transition from sports to medicine.

In 1998, Dartmouth accepted me into its incoming medical school class. It was my first choice, and I accepted. As life goes, within the same week, we also discovered that Maura was pregnant with our first child. We wanted to move closer to Maura's family in the Philadelphia area, so I called Thomas Jefferson University Medical School, whose acceptance I previously declined, and they welcomed me back into the class. While Maura worked full-time as an attorney in Philadelphia, I completed four years of medical school and then a five-year orthopedic surgery residency program at The Rothman Institute, affiliated with Thomas Jefferson's Medical School. The Rothman surgeons work with the Philadelphia Eagles, Phillies, and Flyers; it was the perfect fit. They appreciated my unique perspective as a professional athlete who had endured six sports-related surgeries, and I continued to work with athletes while training within a highly respected orthopedic program. After residency, I then completed my sports medicine fellowship with Kerlan-Jobe Orthopaedic Clinic, in Los Angeles, California. Kerlan-Jobe physicians are the orthopedic physicians for several teams, including the Dodgers, Lakers, Kings, Ducks and USC football.

During my ten years of formal medical training, I had one professional goal: to get back to Notre Dame football. Sixteen years after I walked out of Notre Dame stadium as a player for the last time, and with a lifetime in between, I am back to serve the University that gave me my first start.

Today

Brian Ratigan and his family.

Brian is currently in private practice with South Bend Orthopaedics, in South Bend, Indiana and is the Head Orthopedic Surgeon for the University of Notre Dame football and baseball teams. He and his wife Maura live in Granger, Indiana with their five children: Sean, Conor, Kelly, Austin and Reese. The "family" category that Notre Dame once lacked for Brian is now finally complete.

Brian Ratigan's Lessons from the Notre Dame Value Stream:

- Focus on your grades and your role with the University. Student-athletes have a unique advantage now over non-athletes. Introduce yourself to those who want to be associated with your sport.

- Do not hide from the spotlight. Sports careers are relatively short; make as many connections with fellow students, alumni, administrators, etc. as you can. Most athletes try to just be a student and blend in like everyone else, but do your best to take advantage of the fact that you are a student-athlete and relish that short-lived role.

- Meet people who have similar goals and interests. Let people get to know you. Those will be the people you will want to work with after graduation.

Notre Dame vs. Southern California (USC), 1993. Notre Dame football player Jeff Burris (#9) running with the ball. Photo by Mike Bennett. (Photo courtesy of Notre Dame Archives.)

CHAPTER SIXTEEN

The Football Mentor

Jeff Burris

*J*eff Burris was a highly recruited running back from Northwestern High School in Rock Hill, S.C.; where southern hospitality was the norm and rich history and culture were everywhere you looked. Burris decided to leave the warm breezes of South Carolina and head north to play football at the University of Notre Dame after receiving a challenge from a coach in his home state who was recruiting him. He went on to be an All-American defensive back at Notre Dame, and was also featured at running back in the goal-line package. A first-round pick of the Buffalo Bills in 1994, Burris made the NFL All-Rookie team that year. He went on to play 10 seasons in the NFL before being forced to leave the game because of concussion problems. He started 119 of those 144 games and his career totals included 529 tackles and 19 interceptions. He played in the NFL for the Buffalo Bills, Indianapolis Colts and Cincinnati Bengals before retiring after the 2003 season. Since leaving the NFL Burris has turned his focus to the other side of the ball, coaching. How does a kid from South Carolina leave the warmth and hospitality of the south to play football at Notre Dame, a place that he and his teammates will forever fondly refer to as their second home? This is Jeff Burris' story.

Not the caliber of a Notre Dame football player.

When I was being recruited as a high school running back, I had no idea that Notre Dame was recruiting me. When the whole recruiting process started and various coaches were coming to visit me, this one particular coach mentioned to me that he heard I was on Notre Dame's recruiting list. When you live in South Carolina, you don't hear much about Notre Dame football. Once I found out I was being recruited by Notre Dame, I came to learn that ND was getting the best talent in the country to come play for them. I thought to myself, if I am on their list, maybe they should be on my list as well. This particular coach who was recruiting me went on to tell me that if I went to Notre Dame (instead of his school) that I would never be heard from again, because I was not the caliber of a Notre Dame football player. That really motivated me to prove to him, and everyone else, that I had what it took to be successful in a football program such as Notre Dame's. When I made my recruiting visit to Notre Dame, Tony Rice was my host. When I stepped on campus, I knew that was where I wanted to be. It just felt like home. I knew I could be successful there, that I had what it took to put in the work and be a competitor. The campus was immediately embracing to me. I knew I wanted to be a part of the Notre Dame family.

And without much ado, the Notre Dame Value Stream had already ingrained itself in Jeff Burris and was leading him toward the Golden Dome and Our Lady's University.

There are some numbers at Notre Dame that are legendary. Getting to wear one of these legendary numbers is an honor, but it also comes with a certain amount of pressure. Burris talks about his relationship with former Notre Dame quarterback, Tony Rice, and their conversation about Burris getting to wear the hallowed number nine.

I knew I wanted to be a part of the Notre Dame family.

He made a deal with me when I was there. He told me that if I came to Notre Dame that he wanted me to wear number nine, and that we would start a tradition of South Carolina boys wearing jersey number nine. How could I say no to that? And what surprised me even more was that Coach (Lou) Holtz was receptive to our plan. I may not have had the kind of success that Tony Rice had at Notre Dame, but I did my best to uphold some of the strides that he had gained.

The Notre Dame Years

Most high school football players play on both sides of the ball, but once you reach the collegiate level you settle into one specific position. Like many other football players who had a pretty good idea of which side of the ball they excelled at and wanted to play in college, Burris began his time at Notre Dame as a running back. But head coach Lou Holtz had a knack for making sure his players were in the right place for their abilities and potential; he saw something in Burris that was better suited to the defensive side of the ball. Burris may not have been able to see what Coach Holtz saw, but the Notre Dame Value Stream gave him the ability to trust in Coach Holtz and give his new path his 100%.

> *I started out at the running back position for the first nine games of my freshman year. By the end of the season our secondary was pretty depleted, so the coaching staff held tryouts for the safety position. Since I was a backup running back, I decided to go ahead and take the opportunity placed in front of me and try out for the chance to move over to the secondary. I finished the rest of the season as a safety, and then was given the choice of either staying in the secondary for my sophomore year or returning to running back. I decided that being a starter in the secondary was much better for me than being a backup running back. I had played some defensive back in high school, so the transition was not too complicated. Plus my brother was a starting corner at the University of Arkansas. I immediately got on the phone with him to get his thoughts and advice.*

Some football coaches teach their players how to be the best at their position and how to win games; and some football coaches not only teach their players how to excel on the field, but off the field as well. Notre Dame head coach Lou Holtz was the latter. He often said, "No matter what happens on the field, getting an education makes you a winner." Jeff Burris talks about the special relationship he had with his head coach.

No matter what happens on the field, getting an education makes you a winner. ~ Lou Holtz

> *Coach Holtz was wonderful to me, both as a coach and a person. Prior to the BYU game, I remember him coming up to me and telling me all the different ways I had already scored a touchdown. Then he told me all of the ways I had yet to make a touchdown, and how he was going to help me achieve*

*them and secure my place in Notre Dame History. The fact that he was so
aware of what I had done, and what I had yet to do, was very humbling to
me.*

Every student-athlete at Notre Dame fills their ND years with memories both on
and off the field. But for Burris, one in particular stands out from the rest.

> *It has to be the game we played my freshman year against Michigan. It was
> a Saturday night game and they brought in temporary lights to the stadium.
> Michigan came out to kick off the ball, and we all knew that there was no
> way they were going to kick the ball to Rocket Ismail. Coach Holtz put me
> out there with the special teams unit, and they kicked the ball to me. When
> I got the ball, I didn't really even try to make a big return, I just ran straight
> for the sidelines. All I wanted to do was get to the sideline as quickly as I
> could so that I didn't get hurt, and I didn't drop the ball. It was a terrible
> return! When I got to the sidelines all of my freshman buddies were so excited
> for me. At that moment, the results didn't matter one bit. They were so excited
> that I caught it, returned it and was on TV. Our class was such a close knit
> group. They were my family. That moment really sticks out in my mind.*

**You don't go to Notre Dame to learn something; you go to Notre Dame to be
somebody. ~ Lou Holtz**

> *Being at Notre Dame was a huge privilege for me. To be at a place sur-
> rounded by legendary players and coaches, to be able to walk in such great-
> ness, was an honor for me. When I go back and walk around the stadium, I
> have such great memories. The funny part of all of my memories from school
> is that they are all on-campus memories. We never had to leave campus.
> Everything we needed was right there. It means a lot to me that all of my
> great memories are those which took place within the school walls.*

The night before the legendary 1993 Notre Dame vs. Florida State "Game of the
Century," Jeff Burris had a dream that he'd return an interception for a touchdown. Jeff answers my question: did having two offensive touchdowns during
that game make up for his dream not coming true?

> *Absolutely not. I did have a big game that day from a running back perspec-
> tive, but not from a catching perspective. I always put a lot of pressure on
> myself to excel at everything I do. That was just the way we played.*

Each dorm at Notre Dame has its own personality or reputation. The older
dorms often have unique architectural design along with a tremendous amount
of tradition, while some of the newer dorms might lack in tradition but make up
for that in amenities. One hall in particular, the one that was the furthest away

from everything, was often sold to student-athletes as the dorm you absolutely did not want to be in. But after living there, Burris found out that there was more to Carroll Hall than met the eye.

Typical college life.

Initially when I found out I was living in Carroll Hall I was very disheartened because I had been told that they didn't put athletes out there. I called home and told my family that I didn't think they wanted me because they had placed me in a dorm where athletes were not placed. The majority of my friends on the team were living in Keenan Hall and Morrissey Hall, but I ended up absolutely loving Carroll. It was awesome to be able to get away from my teammates and experience typical college life. It was almost like being off campus, even though you really were on campus.

Professional Career

A student-athlete's career at Notre Dame flies by in an instant and then suddenly it's time see what path the Notre Dame Value Stream is going to set you on next. For most college football players at Notre Dame, the NFL is the prized destination. Burris talks about his NFL draft and what it was like to play football at the next level.

It was very simple for me: I wanted to go home and watch the draft with my family. It was hands down one of the longest days of my life, but also one of the happiest. They had a professional photographer at the house, and he snapped a shot of my mom and me hugging when I was selected (in the first round, the 27th overall pick) by the Buffalo Bills. We'll always have that photograph of me hugging her with the phone in my hand. What an amazing moment. It was such a long day, but absolutely gratifying at the end.

The people that I met playing in the NFL, they were definitely a high for me. I didn't only play with Hall of Famers, but some truly great people. Not to mention that they were from such a wide variety of backgrounds. That really made things interesting. I played with Jim Kelly, Peyton Manning, absolutely humbling to be able to say that you stepped out on the field with those greats. You get to see a side of the "stars" that most people never get the opportunity to see.

The risk of further damage was more than I was willing to take.

The fact that I actually chose to retire after 10 years as a result of all of the concussions I received was a definite low for me. I felt like there were still many things that I could have accomplished professionally, but the health risks were simply too great. With brain stem injuries you don't ever really get a good read on how bad they are, or how much more you can take. I decided that the risk of further damage was more than I was willing to take. Even retiring when I did, I still have some residual effects from all of the concussions. I still have headaches and have a certain amount of memory loss. There are certain timeframes of my life that I have simply lost. But it is difficult to say what is concussion related and what is not.

Despite all of the highs and lows that Burris encountered during his time in the NFL, his season with the Indianapolis Colts in 1999 was a season that memories are made of.

Being a part of a team that had one of the biggest turnarounds in NFL history was a shining moment of my NFL career. We (the Indianapolis Colts) went from being the worst team in the AFC, to the first-place team in just one short year. We were 3-13 in 1998 and then finished 13-3 in 1999. After coming so far, we ended up losing in our first playoff game. It was a double-edged sword. We had fantastic comeback success that year, but we didn't have success when it mattered.

Like many journeys in life, Burris' time in the NFL came to an end and it was time to set off on his next adventure. While at first he didn't know exactly what that was going to be, Burris trusted in all he learned during his time on the Notre Dame Value Stream and knew the path would become clear if he kept his mind open to all the options set in front of him.

It was a very difficult transition, leaving the NFL and moving on to the next chapter of my life. Part of what made it so difficult for me was the fact that I was not completely prepared for what to expect next. You go from organized chaos to this big unknown. Now what? My first post-NFL business venture was a clothing store that I opened, but that became financially costly for me. Then I decided to try my hand at broadcasting. I started out as a radio analyst at Marian University for five years, but if you are not a Pro Bowl or Super Bowl alum, subsequent doors just don't open for you. Then I transitioned into something that was perfect for me. I returned to football as a coach. I began my coaching career at the high school football level. In 2007, I became the defensive backs coach at Fishers High School in Fishers, Ind. Then I went on to coach cornerbacks at Warren Central High School in Indianapolis, Ind. In 2011, Dennis Green, former Minnesota Vikings and Arizona Cardinals coach, gave me the opportunity to try my hand at coaching in the United Football League (UFL). I was the cornerbacks coach for the Sacramento Mountain Lions during their 2011 season.

In 2012, I heard the call to coach at the college level for the University of

Jeff Burris and his children at his daughter's graduation.

Massachusetts. I was their cornerbacks coach and was also responsible for community relations. A big part of my job at UMass was recruiting and I was on the road a lot, but it was a labor of love for me. My recruiting territory was Maryland, Washington, DC, Virginia, my home state of South Carolina, and Indiana. It was the perfect transition into coaching. From the University of Massachusetts I took a coaching job with the Miami Dolphins as their Defensive Assistant, and then from there I became their Assistant Defensive Backs Coach. Coaching for the Miami Dolphins was an interesting scenario for me after having played with the Buffalo Bills for so long, especially when you take into consideration the rivalry between the Bills and the Dolphins. When you think about the rivalry between the two teams, you think about classic games: Marino versus Kelly; those were games you want to sit down and watch. When I took the job with Miami the Buffalo-Miami rivalry lingered on, even within my family. My daughter, who was 16 years old at the time, was born in Buffalo and it was kind of funny. When she and I would talk, she'd tell me, "I'll root for you every week except when the Dolphins play the Bills." I said, "thanks." She better just be kidding.

Today

Burris is currently seeking out his next adventure.

Jeff Burris's Lessons from the Notre Dame Value Stream:

- Attending Notre Dame was a huge privilege for me. To be at a place surrounded by legendary players and coaches, to be able to walk in such greatness, was an honor for me. Treasure those moments in your life.

- Embrace your relationship with your teammates but make friends outside of football. Make sure you take time to get away from you teammates and experience typical college life.

- Ready yourself for life after sports. Football doesn't last forever. Make sure you prepare yourself for the next phase of your journey so that you're not lost when your athletic career ends. The end of sports is just the beginning of your next adventure.

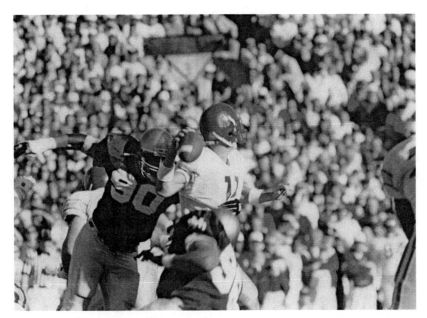

Notre Dame football player Brian Hamilton (#90) pressures the USC Quarterback. Photo by Ken Osgood. (Photo courtesy of Notre Dame Archives.)

CHAPTER SEVENTEEN

The IT Developer

Brian Hamilton

*W*hat's in a name? If you are an avid follower of Notre Dame football and you hear the name Brian Hamilton, your thought process may go one of two ways. If you follow Notre Dame football in the media, you may think of former Chicago Tribune Notre Dame beat writer, now Sports Illustrated staff writer, Brian Hamilton. Or, if you enjoy following the young men whose individual stories weave the fabric of the lore of Notre Dame football, you may think of Chicago native and former Notre Dame football standout, Brian Hamilton. Who is Brian Hamilton the former Notre Dame football player? When I asked one his teammates to describe him to me, the answer was immediate – "he's a leader. He's the nicest guy in the world, and he's still the same guy he's always been. He's the older, wiser guy. He's the one with the old soul." Brian Hamilton, a talented defensive tackle, the product of legendary St. Rita High School in Chicago, had a successful collegiate career at Notre Dame and signed as a free agent with the Atlanta Falcons. How does a Chicago native who aspired to be anywhere but Notre Dame end up playing football for the Fighting Irish? This is Brian Hamilton's story.

Football in Chicago is an intricate network, often starting young men out in the game at a very young age. St. Rita High School produced some of the crown jewels of high school football over the years. Brian, though, did not dip his toes into the waters of football until he was a freshman in high school.

> *I didn't start playing organized tackle football until my freshman year at St. Rita High School. I had a tremendous coach in Coach Quinn and he taught me a lot about the game. I started out on the defensive line, switched to tight end my sophomore year and then switched back to defense my junior and senior years. I actually went to St. Rita to play basketball; that was my sport. I joined the football team to stay in shape. Little did I know where football would take me. It was a great decision. Two years ago I was inducted into the St. Rita Hall of Fame. That was a huge honor for me. I still go back to St. Rita quite often for functions and their annual reunion in April. It's great to reconnect with the guys I played with in high school. When we see each other it's like not a day has passed. It's just like old times.*

When you play football at a Catholic high school in Chicago, it's hard not to have your eyes gazing towards the next level of Catholic football just down the road in South Bend, Indiana. For some people, it can completely turn you away from heading towards Our Lady.

> *Coming from a Catholic high school, Notre Dame really did not appeal to me. I took official visits to USC, Michigan and Tennessee but my family, coaches, and teachers really nudged me in the direction of ND.*

But when he made his visit to Notre Dame, something changed.

> *I really liked the atmosphere at Notre Dame, some of the other campuses were a little bit too big for me. I liked the intimate small campus feel of Notre Dame. I felt it would give me the opportunity to get to know people better as opposed to a large school like Michigan. I met a lot of great guys during my official visit weekend at Notre Dame. There was a great camaraderie between the guys on the current squad and they had a great coach in Lou Holtz. Barry Alvarez was the defensive coach who was recruiting me and I was very much looking forward to playing under him. Unfortunately (for me), he ended up taking the job at Wisconsin that year. That was the only*

downside for me, I would have really liked to have had a chance to play for Coach Alvarez. My host during my official visit was Irv Smith. He was the ultimate Notre Dame salesman. He was responsible for bringing a lot of excellent guys to ND.

The Notre Dame Years

When you become a student-athlete at Notre Dame, you've probably had your fair share of fame as a high school athlete. Especially if you played high school football with the Chicago elite at St. Rita High School, as Brian Hamilton did. You probably had top coaches singing your praise during the college recruiting process, and you probably felt pretty confident in your ability to step in the spotlight and capitalize on all of the opportunities that lie ahead of you. But then you step out onto that field for the first time and something unexpected takes hold of you. This is when the Notre Dame Value Stream wants you to slow down just a bit, take in the sights, sounds, and smells that are all around you, and revel in the moment that is Notre Dame football.

The moment that stands out most in my mind is the first game I played at Notre Dame Stadium. It was our home opener my freshman year. It was a night game against Michigan, the very first night game at Notre Dame and there were a lot of rising stars on both sides of the ball. Running out onto the field with 59,000 screaming fans in the stadium was incredible. We won in a close game (28-24) and it is something I will never forget.

Half of them had left the game to head out to the car to warm up.

The match up against Florida State my senior year was incredible as well. The atmosphere surrounding that game was unreal. It was the first time that ESPN had traveled to a college football site (the beginning of ESPN College Game Day). The whole experience was pretty unique. When you look back at that game everyone talked about Florida State's offense and defense and Notre Dame's offense, but no one talked one bit about our defense. We proved, soundly, to be the difference maker in that game. The other moment that stands out in my mind was my touchdown against Purdue my senior year (1993). For some reason, every time we played Purdue it rained. This game was no different. It was pouring down rain and was scoreless into the third quarter. Jeff Burris blitzed the quarterback and when he hit him the ball popped into the air. I caught it and ran 40 yards for the touchdown and that was the only touchdown of my career. The funny thing was that 20 members of my family had come down from Chicago to watch me play that day. Because of the miserable weather conditions about half of them had left the game to head out to the car to warm up. When they got to the car and turned the radio on, I scored the touchdown! Did I mention it was my only touchdown? We ended up winning the game by a score of 17-0.

Most 18-year-old kids think they have everything figured out. They head off to college confident in their path, be it their major or their aspirations to eventually play professional sports, but more often than not, each one of them is derailed at some point in their collegiate careers. At some schools, you just become another casualty, another college dropout; but not at Notre Dame. The Notre Dame Value Stream at Our Lady's University recognizes the pitfalls that most of Her students will encounter at Notre Dame and sets them up on a path for success. Her professors, advisors and coaches are there to catch them when they fall and direct them on their ascent to the peak of success.

Initially managing my time was a big challenge. It is difficult just to be a student at Notre Dame, let alone a student and an athlete. You have a different set of issues as a student-athlete as far as time management goes. Making sure I got to class, to practice, and got studying done in the evening was a big adjustment for me from high school. We had some pretty long days during football season. But I was able to manage it and I was able to do well in school. That is why I chose Notre Dame. I wanted a challenge. My other big challenge freshman year was trying to get some playing time. When I came to Notre Dame there were some incredibly talented upperclassmen, such as Chris Zorich and Boo Williams. We had some definite stars at that time, so I knew it would be an uphill battle to get any playing time my freshman year. But again, anything that is good is worth fighting for.

It's not the will to win that matters. Everyone has that. It's the will to prepare to win that matters. ~ Paul "Bear" Bryant

Professional Career

When the students of Our Lady's University are ready to set foot into the world and forge their path ahead they are one thing, and that is prepared. Over the course of four years She has done everything in Her power to make sure those 18-year-old high school students have been molded and shaped into men and women who are the future leaders of the world. Their first path may not be the one they are destined to stay on for their entire career or life, but She makes sure that though their journey may shift over the years, they are ready for anything that is brought in front of them. Following graduation, Brian says:

I signed with the Atlanta Falcons and went to training camp. When you get to that next level, as far as talent goes, it's a whole new level. The jump from high school to college is big, but the jump from college to the pros is even bigger. It was a tough time for me. I thought I did well in camp and proved myself but the Falcons ended up re-signing one of their veterans, which ended up eliminating my spot. It was a good experience for me, though, and I'm okay with how things turned out. It was (because of) times like this that I went to Notre Dame and got my degree. I knew that the pros were a possibility but at the same time knew it was not a guarantee. Staying at Notre Dame for my fifth year allowed me to walk out of there with two degrees. I graduated with one degree in business management and one degree in sociology. It was my priority to make the most of my time at Notre Dame.

Today

My wife, whom I met at Notre Dame, went to graduate school in Arizona. When I got released from the Atlanta Falcons I moved out to Arizona with her and got a job with a company called Unisys www.unisys.com/unisys. I began working on a child welfare project where we went in and converted paper cases into electronic files. I managed the effort at the different offices and I did that for six months. Every week I was at a different office working with the contractors that I hired to do the work. I learned a great deal about IT and the system and that's how I got more into the technical side of the business, and from there into development. I worked out there for a year and a half and then ended up being transferred to work on a project here in Indianapolis. I currently reside in Fishers, IN. I worked for Unisys for quite a while in their IT development department. Now I work for Molina Healthcare, which is based out of Long Beach, California. We implement systems for government state contracts that track Medicaid member and provider information. I manage a team of developers across multiple states on the projects. We have an office in Glen Allen, VA, but the majority of my team works remotely anywhere from Florida to Idaho. Technology has definitely helped out in that respect. As long as I'm on my computer, I can do work from any location.

Any school can prepare a young man or woman to head out into the world and create a successful life. Notre Dame not only prepares a young man or woman with the skills to create a successful life, but also teaches them the importance of taking care of your fellow man and giving back. The Notre Dame Value Stream instilled this quality in a young Brian Hamilton and he wears it on his sleeve today.

I met Father Streit at a Universal Notre Dame Night function here in Indianapolis. He was our guest speaker and talked to the group about the work that Notre Dame is doing in Haiti. We ended up being seated at the same table, as we knew some people in common, and we both thought it would be

*a great idea to get the Lou's Lads Foundation involved in the Notre Dame
Haiti Program. We really felt that Lou's Lads would be able to bring some
good awareness to the program.*

Get the Lou's Lads Foundation involved in the Notre Dame Haiti Program.

*I brought it up to Derrick Mayes and Brian Baker (Lou's Lads treasurer) and
they both seemed very interested. We decided that a few of us should go to
Haiti to check out the program first hand. So myself, Jeff Burris, Randy
Kinder and Reggie Fleurima (whose parents are actually Haitian) made the
trip to see the amazing work that is being done in Haiti. What we saw just
blew us away. To see what the program is doing and how they were making
a difference was incredible. They are definitely doing some great work and as
Lou's Lads continues to grow and build our fund we hope to get more
involved with the Notre Dame Haiti Program in the future.*

*We came back and talked to Lou about it. We wanted to get him to go down
there as well but we have not been able to schedule that just yet. He has such
intense demands on his time. It was a great experience. We were only down
there for a few nights but we got to see quite a bit. We saw a surgery, which
was extremely eye opening. Seeing the "hospital" that they use and the environment they have to work in, it really makes you realize how fortunate we
are in the United States. The doctors who work with the program come down
from the mainland and volunteer their time. They are doing some tremendous work in Haiti. It was amazing to be able to sit in and watch a surgery.
For now Lou's Lads is trying to raise money and awareness for the program
in Haiti and in the future we hope to be able to help more charities.*

Coach Holtz did not have many warm and fuzzy moments with his players while
they were playing for him at Notre Dame. But if you asked any one of his players today what their thoughts are regarding their former coach, each and every
one of them are truly grateful for everything he did for them and would drop
everything if he needed them. They may not have "liked" him back in the day,
but Coach Holtz absolutely knew what he was doing in molding his young student-athletes into true Notre Dame men.

*Coach Holtz was definitely a character. I was glad we (the defense) didn't see
him as much at practice as the offense did. If we saw him at practice, that
meant we had done something wrong and were in trouble. We wanted to see
him as little as possible! The defensive coordinators who mostly worked with
us were Rick Minter and Bob Davie. We had the most success under Coach
Minter but we had so much talent on that squad his job was relatively easy.
I wish they would have been a little less restrictive with us and just let the*

Brian Hamilton and his family.

guys go a little bit, and have the ability to do some different things. I really liked playing under Coach Mike Trgovac. He was my favorite defensive line coach. He's in Green Bay now.

My favorite memory of Coach Holtz came after my football career at ND was over. Coach and I talked at an event in South Bend during the Blue and Gold game weekend. He had a gathering for all of his former players that were in town. He took time out to make sure he spoke to each and every guy and their families. At that time, I was President of the Notre Dame Club of Indianapolis. I asked him if he would come and speak at the Universal Notre Dame night for our club. Coach said he would be more than happy to as long as he could fit it into his schedule in the spring. We talked a little while later and he was able to attend the event. Because of his presence we quickly sold the place out. It was just like old times. He spoke for over an hour even though it felt like only 15 minutes had passed. I don't think many coaches would do that for a former player. When he was recruiting his players I guess he truly meant if you give me 4 years I'll give you 40.

Brian now lives in Indianapolis with his wife and three children, he enjoys coaching his kid's soccer and basketball teams and is very active in the Lou's Lads Foundation and the Notre Dame Haiti Program.

Brian Hamilton's Lessons from the Notre Dame Value Stream:

- My biggest take away from my time at Notre Dame is the friends that I made who I still stay in touch with to this day. Some of my best friends are from Notre Dame. Even though we don't live in the same city, or even state, I still talk to a lot of the guys on a regular basis.

- My advice to current athletes would be to make sure that they are preparing themselves during their time in college for life after college. The preparation should not start your senior year. That is one of the biggest mistakes that people make when they are in college. You need to start preparing yourself during your freshman year for what lies ahead.

- Take advantage of the programs that Notre Dame, or whatever school you attend, has to offer. A lot of guys feel that they will for sure have the opportunity to play in the NFL but we know that those opportunities are few and far between.

- Make sure that you keep in touch with the people you went to school with. Being in my position I feel like I'm always looking for good people to hire and the best people usually come from referrals from people I already know. The best way to find an opportunity is through the people you know.

Notre Dame vs. Michigan, 1993. Notre Dame quarterback Kevin McDougal (#15) looking to hand off the ball. Photo by Matt Cashore. (Photo courtesy of Notre Dame Archives.)

CHAPTER EIGHTEEN

The Non-Emergency Transporter

Kevin McDougal

*A*ll Kevin McDougal ever wanted at Notre Dame was a chance to prove himself as a quarterback. McDougal sat for three years behind star quarterback Rick Mirer, then watched as Coach Lou Holtz named incoming freshman Ron Powlus the starter even though he'd never thrown a pass in college. McDougal felt he had earned his shot after leading more than a dozen scoring drives in a backup role and soaking up the offense for three years. After getting the starting nod Powlus suffered a broken collarbone and McDougal stepped in to lead the Irish on a Cinderella journey that some believe should have resulted in a national championship. McDougal completed 105-of-174 passes that season for 1,646 yards, seven touchdowns, and five interceptions.[3] After leaving Notre Dame,

McDougal played in the World League of American Football for the London Monarchs, the Canadian Football League's Winnipeg Blue Bombers, the XFL's Chicago Enforcers, and in the Arena Football League for Milwaukee and Georgia. He retired as a player in 2002 and returned to his home state of Florida, where he and Marci Dorsey are proud parents of their daughter, Haven Dorsey McDougal. How does a young man from Florida go from riding the bench to leading his team into a championship caliber season? This is Kevin McDougal's story.

Convincing a young man who's lived in Florida his entire life to relocate to South Bend, Indiana, is no easy feat, even when the reason is Notre Dame football. But when the recruiter sitting across the table from you is Vinny Cerrato and the Notre Dame Value Stream is doing the talking, heading north to play football for the Fighting Irish suddenly sounds pretty appealing.

> *Throughout my entire life everything revolved around the Florida Gators. Everyone in my family was a Florida Gator fan, so as far as I was concerned I was going to be a Gator as well. When I got to high school, however, I discovered that there were a lot of other choices. During my sophomore and junior years I started getting communications from several different schools that were interested in me, and then my senior year it just exploded. Vinny Cerrato, who was the football recruiting coordinator under Lou Holtz, did an outstanding job of recruiting in the late 1980s, early 90s, and brought many talented players to Notre Dame, but he really hit the Florida area hard. Just in my class alone he recruited Tommy Carter, John Covington, Clint Johnson, Oscar McBride and me out of Florida. To convince a Florida kid to leave the warmth of Florida, the close proximity to home and attend a school in South Bend, Ind., is quite an accomplishment. We were all actively recruited by Florida schools and yet we all left and went to Notre Dame.*

The Notre Dame Years

Notre Dame and head coach Lou Holtz's culture of "give me four years and I'll give you forty" came across loud and clear to these young men.

The Notre Dame Value Stream is easily recognized by prospective student-athletes and their parents, but it is also recognized by the schools and coaches who are competing against Notre Dame.

> *Once Notre Dame started recruiting you, it made you much more attractive to other schools as well. When I was looking at schools I was not only looking at football programs, I was also looking at basketball and golf since I was a*

Stats from http://www.sports-reference.com/cfb/players/kevin-mcdougal-2.html

three-sport guy. I took five official visits: West Virginia, Syracuse, Penn State, Notre Dame, and Michigan (where his recruiting host was Desmond Howard). Back then, Notre Dame brought all of the top recruits in the nation to campus for the weekend the team was preparing for its bowl game. There we were watching the top Notre Dame players get ready for their bowl game the following weekend. To see Rocket Ismail, Chris Zorich and Tony Rice out there on the practice field had me in such complete awe because they were such high profile players. Notre Dame was bigger than just about any pro team, and watching them made me think that this might be too much for me... maybe I should go play basketball. Notre Dame had just gotten the big NBC contract and they were on TV and in the national spotlight every week, which was pretty much unheard of at the time.

Fast forward to my freshman year at Notre Dame: I was the backup quarterback behind Rick Mirer in 1990 and went to Miami for the Orange Bowl, the next weekend I flew back to Notre Dame to play with Coach Digger Phelps and the basketball team in the Christmas basketball tournament. I had badly hurt my ankle during my senior year in high school and I had struggled with bone spurs all of freshman year. After I completed the Christmas basketball tournament, I made the decision to give up basketball and focus on football. I called Coach Phelps and told him that I was going to have to give up basketball and have surgery done to remove the bone spurs. Playing football was not nearly as hard on my ankles as basketball was, I just couldn't take the constant jumping. It was too much pounding on my ankles.

An important component of a successful team is to have a group of guys who support each other and have each other's backs. As a student-athlete you assume that every team you are a part of is going to be like this, but unfortunately that isn't always the case. The 1993 Notre Dame football team truly was.

The camaraderie we had was indescribable.

There was an extremely strong bond between the guys on that team. Notre Dame was a school that brought kids in from all over the country: California, Florida, Ohio, New York, and Lou Holtz and his recruiters, in particular Vinny Cerrato, did a great job at bringing a certain type of kid to Notre Dame. We had just an outstanding group of guys who really cared about football, and each other, and worked really hard. We still have tight bonds today. My senior year, when Coach Holtz told me that I was not going to be the starter, my teammates immediately got behind me to fight for me to be the starter and their leader. The camaraderie we had was indescribable. I really felt the love when the guys stuck up for me, because they felt that it was the right thing to do.

Not only is it important to have a team that is a cohesive unit, it is also important to have a head coach who can take their talents and push them to their full potential. Lou Holtz was one of the best when it came to player development. The hands-on type of coach that Holtz was, especially with his offense, means his players have volumes of stories to tell about their coach.

Clint McHawkins

As a quarterback, we spent so much time with him, so I've got tons of stories! For example, Clint Johnson was lined up at receiver and the cornerbacks were pressing him and the other receivers so as to not let him off the line. The defensive back fell down and I didn't even read the defense and I just threw it to Clint (or maybe Lake Dawson) because they were wide open, but Coach kicked me out of practice because I did not make the read. All I could hear was him yelling, "GET OUT, GET OUT, GET OUT." And the look on his face as he was screaming at me to get out was the look of a crazy man. As I'm walking off the field and he's still yelling at me, I'm thinking to myself, does he want me to stay and fight or does he want me to go to the locker room? These things happened all the time with Coach Holtz at practice.

Another time, Clint Johnson fumbled the ball during a run at practice, right before we played Michigan. Coach Holtz made Clint go stand on the Michigan side of the field and move the first-down marker during practice. Humiliation was something he used often. Clint Johnson and B.J. Hawkins were also quarterbacks, and our playbook was so big that it was often hard to remember all of the plays. We were having a particularly bad day at practice, and Coach Holtz got so mad at us that he combined all of our names together when yelling at us, "Clint McHawkins!" Another day at practice, Michael Miller was returning punts, and he kept fumbling the ball. Holtz was so frustrated that he went out there and said, "let me do it!!" The wind was blowing particularly hard that day, and he caught the ball, but the force of the ball hitting his hand broke his finger! He sure showed us.

The ability to multi-task and manage your time in high school is one thing. At the college level it is combined with being on your own for the first time and being completely responsible for taking care of and managing yourself. This may sound freeing and pretty fantastic to an eighteen year old kid, but the realities of what that entails can be quite eye opening. Add on the complexities of football and the competition that goes along with it, hold on… it's going to be a wild ride. Thankfully at ND you have the Notre Dame Value Stream to help keep you above water.

I think my whole college football career was a challenge. When people recruit you they tell you that you will have the opportunity to play. They tell you, "We only have this one person at your position so if you work hard you can be a starter." I had no idea how good Rick Mirer was and after seeing him play I thought I was never going to get the chance to play. Recruiting me, they told me that they were expecting Mirer to leave early, so I always felt I was going to get two good years. It was a huge blow to me when he decided to stay for his senior year.

Once I was a senior and thought that my time was finally here, that's when the Ron Powlus Era began. In comes this phenom whom everyone was touting as the best quarterback to ever come out of high school, and he got the start over me. I was devastated. I had played tremendously well up to this point and really felt that it was my turn to be in the spotlight. During my junior year, every time I would get into the game with the second team we would score, so I thought I would be the next starter. It was definitely a hurtful time for me once Lou decided to start Powlus. Then after he suffered an unfortunate injury, I finally got my chance to start and we did really well that year. In fact, we almost won the national title. That senior year was tough for me though, because I always felt like I wasn't wanted, especially by the coaching staff.

McDougal took the opportunities he received at Notre Dame, and the unwavering support of his teammates, and used them to his full advantage. The game that he is most remembered for is also one of his most cherished memories at Notre Dame.

The Florida State game was unbelievable for so many reasons. To begin with we had just become the number one team in the nation, so for a week I quarterbacked the number one team in the nation and not many quarterbacks can say that. There was so much media hype surrounding that week. It was the first ESPN College Game Day ever. So many big people were there, including Bob Costas. Very surreal. My breakout game was the Michigan game my senior year. We were expected to get clobbered and instead we upset them (27-23). It was the second game of the year and we had just beaten Northwestern at home. It was a huge win for us.

As with the butterfly, adversity is necessary to build character in people.
~ Joseph B. Wirthlin

Every athletic career is filled with ups and downs. McDougal's was no different. After not getting the starting QB job, then getting it and leading his team to an outstanding regular season capped off by a bowl game win, having the national championship snatched out from their grasp was heartbreaking.

Immediately following the (bowl) game, we definitely felt we would at least share the national title. We beat Florida State, and even though we lost to Boston College the next week, we still beat Florida State the prior week. How could they give the title to them (Florida State) when we beat them during the regular season? If they (the voters) didn't want a shared title between Notre Dame and Florida State, they should have given it to someone else. It just didn't make sense. The whole thing was very upsetting to us. I was on my way back to the airport with Coach Holtz to go back home when we found out and it was really sad. We could taste it, and then to have it taken away like that was devastating. At a minimum we thought we'd share it.

Professional Career

Every student-athlete who plays football at the collegiate level dreams of playing football in the National Football League. But once they are there, they soon learn how different the atmosphere is from what they've experienced at their alma mater. The family vibe and camaraderie is gone and is replaced by fierce competition in careers that are often short lived. They don't call the NFL "Not For Long" for nothing. McDougal was confident that following the successes of his 1993 Notre Dame football season his obvious next step would be the bright lights and spotlight of a NFL career. His path, however, would take a different turn.

Of course I was hurt. I didn't get invited to the NFL combine. I didn't get invited to any senior bowl games. Half of our coaching staff had left at the end of that season and they really didn't follow up with the NFL scouts to help us find our way to the NFL. Once I got to the Rams they were going through a transition as well, and unfortunately they decided that I was not part of their plan moving forward.

You learn so much about how to live your life from sports.

When I got to the Canadian Football League, I just fell off the radar. Back then TV was not like it is today where you can pretty much watch everything, and the CFL games were not televised in the U.S. The way the system worked was that you had to play a few years in the CFL and prove yourself before you could get the chance to come back to the NFL. I was very unhappy in Winnipeg. When you have to go backwards in order to move forward, you really need to be in a good state of mind to stay motivated. I got to the Winnipeg Blue Bombers and got stuck behind Canadian football legend Matt Dunigan, and at the time he was the second-best player in the whole league. They loved me but I never got a chance to play. There were positive aspects of my time playing in the CFL, World League and Arena Football. I'm still friends with a lot of those guys, and we still talk quite often. The friendships that I took away from all those years of playing football are something that I'll always treasure. It never was about money. It was about the fun of the game and being able to continue to play, meet people and grow in life. You learn so much about how to live your life from sports; especially teamwork and camaraderie.

Today

Kevin McDougal

All Notre Dame student-athletes walk out of Notre Dame prepared for life after sports. While they may all dream of professional careers, the reality is very few make it at the next level of sports. This is where the Notre Dame Value Stream points them in the right direction and carries them through the sometimes difficult transition.

Following my playing time in the CFL, World League and Arena football, I was heavy into real estate and I did that for a few years. Currently I own a transportation company, KCD NonEmergency Transport Corp., and I've been doing that for several years. We transport people in wheelchair vans and regular vans to their doctor appointments. We do a lot of work through rehabilitation facilities and we are constantly looking to expand and grow our business. We have big plans for our road ahead, and being located in Florida we have a booming market.

Kevin McDougal's Lessons from the Notre Dame Value Stream:

- Never give up. No matter how successful you are, sports only last for a short period of time. You may feel like you've been in it forever, but when you are done, your life is just beginning. I've been out of sports for 10 years and I'm 40 and I feel like I have my whole life ahead of me.

- Definitely enjoy playing sports, practice hard and soak up every moment but know that it's only a temporary thing.

- Prepare yourself for life afterwards. I think a lot of athletes believe they are going to play for a long time and they are going to make it to the pros and that is so false. Even while you are still playing, (you) always need to be thinking about what you are going to do when you get out because you are still going to be a young man.

- Enjoy every day.

Portrait of Notre Dame football player Shawn Wooden, 1993.
Photo by Bradley Photographers. (Photo courtesy of Notre Dame Archives.)

CHAPTER NINETEEN

The Financial Manager aka Mr. Hollywood

Shawn Wooden

*F*or a young man whose lofty dreams included attending an Ivy league school and receiving an Ivy league education first and foremost and secondarily competing as a NCAA athlete, Shawn Wooden's successful nine-year NFL career may seem to be something of a surprising accomplishment. Wooden ran track, which was his first love, and played running back at Abington Senior High School just outside of Philadelphia. The eastern Pennsylvania native then went on to play cornerback at Notre Dame, which at one point was in jeopardy when he needed back surgery following his freshman year. Shawn overcame the odds and went on to memorably bat down a pass from eventual Heisman Trophy winner Charlie Ward which preserved an epic 1993 win over Florida State, coined the "Game of the Century." He moved on to play defensive back for the Miami Dolphins and Chicago Bears, eventually retiring in 2004 because of a back injury. How does a young man go from being Ivy League bound, to having an electric football career both at the college and pro level, to being a successful financial planner? This is Shawn Wooden's story.

Life is all about timing. ~ Carl Lewis

Being a Pennsylvania kid, Penn State was on my radar, but I was actually looking more at Ivy League schools. Football wasn't my first love, I really wanted to run track at the collegiate level. My dream was to go to the Olympics and be like Carl Lewis. My two races were the 100-meter and 200-meter dash. As my high school football career evolved, I was getting a lot of (college recruiting) interest. I took five visits my senior year: Notre Dame, Penn State, Georgia Tech, Duke and Syracuse. When I made my visit to Notre Dame my host was Tony Brooks because at the time I was predominantly playing running back. Once I stepped foot on Notre Dame's campus, I realized how special a place it was. It wasn't just the football program or the excellent academics; there was something bigger that drew me to Notre Dame. When I took my visit to Duke I was told you can come here and be a star, or go to ND and be another brick in the wall. But once I made my visit to Notre Dame, I knew it was not just any ordinary wall.

Many young men and women head off to college with a clear vision of what they want their path to be; but so many of them arrive at college and quickly realize that their vision and reality are two different things. This is where the Notre Dame Value Stream guides its student-athletes through those rough and uncharted waters and steers them in the right direction.

That flanker mistake my freshman year was one of the best mistakes I ever made.

At the beginning of my freshman year I was a flanker. During a game, just a few games into my freshman year, I ran the wrong route and got Rick Mirer hurt. When I went over to the sideline Coach (Lou) Holtz looked at me and said, "See you in the spring. You are not going to play anymore." I looked at Coach Skip Holtz and said, "Is he serious?" And yes, yes he was. When one of the defensive backs got injured, I went ahead and offered to switch from flanker to cornerback, and that change ended up turning into a nine-year career in the NFL. That flanker mistake my freshman year was one of the best mistakes I ever made.

A career at Notre Dame as a student-athlete is not just about books, classroom time and work on the field. It's about developing the whole person and preparing

Her students for the long road ahead. It's not just about the four years at Notre Dame, but much more about the 40 years ahead. Wooden's successes and failures on the field did just that: they prepared him for the ups and downs that he would face in his life.

I look at it as a whole experience, an entire body of work. The experience of getting to play football at Notre Dame was such a joyful one for me. The '93 Notre Dame–Florida State game when I broke up Charlie Ward's final pass and secured the win is probably what most people remember me for, but that moment was a high and a low for me. Yes, we won the game, but I also tore my ACL during that game. An extreme high, and an extreme low all at once. Seeing the number one sign lit up on the top of Grace Hall was a pretty great memory for me too, even if it was only for one week. That right there is the reason why you play college ball – to have those great moments.

As a high school student-athlete, being able to manage academics and athletics is usually not much of a challenge. But when you get to the college level, it is a whole new ball game and is a stumbling block for many. The Notre Dame Value Stream does a great job of teaching Her students the valuable skill of time management.

Being able to manage your time was quite a challenge for me. My freshman year I was an electrical engineering major and my first semester I took 18 credit hours in addition to playing football. Not only was I adjusting to being away from home and trying to keep up with my engineering classes, you also have to factor in football practice, meetings, traveling, and games. When I was at Notre Dame they didn't have that 20-hour a week practice rule. If a particular practice wasn't going the right way, we could be on the practice field for hours.

Go confidently in the direction of your dreams. Live the life you've imagined. ~ Henry David Thoreau

Having a certain level of poise and confidence pretty much goes hand in hand with being successful in athletics at the collegiate level. Mr. Shawn "Hollywood" Wooden certainly had the confidence and a maturity that was well beyond his years. How did Shawn become known as "Hollywood?"

Hollywood

Partly it came from my last name, Wooden. The rest came from me trying to teach the younger guys how to have a certain level of confidence on the field. This got misconstrued as me showboating on the field and from that came the nickname "Hollywood."

Professional Career

The NFL draft is a mystical beast. It can bestow on you your greatest wishes and then without warning crush your dreams. For Wooden, it was the stepping-stone to something great. It was also a time for him to reflect back on his Notre Dame career and look forward to what was yet to come.

> *It was kind of a bittersweet moment for me. I didn't get drafted until the sixth round and though you are happy enough to be drafted, you always think you will be drafted higher than you are. I had back surgery and knee surgery during my career at Notre Dame, so I was happy that a team was able to look past that and select me. It is a great feeling to be picked; to know that someone wants you. But I did have a little chip on my shoulder because I went so late in the draft. I was drafted by Jimmy Johnson of the Miami Dolphins and I really enjoyed playing for Johnson. He was an upfront kind of head coach. Just an all-around quality guy. He gave me a chance when a lot of people probably would not have.*

> *My first game in the NFL has got to be the biggest high I ever experienced. The atmosphere on opening day (and) the realization that you made it. It was not necessarily a dream of mine as a kid, but that first home game when we took field against the Patriots; to be playing for a team that had football legend Dan Marino at the helm, it was amazing. You realize that you've made it. You are a player in the NFL. You are playing with these sports figures that you've looked up to all your life. Truly unforgettable. One of the other greatest highs of playing in the NFL was playing on Monday Night Football. Not only were you playing in front of millions of fans around the world, but you also knew you were being watched by your peers (who were) checking you out. That was a great feeling. The risk of injuries was one of the biggest lows for me in the NFL. The uncertainty. The high stress level. Worry about who is the next one to get cut, who is the next one to get injured. Watching your back because they were always looking for someone to replace you who is younger, faster and cheaper. But at the end of the day, you just needed to make sure that the highs outnumbered the lows.*

Today

The transition from the NFL to the next chapter of your life is always difficult. Whether you played two years or nine years, you are never really ready to retire.

> *As an NFL player, you are often taken advantage of if you don't know how to wisely manage your money. I made it a point to educate myself on how best to manage my money and I decided after my NFL career that I would take my financial knowledge and use it to help others. I knew that I could not get*

back into computer science (I switched majors from electrical engineering to computer science after my freshman year) without going back to school, so I went ahead and got my financial planning license, and started my career as a Financial Planner. I keep myself at the top of my game by continuing to educate myself, as tax laws continue to change and I need to be well versed in how they affect the financial market. You have to stay on your toes when you are in charge of someone else's money, so you do have to make sure that you are well educated and detail oriented. I love my job and can see myself doing this for years to come.

The role of a head coach at Notre Dame is tricky. You are expected to have your players prepared to hit the field each week and achieve the highest pinnacles of sports success. You are also responsible for molding these young men into the leaders of the future. No easy feat for anyone, but head coach Lou Holtz did it. It was the fabric of who he was as a coach. His players may not have loved him for it back then, but you can see it in their eyes when they talk about him; he has a special place in their hearts forever.

Shawn Wooden and his family.

Coach Holtz and I had an interesting relationship. We most certainly did not have a love affair. He did not hate me, but we definitely had our differences and battles. He was more of a psychological guy. He really tried to get into your head. Some guys he babied and some guys he challenged. I was one of the ones whom he challenged. He wanted to get into your mind, break you down and see what made you tick. He was a good coach though. We had words one time in his office and it came to a point when I threatened to never play football again. But I had such a love for the game and wanted to play, and he knew that. He knew that I was not going to quit. He was just pushing me to be the best that I could be. I became a leader on the team, and eventually a captain.

A telegram! Who sends a telegram?

When I officially made the 53-man roster, after being drafted by the Miami Dolphins, I got a telegram from Coach Holtz congratulating me. A telegram! Who sends a telegram? But he was so proud of me, and he didn't have to do that. That telegram meant so much to me. Not only did he demand respect from his players, but he respected them as well. As a head coach, if you don't win that locker room, and the guys don't respect you, you'll never have control of the locker room. When you are respected you have complete control. You get the guys to buy in to what you're selling. Your team becomes a cohesive unit. Coach Holtz may have torn you apart, but he didn't break you down. You knew he cared about you. You may not have liked him, but you knew he truly cared about you and you wanted to do your best for him.

Enjoying life as a financial planner, Wooden lives in Fort Lauderdale, Fla., with his wife and four children. Find out more about Shawn's business at www.WoodenWealth.com

Shawn Wooden's Lessons from the Notre Dame Value Stream:

- Get the most you possibly can out of college. College isn't just about preparing your mind academically for the future, it is also about preparing you as a total person for wherever you go in the world.

- Make good choices when it comes to your education. When you say you are a graduate from a school like Notre Dame, people look at you differently. It is not just a four-year benefit, but a lifelong one.

- When you have Notre Dame on your resume, your resume all of the sudden rises to the top of the pile. Use the alumni network to your advantage.

- Being part of an institution such as Notre Dame prepared me to be a good father, a good husband and a good businessman. That is a direct result of what I learned at Notre Dame. Being a Notre Dame student-athlete, you are a student first before you are an athlete. Your time as an athlete will end one day. Remember that being a student is the most important part of being in college.

Portrait of freshman Notre Dame football player Bertrand Berry, 1993. Notre Dame University Photographer. (Photo courtesy of Notre Dame Archives.)

CHAPTER TWENTY

The Sports Radio Analyst

Bertrand Berry

*F*ormer Notre Dame and NFL defensive end Bertrand Berry was a three-sport standout from Humble, Texas, not exactly the type of city name one would associate with most professional athletes. He was great at every sport he played in high school – a two-time all-district selection in basketball, that also set new records in track, but football was his dream. Berry was a four-year letterman in football at Notre Dame, finishing his college career with 187 tackles and 16.5 sacks. In 1997, Berry was selected by the Indianapolis Colts in the third round of the NFL Draft. He was with the Colts from 1997-99, then had a short stint in the Canadian Football League with the Edmonton Eskimos before returning to the NFL with the Denver Broncos and later the Arizona

Cardinals. He finished his NFL career with 229 total tackles, 65 sacks, 14 fumble recoveries and 14 forced fumbles, earning a Pro Bowl spot in 2004, the same year he led the NFC in sacks. How does a three-sport standout hailing from Humble, Texas end up in frosty South Bend, Indiana? This is Bertrand Berry's story.

When you play high school football in Texas it is pretty much assumed that you will play college football at a school in Texas, or at the very least at a school in the south. But to leave the big football atmosphere of Texas and head to some small town in Indiana; that decision came as quite a shock to those following Bertrand Berry's young football career.

I was a momma's boy.

My plan was to go to Texas A&M. My mother grew up 20 miles from College Station and I loved their defense, known as "The Wrecking Crew." They were dominating their conference. Then in 1993, Texas A&M played Notre Dame in the Cotton Bowl. Texas A&M was undefeated that season and Notre Dame had one loss. Everyone in A&M country was very disappointed that they had to play Notre Dame. They thought they should have been playing for the national title, and then Notre Dame came in and absolutely manhandled them. It really made me stop and think. If I go to A&M, they really don't have a chance to win a title. But, if I go to Notre Dame, my chances may get better. Plus, I really needed to get away from Texas. I was a momma's boy and really needed to set out on my own.

The Notre Dame Years

Every Notre Dame career is filled with highs and lows. Some careers, however, are blessed to have one special high that will truly go down in college football history. Bertrand had the chance to experience a historic moment during his freshman year at Notre Dame.

When we beat Florida State my freshman year (1993), the "Game of the Century," everything about that game was truly memorable. The energy on campus that whole week before; the media hype surrounding the game; watching the students rush the field after the game. It was simply amazing. We had a bye the week before and there were so many people on campus that week. It was tough going to class with all of the news media around. It was like nothing we had ever experienced before. That was the very first ESPN College Game Day. When I think back to that moment, all of the students on the field, watching the clock hit zero, we felt that we were so disrespected going into the game and finally we were going to get the respect we felt we deserved. Winning was great, but we should have beat them by a lot more (the Irish beat the Seminoles 31-24). The score didn't really represent how good we really were.

As a collegiate student-athlete, your relationship with your coach is crucial. It can either make or break your athletic career. When your head coach is Lou Holtz, he's not only concerned with your on-the-field success; he's also concerned with preparing you for success off the field for your next forty years. Lou Holtz was the heart and soul of the Notre Dame Value Stream that carried his players through their careers at Notre Dame.

When we played Stanford my sophomore year, we put a pretty good beating on them. Bill Walsh was head coach for Stanford and Steve Stenstrom was their quarterback. I got to know Stenstrom pretty well that day, and he spent a lot of time on his back. At the end of that day a couple of the guys on Stanford's offensive line had just about had enough of me. They were giving me the business after one of my big plays and I got frustrated and dished it back. They were shoving me back and forth like a pinball when I hit one of the guys in the face. Of course, the ref saw me and I got thrown out of the game. When I got to the sideline, Coach Holtz was waiting for me. In his signature move, he grabbed me by the facemask and shook it. (He) told me, "Don't ever do that again," and then patted me on the head. Had I had a bad game that day, he probably would have said more, but because I had a good game he just left it at that. I got a lot of phone calls that day because it was on national TV. Coach Holtz was definitely a disciplinarian. I appreciated that because I wanted to be great at football and I knew that I needed that type of coach.

My time at Notre Dame was filled with good memories of Coach Holtz. Being from Texas, I was used to tough coaches. What I loved most were his pregame speeches. They were some of the best I've ever heard. I wish I had recorded the FSU pregame speech. After that one, I think we could have beaten any pro team. He masterfully played on our emotions. They never had a chance to beat us that day. I hope someone has a recording of that.

Bookstore Basketball

Football is life at Notre Dame, but what you might not know is that basketball - or rather Bookstore Basketball - carries a great deal of bragging rights at Notre Dame as well.

Playing football at Notre Dame was amazing, don't get me wrong. But my Bookstore Basketball win is something truly special to me. My team got beat my sophomore year to (all-stater) Owen Smith and his team, and that burned me up all year. I think I wanted to win Bookstore more than a national championship. I got teased so much for losing my sophomore year.

The next year when we (Dos Kloskas) won, it was raining cats and dogs. It was a really sloppy game, and the team we played in the finals was a team we had played many times out in the lot. They were an infamous team (Show-time) and they had been together for a couple of years like we had. Beating them was awesome. One of the things that I like most about the whole Book-store Basketball tournament are the costumes at the beginning. The girls' teams who came out in high heels; just awesome. My freshman year I was pretty annoyed with that, but when I saw how much fun they were having, I really grew to enjoy them.

We may encounter many defeats but we must not be defeated.
~ Maya Angelou

Almost every journey encounters a bump in the road. How you handle it says a lot about the person you are and how your journey continues moving forward. When a student-athlete at Notre Dame happens upon this inevitable bump in the road, the Notre Dame Value Stream rises to the occasion and gracefully carries them through and shows them how to overcome the adversity staring them in the face.

Academically ineligible.

I got caught cheating on a paper my freshman year and became academically ineligible to run my first season of track. It was the last paper in that partic-ular class, in late December, and I ended up getting an "F" for the entire class (Composition & Literature). I was doing so well in that class. I had knocked all of the tests out of the park, but I just didn't feel like writing this paper. The paper that I ended up using, I got from a guy who had taken the class three years before, and the professor recognized it right away. After not running track that first year, I just decided it was smart of me to focus on football, and doing well in my classes!

Tradition is a big part of the Notre Dame experience. Living on campus in the dorms is a big piece of that Notre Dame tradition. As a school where there are no fraternities or sororities, Notre Dame dorm life fills the void and creates cama-raderie. Bertrand spent his time at Notre Dame living in Carroll Hall, which is across the lake and the furthest possible dorm from the stadium; but that ended up being a welcome oasis.

I absolutely loved it. It was the best dorm for me, for my personality. I am a low-key guy and it was perfect for me to be able to get away from my team-mates after practice. I have great friends that I made during my time spent hanging out in Carroll Hall. I didn't room with football players, which was great for me. You're with them all day long, Carroll was my sanctuary. I just wanted to go to my room after practice and chill and relax. Not have to worry about talking football. My time at Carroll was awesome.

Professional Career

Today the NFL draft is a circus tent event where everyone goes to New York City to see where their future lies, but when Bertrand Berry was drafted that was not the case.

I watched the draft at my brother's house in Texas. It was a very long day. I ended up getting drafted in the third round, a couple of picks before the end of the first day. It was a day filled with anxiety, anger, and frustration. I started the day with this plastic cup in my hand, and my brother had to eventually take the cup from me. I was taking sips from it and there was nothing in it. When my brother took the cup from me, I had this death grip on it. I guess that was a result of thinking that I was going to be selected much earlier. Kinnon Tatum was drafted the very next pick after me, and that was special for me as well. The fact that the two of us got drafted back-to-back was a special moment, and we'll always share that. I went to the Indianapolis Colts, and he went to the Carolina Panthers.

When the direction of Berry's new journey was revealed it wasn't exactly the path that he was expecting, but the Notre Dame Value Stream helped him find clarity and realize that this was his true path.

I didn't ever think I'd go back to Indiana once I left Notre Dame.

The funniest thing about being drafted by the Colts was that I didn't ever think I'd go back to Indiana once I left Notre Dame. Sitting at my brother's house on draft day I was thinking to myself, "It's been really great Notre Dame, now let's get out of the snow." And then I get drafted by the Colts! Are you kidding me? But then I remembered that my dream of playing in the NFL had just become a reality, and the location didn't really matter anymore.

When you finally reach a dream you've been chasing for much of your life the expectations are high. But in reality, even dreams are filled with highs and lows.

Playing on Sunday was a definite high. It was what got you through the week. There is nothing like running on the field and competing at the top of your profession. For 13 years, there was nothing better for me than putting on that jersey and representing my family and the NFL. I wore "Berry" across the back of an NFL uniform with great pride. It had a lot of hard work behind it and a lot of pitfalls along the way. The business aspect of the NFL was definitely a low. Everyone knows that it is a business. That's what provides your paycheck every month, but it does take some of the fun out of the game. Sunday was an escape from that business side. Time spent with the guys in the locker room, clowning around, getting to know your teammates, was great. But you also knew that at any moment they could be traded or cut. No notice. No warning. The mental side of that is really tough. But even more challenging than that was losing guys like Junior Seau. It is just not fair to see such wonderful men being taken from us much too early.

Two NFL moments stick out in my mind. The first was being selected to the Pro Bowl in 2004. It is obviously an honor when you are voted in by your peers for being the best in your profession. Especially because of the way my career had progressed, and the bumps in the road that I had encountered prior to that year. Secondly, was playing in Super Bowl XLIII. Even though we didn't win the game, we played our hearts out and it was an awesome experience. I would not trade it for anything. It was incredible to be a part of something as huge as the Super Bowl. We got these impressive looking NFC championship rings. I have no regrets at all. It was one incredible ride to get there, and I will never forget that time of my life.

When football has been such an integral part of your life for so many years, the transition from football life to the regular world can be challenging. And then some people like Berry are more than ready for the move and it is nearly seamless.

Get out while you have a little something in the tank.

The transition was not difficult for me. Mentally I was ready. Once playing in the NFL became work, it was time for me to go. I really was OK with leaving. Thirteen years was more than I could have asked for from an NFL career. I was healthy and all in one piece. I did everything I set out to accomplish. I got to play in a Pro Bowl and a Super Bowl. I retired on my terms and I will always be proud of that. The transition for me was seamless. I knew I would survive without the game because I had already proven to myself that I could survive without the game when I was not playing in 2000. Plus, you always want to get out while you have a little something in the tank.

From a fan's perspective.

At first I did some work with a local TV show here in Phoenix, and that was a blast for me, but it was just a little segment here and there, a web-based show. I enjoyed it, but it really was not what I wanted to do moving forward. Following that, I got the opportunity to get my own radio show, which truly was a blessing. I get to talk sports on a daily basis without having to tear my body up. It has challenged me to get out of my comfort zone because I talk about all sports, not just football. It keeps me involved in the sporting world, but at the same time it holds my interest. I have the chance to grow in my relationships with other sports. With our hockey team's success, I really have learned about the game of hockey. I see sports in general from a completely different point of view now, from a fan's perspective. I have enjoyed the transformation.

In 2005 I founded the Bertrand Berry Foundation primarily in honor of my wife, who is a survivor of childhood cancer (leukemia). We wanted to give back to something that gave her a chance at life. I have always been community oriented and have always given back when I was able. The fans are the ones who put their money up to come watch the games. Even at Notre Dame, I thought football was entertainment as much as it was a competition. You have to be able to play to the fans. But I also feel a responsibility to give back to the fans, as well as the community at large. I have always been quick to jump on opportunities to go speak to elementary school and high school kids. I wanted my foundation to not only give back to something that gave my wife a future, but also to help kids. I have a soft spot for kids. Nothing burns me up faster than someone taking advantage of a child.

Berry's foundation supports the Leukemia & Lymphoma Society, Childhelp.org and Big Brothers Big Sisters of Central Arizona: *www.bertrandberryfoundation.org*

Bertrand Berry

It's all about helping out young kids. They are a group that cannot help themselves. We have also added a scholarship in my mother's name. She was a teacher for 30 years and when I went to Notre Dame she made me promise to get my degree. I am most proud of my Notre Dame degree. It is one of my most prized possessions.

Berry now lives in Phoenix, Arizona with his wife, whom he met in middle school, and their three children.

Bertrand Berry's Lessons from the Notre Dame Value Stream:

- Do your best. Don't ever just "phone it in."

- Make sure that focusing on school is a priority.

- As an athlete, be sure to build relationships with both athletes and non-athletes alike. Life is a diverse endeavor.

Notre Dame vs. Michigan State (MSU), 1993. Notre Dame football player Randy Kinder (#25) running with the ball. Photo by Ken Osgood. (Photo courtesy of Notre Dame Archives.)

CHAPTER TWENTY ONE

The Investment Trust Manager

Randy Kinder

Randy Kinder grew up in the heart of Spartan Country where the winters were long and snowy, everyone's closet was filled with green and white, and in a house where everyone knew the MSU fight song by heart. Even with such strong influences, Randy was not a college football fan. He did not even know where Notre Dame was, let alone that it was only a mere two and a half hours away from East Lansing, Michigan. But after some football success in high school and being on the receiving end of attention from several Division I football schools, Notre Dame very quickly jumped into the picture. After his time at ND, Randy had a brief but exciting NFL career with the Green Bay Packers and Philadelphia Eagles. Kinder had the opportunity to play for such legendary coaches as Mike Holmgren, Fritz Shurmur and Ray Rhodes, and to play with childhood role models Reggie White and Brett Favre. How does a young man destined to play football in Spartan country end up a running back for the Fighting Irish of Notre Dame? This is Randy Kinder's story.

I was not a huge college football fan.

As a kid growing up I had no knowledge of Notre Dame and I was not a huge college football fan. I was born in Washington, DC and when we moved to Michigan when I was five years old I brought my Washington Redskin fandom with me. As I got to middle school I became a Spartan fan. Everyone around me knew the Spartan fight song. My mother went to graduate school at Michigan State and worked at the university for a while, and we lived just a mile from campus — it was very present in our lives. When I realized I was pretty good at football, I started to pay attention to what other schools were out there. I knew of Notre Dame but was not really interested. I was shocked when I found out it was only two and a half hours away. I never thought it was a possibility for me to play somewhere like Notre Dame until the recruiting process began. I went down to Notre Dame for the Michigan game when Reggie Brooks scored the unconscious touchdown and I thought to myself, this is the coolest place ever. That was a huge deal for me, when I saw that play. If you grow up a Michigan State fan, you hate the Wolverines. It was awesome to see a running back give their all like that and just fall into the end zone.

I remember the Cotton Bowl game in January of 1993 against Texas A&M. Jerome Bettis scored a touchdown on a Rick Mirer pass late in the third quarter. After he scored he got into somewhat of an altercation with a few of the A&M players in the end zone. When he got to the side lines you could see Coach Mosley talking to him, telling him that he needed to chill out. After the coach was done talking to Bettis the camera was still on Jerome and you could then see him mouth, "I still got six." I wanted to be on the team with that guy.

For a kid who had hardly any knowledge of Notre Dame or any understanding of what Her Lady's University stands for, the Notre Dame Value Stream quite swiftly took hold of him and swept him away with all the mystique that makes us love this University so dearly.

During the recruiting process my senior year, I also got to attend the ND football banquet where I had the chance to see the caliber of guys who were leaving: Rick Mirer, Devon McDonald, and Demetrius DuBose. I also had the opportunity to meet some of the guys that I would be playing with if I came to Notre Dame, including Derrick Mayes who was my host and would later be my roommate. He was the best salesman for Notre Dame. It was a typical snowy South Bend weekend when I was there, but the weather did not scare me being from East Lansing. I absolutely fell in love with the guys on the team and the coaching staff (Tom Clements and Skip Holtz). I went to all of the functions that weekend and then the last person I met with was a one-on-one meeting with Lou Holtz. He asked me if I wanted to be a part of "this" (Notre Dame) and without hesitation I gave him my verbal commitment right then and there. Outside of a short flirtation with Stanford, I never really wavered in my interest of attending Notre Dame. I knew after that weekend that Notre Dame was where I wanted to be.

I took official visits to Michigan, Michigan State, Boston College, Stanford, and Notre Dame. My parents had given me an "approved list" to choose from. They wanted to be sure that academics came first and football came second. Michigan State had an excellent Public Policy program and the academics at Stanford were fantastic. The schools I was looking at had some excellent football coaches as well including Bill Walsh at Stanford, Tom Coughlin at Boston College, and George Perles at MSU. I really could not have gone wrong at any of those places.

The Notre Dame Years

The Notre Dame Value Stream is not show-stopping or attention grabbing, and it's not something that glitters in the sun. The Notre Dame Value Stream is about hard work, core values and treating others as you wish to be treated. It's about learning how to live in a fashion that takes care of yourself and others.

My weekend at Notre Dame was not a weekend of entertainment and fine dining. It was a real weekend. There was not a lot of pomp and circumstance. I had the chance to spend time in the dorm and get to know the students. It gave me a great feel for what the place was really like. My parents really enjoyed it as well and were happy that it was only a couple hours from home. Notre Dame pretty much checked off every box that we had made as a family beforehand and it did so with flying colors. I felt honored that Notre Dame was even considering me.

My freshman class was a top-ranked recruiting class. We had such names as Ron Powlus, Bertrand Berry, and Marc Edwards. The freshman football players arrive on campus five days before the rest of the team comes in and have a freshman orientation. We really came in as a cohesive unit. We had such pride in each other and were very excited to be a part of this thing called Notre Dame football. The camaraderie that we built those five days was incredible. We were so happy, so excited. We all knew we were going to at least attempt to accomplish great things during our time at Notre Dame. That feeling alone is one of my best Notre Dame football memories.

Those feelings of unity and camaraderie then translated into teamwork and wins on the field.

As far as on-the-field memories go, the win over Florida State my freshman year was amazing. To go into that game as an underdog and come out on top was a great feeling for us. For me personally, the comeback over Purdue late in my junior year was a huge accomplishment. I scored the winning touchdown in the final minutes of the game (Randy Kinder's 52-yard touchdown run stalled a strong Purdue rally in the 1995 35-28 thriller). All the trips we took: Air Force, BYU, the trip to Ireland my senior year, we had so much fun as a unit traveling together, getting to visit places we'd never been before. It was a huge part of the experience of playing Notre Dame football. There are some guys who remember every single detail of every play. I am the kind of guy that when the play turns on, my memory turns off. During that Purdue comeback, I remember that Purdue had just scored the go ahead touchdown on a turnover, and when we got the ball back I remember Ron Powlus coming into the huddle and telling us, "We've got to get this game back. Let's do this right now." And on the next play we ran, I scored the winning touchdown and we took the game back.

Football is by nature a violent sport. It is a sport of aggression. In the heat of the moment that aggression can lead to injuries. In September of 1996 Notre Dame played the University of Texas and Bryant Westbrook put an intense hit on Kinder. He talks about the hit:

It's funny, I have a brother who is much younger than me. I was on his Facebook page not too long ago and his buddies were giving him a hard time about the big hit I took during that Texas game in 1996.

Any time someone new comes into my office, the first thing my boss does is rush them over to the computer to show them the play. But my only thought is this: we won the game. If you look at the play, for years and years people have said to me, "Aww man, you must have been mad at Ron (Powlus) because he hung you out to dry." A couple of years ago Malcolm Johnson sent me an apologetic email saying that he was supposed to block Bryant Westbrook on that play.

When I went to the NFL combine Bryant was there as well. He ended up getting drafted in the first round by the Detroit Lions. We ran into each other at the combine and just cracked up laughing. I told him "You're welcome" because that play was run so many times on ESPN that it probably helped catapult him into his NFL career. I don't have an active memory of that play. I was pretty much done after it. I went in for one more play. A play that I had nothing to do, but I knew my mother was watching the game on TV in East Lansing and I was sure she was thinking that her son had died so I wanted to make sure she could see that I was okay. I knew it was bad when on the flight home they kept telling me, "you should probably stay awake for a while. No sleeping on the plane."

Being a student-athlete at Notre Dame is a challenge. Most student-athletes at Notre Dame are used to balancing busy schedules, as many of them were multiple sport athletes in high school and excelled academically. But time management at the college level is different than what was expected of you in high school. The Notre Dame Value Stream guides its students and shows them how to avoid the pitfalls that can happen when you are on your own and away from your parents' guidance. What was Kinder's biggest challenge?

I was not a great student but I always loved school.

Keeping my focus. It is so hard to stay focused and you don't realize it until you are in a situation which requires focus. To be able to remember, as Lou Holtz always said to us, "WIN — What's Important Now?" What is the most important thing to do first and what gets you to your goal. It's the first time you are away from home. There are so many distractions outside of football and school, it is easy to lose your direction and get knocked off your path. I got caught up with things that had nothing to do with what my goals were or what should have been my priority. It led to off the field issues with student affairs that were unnecessary and mistakes, but they could have been completely avoided. They came from a lack of focus. In the classroom I had the same issue. I loved school. I was not a great student but I always loved school.

There are so many demands on you and it's so easy to let something fall by the wayside. I did not manage my time well at Notre Dame. What I can say now is that through all I experienced as a student at Notre Dame I have learned a great deal and am much more organized and efficient as an adult. I think about Tim Ruddy. He had over a 4.0 grade point average, was the starting center and was a high NFL draft pick. He was a brilliant guy, a good guy who didn't suffer on the personal side of things. We should celebrate student-athletes such as that. There are so many ways to take short cuts in life. Any time I hear about student-athletes who make Academic All-American, I think we should do more to recognize those students. We should provide more services to the student-athletes to help them better manage their time and their lives. The more we do to help student-athletes early on, the better. When we arrived at Notre Dame, staff from the student affairs and counseling offices would meet with us and explain, "You're about to face a lot of demands on your time," but we had no idea what was really about to happen. I was so invested in football practice I just blew off the academics. There is so much we can accomplish in college; it's a shame when a student does not take full advantage of all that is offered. I feel bad that I did not take advantage, academically, of all the things that Notre Dame had to offer.

Many of us were disappointed in the way that Coach Willingham had been dismissed.

When the university hired Reggie Brooks to be the liaison between the alumni football players and the current football players it sent a huge message to the rest of us. Many of us were disappointed in the way that Coach Willingham had been dismissed and had lost our connection with the University. Coach Holtz had a reunion with us somewhere around 2005, and as we were sitting there in South Dining Hall he reminded us that we own this University, through the blood, sweat, and tears that we put into it; and that we all needed to be active participants in it and not hold on to the bitterness. This message from Coach Holtz along with the hiring of Reggie Brooks (one of us) helped show us that the University was not only interested in reestablishing a relationship with Her football alumni, but was also interested in getting us involved in mentoring current student-athletes. To get us to come back and help make the University what we want it to be. Reggie's hiring was instrumental in making that happen. As a student-athlete you need to have a place where you can go and get some real advice on how to deal with what you are experiencing, from someone who has already experienced it; to have trusted people that you can get advice from. This is what Notre Dame is doing today.

Coach Holtz did his part with the Notre Dame Value Stream to keep his players on the straight and narrow and develop them into the young men he knew they could be.

I was the dumbest player recruited out of the state of Michigan.

Coach Holtz had this way of breaking you down so that he could build you back up. He was a psychology major in college and he used every ounce of that degree in coaching. My freshman year he had me convinced that I was the dumbest player he ever recruited from the state of Michigan. We had worked on my stance and it was still a half-inch off and he kept yelling at me — why could I not get it right? Then one of the upperclassmen Pete Chryplewicz told me not to worry, *that he was the dumbest player recruited out of the state of Michigan the previous year.*

My favorite Coach Holtz story happened the week before the Florida State game in 1993. It was the Wednesday prior to the game and I don't think one pundit had picked us to win. They were this gargantuan power and we were the lowly guys who should not even be on the same field as them, with a quarterback who did not even come close to competing with their amazing Charlie Ward. Coach Holtz called us in to the defensive meeting room in the ACC. He then started going through our team, player by player, down the starting lineup and compared each one of our guys with Florida State's corresponding player. He explained why Florida State had no business being on the field with "us" and how our players were more talented than each one of their players. It was the best psychological exercise I'd ever seen. It was so clear to us. I think every one of us walked out of that meeting convinced that we had already won the game and that we didn't even need to play it. We knew that we could beat them and that we would beat them. We meditated before every game. Coach Holtz was big on making sure you were in the right mental space before taking the field to play the game. The power of your mental psyche over what you can do physically is amazing. It's like flipping on a switch in your head. At that meeting before the Florida State game I saw really how good he was as a coach.

Professional Career

Notre Dame's mission and purpose with its students is to "foster the development in its students of those disciplined habits of mind, body, and spirit that characterize educated, skilled, and free human beings." This mission, implemented through the Notre Dame Value Stream, prepares students for the long and winding road ahead. Kinder's journey beyond Notre Dame started with the NFL Draft.

I sat at home with my family and we watched both days of the draft. There was some wishful thinking on my part that I'd get picked somewhere in the middle rounds but it didn't happen. I did get calls from several teams who expressed interest in drafting me and told me that if I did not get drafted that I would get invitations to camp. Ron Wolf, the general manager of the Green Bay Packers called me in the middle rounds of the draft and said, "We like you and we have a plan for you." He explained to me that they were very interested but were not sure that they wanted to keep me in the running back position, but possibly move me to defense. He was quite a legend, so getting that call meant a tremendous amount to me. Shortly after the draft, I received calls from several teams inviting me to their training camps. Mr. Wolf called me again wanting me to come to camp, and there were three other Domers already on the team (Aaron Taylor, Craig Hentrich and Derrick Mayes) so it was a great fit for me. I was very familiar with the team, and they were coming off a Super Bowl win, which made them very attractive. Green Bay has a college town feel to it, which I liked. They wanted me and they had a plan for me, and so I went up to Green Bay and signed with them.

We love your enthusiasm, but don't do that again.

They decided that they wanted to switch me to defensive back and I agreed because I wanted to be a part of their organization. They had done it successfully with several other guys, so seemed like a great opportunity for me. I would spend a year or two on the practice squad and then I'd have the opportunity to join the 53-man roster. After the first game of the season Craig Newsome, their starting cornerback, tore up his knee and so they bumped everyone up on the depth chart. Suddenly I was the sixth corner and was added to the active special teams unit. This gave me a chance to learn more about the system and they'd have the ability to move me back to the practice squad if needed. In my very first game (which was week two of the season), on my very first play, I was one of the gunners running down field towards the kicker. As I got down there I was completely in the zone. I was running full speed ahead and when the punt returner sees me coming he throws up the fair catch signal. I tried to change up my momentum but by that point I was already too close and I ended up slide tackling into him. I headed over to the sideline, sure that I was going to be cut or sent home, but they were totally great with me. "Randy, we love your enthusiasm, but don't do that again."

I played a lot of special teams in Green Bay. In November of that season I was moved back to the practice squad and was then picked up by the Philadelphia Eagles. This was great for me because my Dad was from Philadelphia and my grandparents lived there and were able to come to every game, along with my cousins and Uncle and Aunt. I spent the offseason in Philly and then was cut at the end of the following training camp, and aside from a short offseason stint with the Indianapolis Colts that was the official end of my NFL career. I could have gone and played in Europe or Canada, but I decided not to pursue that and to begin the next chapter of my life instead. I can't complain at all. I got to play with Reggie White and Brett Favre, two of my childhood role models, and a lot of my childhood dreams came true. It was a wonderful opportunity/experience for me.

Some of Our Lady's student-athletes get to play their sport at the professional level. But all of Her student-athletes get to play the game of life. What they learn during their journey on the Notre Dame Value Stream readies them for the roller coaster ride of life that looms in front of them.

After my time with the Eagles, I lived in Chicago for a bit but eventually settled in Washington, DC with my wife. I work for a company called the AFL-CIO Investment Trust Corporation. I work in marketing and investor relations for a series of funds that invest union pension dollars into commercial real estate and into the stock market. Our whole main idea is to use union pension dollars to create jobs and a secure retirement for our workers. In our commercial real estate fund, if we build anything, it is built with union workers. And if we own buildings, they are serviced by union workers.

There is a big industry conference that I go to every year for union trustees, the International Foundation, and a few years back it was in New Orleans and Lou Holtz was the guest speaker. Within ten minutes of the big announcement that Coach Holtz was going to be the speaker I already had several emails from colleagues, "can you introduce me to Coach Holtz?" So I sent an email to Coach Holtz' secretary, Jan, letting her know that myself and Bryan Flannery both work in the industry and that we'd love to have dinner with Coach Holtz after his speech. Almost immediately Jan emails me back saying, this is great but it's too far off in the future. The next day I get an email from Coach Holtz, "Randy, whatever you and Bryan need, I will do it for you." And that was Coach Holtz.

Give me four years and I'll give you forty. ~ Coach Lou Holtz

He was coming to the conference from Bristol, Connecticut (he had been working at ESPN headquarters) but because of a blizzard his flight out of Hartford was cancelled and so he had to drive to NYC to fly out of LaGuardia. They were closing roads left and right on his route and a state trooper ended up guiding him down the road. He makes it to his flight and gets to our luncheon and could not have been more gracious. He stayed with us for 90 minutes after his speech, signed autographs, never once complaining that he had been up all night trying to get there. And for him, we were able to raise money for his foundation, Lou's Lads. Years later he is still very much a part of our lives, and we are in his as well. When he arrived at the conference, the first thing he said to me was, "How's your family? How are your folks? How's your sister?" Even years later, he still had a vested interest in your life, success and well-being.

Lou's Lads

The impression that Lou left on his players has stuck with them long after their time at Notre Dame was complete. They have now joined together to form the Lou's Lads Foundation, of which Kinder is an active participant. They feel a deep connection to their former head coach and have banded together to do good works in his name.

Lou's Lads is a charitable foundation set up by his players, dedicated to Coach Holtz and designed to preserve his legacy. He did so much for us, we are more than happy to give back to him through this foundation. We based the foundation on the same idea as Leahy's Lads. Their foundation started out mainly as a way for them to stay together — to get back to campus and stay in touch. We started not only with this concept but directly with the idea of doing charitable work and giving back to the students. We wanted to not only take care of each other, but to give back as well.

Our Mission: *Lou's Lads Foundation, Inc. is a 501(c)(3) charitable organization dedicated to preserving and supporting the legacy of Coach Lou Holtz and his players, while providing a platform to provide financial assistance for the educational needs of underprivileged students and legacies as well as support charitable and educational activities and organizations within the communities of its members.*

I have been involved in a project that the foundation is supporting in Haiti. Reggie Fleurima, Jeff Burris, Brian Hamilton, and I made the trip to visit the ND Haiti Program to see how we could use our influence to help an existing program at the school. We had been introduced to the program through Brian Hamilton and it's director Father Thomas Streit and we got a chance to see firsthand the amazing work they are doing down there. There is so much work to be done in Haiti you have to force yourself to be extremely focused. The Notre Dame Haiti Program, founded in 1993, seeks to achieve the historic goal of eliminating Lymphatic Filariasis (LF) in Haiti by 2020. In an area where there are issues with clean water, the disease is spread through mosquito bites. The disease is the second leading cause of long-term disfigurement and disability worldwide, which primarily presents itself as elephantiasis. The social stigma associated with the disease is often as bad as the disfigurement itself. Once you contract the disease it is not reversible, however it is possible to eliminate it through mass drug administration and the distribution of co-fortified salt.

What the Notre Dame program is trying to do is get the medicine to the people. Haiti is one of the few countries that does not have an iodized salt pro-

gram, so they decided why not put the medicine along with the iodine into the salt and you're killing two birds with one stone. The work that Notre Dame is doing is remarkable, and once successful in Haiti they hope to use their model in other developing nations. After we had a chance to see the work that Notre Dame is doing in Haiti firsthand, we are now trying to figure out how we can be ambassadors for the program and get Lou's Lads behind it. The potential of what we can do is limitless. I am very excited about what lies ahead.

Today

Today, Kinder lives with his wife in Washington, DC, and recently completed his MBA from Robert H. Smith school of business at the University of Maryland. Kinder works for the AFL-CIO Investment Trust Corporation and keeps in close contact with his former Notre Dame teammates and Coach Holtz through his work with the Lou's Lads Foundation, and the ND Haiti Program *www.haiti.nd.edu/* .

Randy Kinder and former Notre Dame head coach Lou Holtz.

Randy Kinder's Lessons from the Notre Dame Value Stream:

- Focus on "What's Important Now." It is important that young people are able to focus in on, as Coach Holtz says, "What's Important Now," but I think in order for these young men to get the fullest out of their experience in college they have to make it a priority that they get the most out of each part of their collegiate life.

- Don't sacrifice one for another. Football is important, but it's just one facet of college life. The opportunity that you get to attend a University such as Notre Dame goes way beyond just playing football.

- Take advantage of everything that college has to offer, the services, faculty, fellow students. I did not take advantage of all that Notre Dame had to offer when I was a student.

- Meet new people. In college you are becoming the person that you are going to be in the future. Student-athletes need to really explore that in their personal lives — to meet other people and to figure out what kind of person you want to become.

- Develop all areas of your collegiate life. If you put one of the facets of college life aside, if you let any one of these fall by the wayside, you'll know it and regret it later on. The only person you hurt by not taking advantage of all that college has to offer is yourself.

Portrait of Notre Dame football player Tim Klusas, 1993. Photo by Bradley Photographers. (Photo courtesy of Notre Dame Archives.)

CHAPTER TWENTY TWO

The Entrepreneur Juggler

Tim Klusas

Notre Dame fans have read about the favorite experiences of Notre Dame scholarship student-athletes, especially from the legendary football teams. Stories about the famous "Play Like a Champion Today" sign and the ritual of touching it on your way out of the locker room, of running out of the tunnel for the first time and into Notre Dame Stadium, and of that moment when your cleats hit the cushion and you look up to see the thousands of cheering fans. We've heard lots of stories about top players coming in and loving these moments, but what about those other guys that put in the blood, sweat, and tears - the walk-ons. Are they welcomed? Are they treated like outcasts? Are they embraced and share those great experiences in the same manner, or are they shunned? This is Tim Klusas' story.

> As I grew up we moved around a lot as my dad's career in corporate finance advanced. I lived in Illinois, Minnesota, Indiana, and New Jersey, with Indianapolis my final stop and where I finished high school. Notre Dame was a school that I always wanted to attend. When I was in high school my parents told me if I got into Notre Dame – don't even think about it – just go. "Go anywhere you get accepted," they said, "…but if you want us to visit and if you want to come home during the holidays, go to Notre Dame." Although I was an All-Conference and Honorable Mention All-State football player in high school, I wasn't getting any attention from schools like Notre Dame. I was recruited by several in-state non-Division I schools such as Wabash College, DePauw University, Butler University and Earlham College, in addition to the Ivy League schools. I also received some preliminary interest from some Division I schools such as the Air Force Academy and Stanford University. However, I think they were looking at me for football because I passed the screen for their academic requirements.

I'd rather take the risk of going to Notre Dame and trying to be a walk-on for the football team and graduate with a degree from ND.

> I was pretty serious about the Air Force Academy, but once I was accepted at Notre Dame I stopped pursuing the Academy. In order to attend the Air Force Academy you have to obtain a letter of recommendation from your congressman and I didn't want to take that recommendation away from someone else in my district, if I was leaning toward attending Notre Dame. While I had some football scholarship opportunities from some of the schools who were looking at me, in the end a degree from Notre Dame was a much more attractive proposition for me. I decided I'd rather take the risk of going to Notre Dame and trying to be a walk-on for the football team and graduate with a degree from ND than go elsewhere to be a starter on the football team.

Once the Notre Dame Value Stream catches your attention, it's very difficult to look away, let alone not follow it. And that is exactly what Klusas did!

The Notre Dame Years

A scholarship athlete on a Division I football team at Notre Dame requires a great deal of determination to get there and an extremely focused work ethic in order to stay there. Try doing this as a walk-on, and you've just raised the level of difficulty. You not only need to show you belong on the team, but you need to show you can compete with recruited athletes who already have proven themselves while you seek a place for yourself. The Notre Dame Value Stream provides the support needed in order to dig in and accomplish the task at hand.

I wanted to come on as a kicker in the fall so I went on a one day tryout at the beginning of my freshman year. They already had a lot of kickers and so I was told to stay in shape and come back for winter conditioning and try out again in the spring. I did my best to stay in shape and participated in winter conditioning with the team, which consists of running and conditioning drills, but of course no ball work with the football. Then we had spring practice and that is when I got another tryout. In high school I was a kicker, defensive lineman, and a running back. I talked to the running backs coach and he encouraged me to try out as a running back instead of as a kicker as I had the previously fall. He was very clear about not making any promises. I went through spring practice with the team, which was a remarkable experience. It was great to be with people that you had seen play football on television and now you're right next to them, playing alongside and against them.

Even though I was outmatched as far as size, speed, and strength, I made the team as a walk-on running back. I really can't explain why the coaches kept me on the team. I guess because I kept showing up for practice day in and day out while others were dropping off. I'm sure the coaches were thinking "maybe someone forgot to talk to him - he's back again!" (laughs) My sophomore year I was in the backfield with Jerome Bettis and Reggie Brooks and my classmates Ray Zellars and Lee Becton. My junior year, the incoming freshmen included Randy Kinder, Marc Edwards and Robert Farmer. They were all Players of the Year in their hometowns. It was an honor for me to be able to have a chance to play with that caliber of football players and people. I think athletes come to Notre Dame to compete with the best of the best. I was on the scout team which lined up as the opposing team against our defensive starters. I can tell you from firsthand experience how great the talent was on the defensive side of the ball: Demetrius DuBose, Junior Bryant, Bryant Young, Pete Bercich. When you are a walk-on and you're trying to hit the hole and you see Demetrius take six steps toward you before you even take two toward the hole, it was scary – he was an amazing talent.

What is it like to be a walk-on? Football fans have heard starters and the star players talk about what it was like to don the golden helmet for the Fighting Irish, to bask in the spotlight and hear the deafening sound of eighty thousand cheering fans. What is it like to sit on the bench and pray to get your chance as the "next man in?" Did the coaches make you feel like a walk-on?

Coach Holtz made me feel like I needed to watch game film and make sure I was prepared in case the "six guys ahead of me" couldn't dress for the game.

Maybe some of the other position coaches were focused on their position play-ers, but not mine. Coach Holtz also made everyone feel as if they were not only important to the well-being of the team but also a direct contributor towards the outcome of the game. As a player I was an inconsequential part of the team yet Coach Holtz made me feel like I needed to watch game film and make sure I was prepared in case the "six guys ahead of me" couldn't dress for the game for some reason. I was one of the few walk-ons that traveled with the team and dressed for the away games. I got the ball a few times at the end of a game to run out the clock. I was told whatever happens, don't fumble, don't run out of bounds (that stops the clock), and in case you forget, don't fumble. I never wanted to miss a practice for any reason because I was a walk-on who traveled with the team, and I wanted to do everything in my power to earn that privilege!

Coach Holtz knew who each and every one of us was, me included. He would always take a one-on-one meeting with me, even on short notice. I could never give him enough credit for what I learned as a player. He comes off as such an entertaining guy and many people mistake his sense of humor and simple sayings for being aloof at times, but Coach Holtz knew every detail of every play. If your foot was angled the wrong way, he knew it and pointed it out. If your split (distance between you and the person lined up next to you) was three inches off, he knew it and would have a yardstick/ruler on the practice field to measure your splits. Sometimes if you were right you actually got the benefit of having a yardstick to prove your alignment was cor-rect. I took away many things from Coach Holtz. He made me feel important and that is why I tried to give as much effort as I could. I learned how pow-erful it was to engage people and make them realize their attitude determined success or failure in any process. Coach Holtz had his three standard ques-tions: "Can I trust you? Are you committed to excellence? Do you care about me?" I try to use these questions as a model to evaluate team members in our business every day.

I learned how powerful it was to engage people and make them realize their attitude determined success or failure in any process.

There are dynamics on the team between the starters and the walk-ons. In addi-tion to the dynamics between the coaches and the starters, and the coaches and the walk-ons; there also are dynamics within the team between the starters and the walk-ons. Klusas talked about the relationships between the various players on the team and the camaraderie which existed among them; and whether or not the walk-ons were treated any differently by their starting teammates.

Not really, the other players were great. They were gracious to me in making me feel like I was an integral part of the team. I don't remember anyone really caring about who was on scholarship and who wasn't. What I appreciated was this: here you have a group of 18-22 year old young men. They are thinking about a million other things that they'd rather be doing other than being at practice having coaches scream at them and criticize their mistakes. They are black, white, Hispanic, Catholic and not Catholic. We could not have been more different but we were all part of the team and we were a cohesive unit. We were all focused on becoming the best team that we could be, on winning games and living up to the high standard that was placed on us by the privilege of playing football at Notre Dame. Play smart, play tough, and give your best effort.

Play smart, play tough, and give your best effort.

Even my fellow running backs were all there to help each other out. It was a well-functioning team. It makes you aspire to be part of something like that again. There was so little fighting, no politics even though we spent many hours together, and everyone was supportive both on and off the field. Whether you were having trouble with a class or a certain subject, there was always someone there to help you. There was always someone there supporting you, and then later in life, "can you make an introduction for me? Can you put in the good word for me?" You appreciate that more the further you get away from it.

Every coach has a personality all their own, but Coach Holtz's personality and the way he led is something his players always remember. Coach Holtz 100% embodies the Notre Dame Value Stream and took it upon himself to instill it in each and every one of his players. None of them forget the many lessons they learned from Coach Holtz at practice.

I missed one practice, one, during the time I was on the team because I suffered a hamstring injury. Coach Holtz walked up behind me, didn't stop, didn't even look up from the ground, and said as he walked by, "I didn't think you were fast enough to pull a hamstring" and just walked off like that. I got the message. That was the one and only practice that I missed during my playing time at ND. Coach Holtz used to always tell me, "I always liked you, you're one of the few guys I can look in the eye when I talk to you"' (Coach was shorter than most everyone else on the team).

One of my favorite Lou Holtz experiences occurred during the 1993 season: the Florida State game, the whole outcome at the end of the season; he really taught us about dealing with both success and failure. Two weeks before we played FSU we played Navy in Philadelphia. We were heavy favorites in that game. Navy was up at halftime. In his halftime speech Coach Holtz said to us, "We've got to be more focused. Just do your job and it will take care of itself." We went out and beat Navy decisively in the second half. The next week we had a bye-week, so the two weeks we had to prepare for the FSU game was Coach Holtz at his very best. He was "Dr. Psychology". He started in the locker room after the Navy game in Philadelphia with "our next opponent is the best team EVER". He continued that theme when we got back to ND, "They are so good, and us, we are just OK at our best. I don't know how we are going to even come close to playing with these guys - let alone win." Then on Monday (ten days before the game) we looked at film and he said, "There is no way we can play with these guys, but there are a couple of things we can do so maybe we won't get embarrassed on our home field." Then on Tuesday he says, "Well, we had a good practice today and maybe we can keep this game close." On Wednesday he says, "We had another good practice today and I think we might, might, have a really, really long shot at winning this game in the second half." Of course we were all wondering what he was seeing to change his mind. By the time we get to the weekend before the game he says, "Wow, you are not going to believe this, but I think we really might have a halfway decent shot at winning this." The week of the game, "We are going to win this game because we are going to play our game, and when such and such happens they are going to react in such and such way that they are not accustomed to reacting."

Coach Holtz had a knack for telling us exactly what was going to happen in a game, and sure enough it would.

William Floyd was FSU's All-World fullback, so during practices in preparation for the FSU game I was playing "as" William Floyd. I had to watch the film and be able to stand just the way he stood for each different play that he made. I did everything I could to prepare my teammates for every play they would see from Floyd. A couple of times they ran a play in the game that our defense recognized immediately and stuffed. This was what Coach Holtz did: prepare us for every facet of the game. Coach Holtz had a knack for telling us exactly what was going to happen in a game, and sure enough it would. In preparation for the FSU game he told us, "They are going to come out and score on us really quickly but then this is what is going to happen next." And that is exactly what happened. They didn't know quite how to handle us when we were ahead as the game wore on, and that is exactly what Coach Holtz said would happen.

The Plan

Coach Holtz had what he called "The Plan." The day before the FSU game he told us, "Follow The Plan, The Plan is infallible." The Plan is: "We're not going to turn over the ball, we are going to hit them harder than they hit us, and this is how we are going to beat them because we follow The Plan." Of course we had all bought in and The Plan had gotten us this far. The night before the game at team meeting Coach Holtz told us, "I have a confession. (Long pause - dead silence.) I've known Bobby Bowden (FSU Coach) for a long time and once when we were both young coaches, Coach Bowden called me for some advice; (pause) and I gave him The Plan." (We all gasped – really long pause. How are we going to win if Coach Holtz gave him The Plan? This is terrible!) Then Coach Holtz continued, "but I just want you to know I only gave him half of The Plan, so that's why I know we are going to win." It was like a wave of confidence that crested at that moment.

The week following FSU we played Boston College and lost in the final seconds of the game. We were a sure bet to win the national championship by defeating Boston College and then winning our Bowl game, but not after the loss. After the game everyone was in the locker room sobbing and looking distraught, because we knew a national championship was a long shot. Here comes Coach Holtz. Instead of telling us that it was going to be okay he said, "You should feel how bad this feels. It hurts. It should hurt. It hurts me, it hurts you. This is what it's like when you come up short. You remember this. You remember this after football, after Notre Dame, this is what coming up short feels like; and it hurts. When you get a chance to finish something, you finish it." Here we are at a massive disappointment at the pinnacle of our lives to this point and Coach Holtz is telling us that we will go on and do great things because of this failure. Every time you think "I can do a little bit more to prepare," do it.

When you think of walk-ons at Notre Dame the first person who probably comes to mind is "Rudy" Ruettiger, but Klusas didn't even know who Rudy was when he set off to begin his journey as a walk-on for the Fighting Irish of Notre Dame.

Rudy

I had not heard of Rudy when I was looking at Notre Dame, but the movie was filmed while I was a student. Rudy spoke at one of our insurance meetings and he and I realized we have something in common: Rudy is from Joliet, Illinois, which is where I was born.

Professional Career

Klusas made the most of every moment during his time at Notre Dame, and after four tremendous years of learning both on and off the field, he was ready to set out on the next journey. One of the primary goals of the Notre Dame Value Stream is to make sure that at the end of your time at Notre Dame you are prepared for anything put in front of you, and Klusas was just that: prepared.

> *After I graduated from ND I worked at a bank doing the credit analysis for commercial loans and developed business relationships with small business owners. I went on to become a lender making loans to small business owners. I loved that job. I got to be their confidant and their advisor, beyond just their lender. Then I went back to school to get my MBA from Cornell University to gain the tools and knowledge to be able to get even more involved with entrepreneurs and small business owners. After my MBA, I worked at a global manufacturing company, Eaton Corporation, working on projects from corporate strategy to divestitures and acquisitions. I was working at Eaton when I was contacted about The Marketing Alliance opportunity, to be the President/CEO. The Marketing Alliance (TMA) was a chance for me to work again with business owners and entrepreneurs through a company that distributes life insurance products.*
>
> *I love working with small business owners. I think my Notre Dame experience prepared me for that. Business owners look for more than just a vendor; they need to know you are invested in their success. During the interview process, when we (The Marketing Alliance and I) discussed my background and how I benefited from playing football at ND as a walk-on, I'm sure they looked at my physical presence and thought, "You must be an overachiever. If you can hang in there and do that, you could do this!" Besides insurance distribution, we have two other businesses. The first is an agricultural terrace and tiling business (Empire Construction) in Iowa. We help farmers and landowners by building underground drainage. Our service increases the growing days which increases the yield of the crop on that farmland. It also reduces soil erosion and maximizes the acreage that can be farmed. The service pays for itself in relatively few years through better yields and more tillable acres. The second business is nine franchised locations of a children's entertainment business.*

Life for Klusas is not dull, that is for sure!

Always be prepared. Juggling the schedule of a Division I student-athlete at a school like Notre Dame teaches you how to be prepared and how to adapt to any situation placed in front of you. The Notre Dame Value Stream places the lessons of preparedness at the top of things that must be mastered before you leave Our Lady's University. It is one skill that will serve you in everything you do for the rest of your life.

Timothy Klusas

Being able to balance the demands of academics and athletics at ND really prepared me for life after college. You knew on the athletic field that you were competing with the best of the best. I had to take the time necessary to be ready to compete, which took time. Then I was expected to walk into the classroom and compete with the best of the best there as well. You knew your peers in the classroom had more time and more energy because they didn't have the life beat out of them every day at practice like you did, not to mention the work required to learn the game plan that week. I had to be extremely focused to keep up. When I was doing football, I did football. When I was preparing for a test, I was studying. Time is finite. You have to be extremely focused and organized when you are a student-athlete at a place like Notre Dame.

In my freshman English class my professor asked, "How many of you were valedictorians?" and it seemed like half of the class raised their hands. I thought, "Whew, only half." Then he asked, "How many of you were salutatorians?" and it looked like the other half of the class raised their hands. As a student-athlete, sometimes you couldn't go to every review session for exams because you were at practice, or you were travelling. Everyone has challenges. I struggled — it was hard. I did a much better job with my studies in graduate school than I did as an undergrad because I could dedicate all of my time and energy to academic life. At ND you just knew you were with the best of the best in everything you did, both on and off the field.

Today

Tim currently lives in St. Louis, Missouri, with his wife Beth and their three daughters. Find out more about Tim Klusas' business ventures:

- The Marketing Alliance: www.themarketingalliance.com
- Empire Construction and Trenching: www.empireconstructionandtrenching.com/tiling
- Monkey Joes: www.monkeyjoes.com

Timothy Klusas' Lessons from the Notre Dame Value Stream:

It's hard to imagine me giving anyone advice, but if pressed I would say:

- As a student-athlete at ND embrace the fact that you are among the best of the best.

- It's okay to fail as long as you learn something from it.

- Keep your college years as a student-athlete; build a unique experience and you will gain skills you will use for the rest of your life. You will draw from it for years afterwards.

- Succeeding, failing, preparing, working with others to accomplish a common goal: learn from these moments because you will truly draw on it for years to come, and I think it puts you at an advantage over others who have not had those experiences.

Notre Dame vs. Purdue, 1996. Notre Dame football player Kinnon Tatum (#2). Photo by Joe Raymond. (Photo courtesy of Notre Dame Archives.)

CHAPTER TWENTY THREE

The Lifetime Wealth Planner

Kinnon Tatum

*W*hen football was a hard-hitting, rough, physical, my-job-is-to-kill-you sort of game, there was a country boy named Kinnon Tatum. He was a rough and tumble, I'm-coming-to-get-you, head-banging kind of player and he loved it. He turned down offers from UNC and Georgia Tech and left the warm comfortable environment of Fayetteville, North Carolina, to play football in the lake effect tormented town of South Bend, Indiana, for the University of Notre Dame. Playing football at ND was no walk in the park for Tatum, but he learned a great deal from Coach Holtz and his on-the-field experiences, and eventually moved on to play football in the NFL for the Carolina Panthers and the Tampa

Bay Buccaneers. Kinnon has taken a path with several twists and turns since his NFL playing days. This is Kinnon Tatum's story.

Like many other guys I didn't know anything about Notre Dame. I had never watched an ND game on TV until I was recruited by them. I didn't even know where the school was. I thought Notre Dame was in England because it kind of had a "holier than thou" look to it. During the recruiting process when I told people who I was being recruited by, every time I mentioned Notre Dame you could see people's eyebrows raise. I was just a country boy, and I had no clue that ND was so highly regarded. All I knew was my attending Notre Dame seemed to really, really matter to my coach and my parents. At that point I did my research to see what Notre Dame was all about. During the recruiting process I was pursued by Georgia Tech, North Carolina, and Notre Dame. I wanted to get away from home and out from under the grips of my parents. I was ready to get the heck out of dodge and so I ended up choosing Notre Dame.

The Notre Dame Years

If you can come here and fall in line, you might be able to fit in.

Back when I was recruited, you didn't make your recruiting visits until the beginning of December. When I got to Notre Dame I fell in love with the school. It felt different to me than the other schools when I was talking to people on campus. What really captivated me about Notre Dame was the following: when the other schools were talking to me, they made it feel like I was going to come to their respective school and make THEM better, that it was all about me. But at Notre Dame it was different. Coach Holtz sat me down and told me, "Here is what we can offer you. If you can come here and fall in line, you might be able to fit in." They expected you to come, work hard, and make a commitment to give your all to Notre Dame. Sitting in Coach Holtz's office, we sealed the deal right then and there. He told me that if I came to Notre Dame and did what he wanted me to do on the field, and got good grades off the field, that I may get the chance to play by my junior year. I thought to myself, "This little man is out of his mind. He must be smoking something else in that pipe." I loved the challenge though and I was headed to play football at Notre Dame.

My host during my visit to Notre Dame was Lee Becton, which was a great fit for me because he also was from North Carolina. Lee (Mr. Smooth Operator) played offense and I played defense but we really jelled together. We were like yin and yang. Everyone that I came in contact with that weekend was so very welcoming. Lee let me know what it was going to be like if I came to

ND. He didn't sugarcoat anything — he wanted me to know what South Bend was all about. South Bend is not a big city; there is no extravagant night life. It is card games and playing pool but that fit me well; I'm a very low-key guy.

Kinnon accepted the challenge and headed to Notre Dame. He played the game of football with an intensity that is difficult to duplicate and quickly made a name for himself in Notre Dame football lore.

I just knew that play was going to be all over SportsCenter that night.

Without a doubt my best Notre Dame football memory is the one that made me immortal; in the 1995 game against USC. The huge play that was violent, destructive, and absolutely game changing; that was the moment, USC was coming in and talking up a big game. They were making all kinds of noise about how they were going to come into our house and beat us. Yadda yadda yadda... bring it on. I have slingshots in reserve! (Kinnon laughs) Yes, they were coming to town and it was a big matchup, but we were ready. That play could not have been any bigger as far as turning points in games go. We were actually down 7-3 at the time, and after that play we went for 35 straight points. It was hands down the turning point in that game. I wish they would have shown me walking off of the field. You think Johnny Cash is cool? The way I walked off the field, I just knew that play was going to be all over SportsCenter that night and that little red light was going to be blinking on my dorm phone when I got back home. That was my moment. I'm so glad that I played football when I did. My job was to be a "trained assassin." I was trained to "kill" people in games. Nobody was protected. Today I would probably be ejected from every game. (laughs)

How did Tatum get himself pumped up and ready to play with the intensity that he did?

Top Authority

Top Authority was the most extreme music a person could listen to, back at the time, without actually doing bodily harm to someone. It really pumped you up. Whatever kind of levels you had, it brought you to your absolute top-level, to the top of your game. You were definitely all fired up and after you listened to them you needed 30 minutes to catch your breath. That was our pregame ritual.

There are football coaches, and then there is former Notre Dame head coach Lou Holtz. Explaining Coach Holtz is like the quote that coach uses to explain Notre Dame:

For those who know Notre Dame, no explanation in necessary. For those who don't know Notre Dame, no explanation will suffice. ~ Lou Holtz

Up until, and including, playing under Coach Holtz at Notre Dame, all of my coaches were basically the same kind of guy; where fundamentals were key. They made you outwork your opponent. They instilled in you to never quit by the way they taught you at practice and when watching film. They always made you feel that you could not lose. I felt like a gladiator each and every week that I played. I never thought that I was going to lose. And I'm not just talking about winning as a team; I'm talking about one-on-one battles, too. A lot of the time you would find yourself going up against one certain player. Never did I think I'd lose the battle.

Ask any player who played under Coach Holtz and each and every one will tell you that practices were a living nightmare, but the purpose of that was to make sure that you were 100% prepared for any situation you could face during a game. This also meant that if you put in the work at practice and were prepared, game time was a walk in the park compared with practice.

Here was all 125 pounds of him showing you how to be tough.

When we made the trip to Ireland, we were out on the field practicing one day. Coach Holtz always had this thing about demonstrating the correct way to do something when you weren't doing it correctly. Here was all 125 pounds of him showing you how to be tough. So we're in Ireland, we're feeling pretty laid back because we're playing Navy. We are enjoying our trip. We get to game day and you know Coach Holtz, he's always on the edge when his teams are too loose. He's down with the offense getting them ready for the game. Coach Davie is with us, the defense, and he's feeling pretty relaxed, too. It's Navy! All we have to do is not get into too much trouble and we're all good. Meanwhile Coach Holtz is down there yelling at the offense like it's training camp or something. We're still warming up and trying not to watch what's going on with the offense too close. We go back into the locker room for the pregame speech and guys are running around, laughing and snickering, "Did you see that??" Coach Holtz walks into the training room with a big bandage on his nose. Apparently he was demonstrating to the offense how to put your face into a guy's chest when you're making a tackle and when he did it he cut his face from the top of his nose to the bottom. I guess he forgot that he didn't have a helmet on. (laughing)

He was the king of breaking you down and building you back up again. He tried to break me one day but I'm unbreakable. Heading into my sophomore year I was feeling pretty good about myself. I had played a handful of games as a freshman and I was competing with an unproven senior for my position so I figured I was in pretty good shape. That summer Anthony Sweeny, Lyron Cobbins, and I all stayed home to work summer jobs so that we could buy a car and did not go to summer school on campus. We were only three out of 80 people who weren't on campus for the summer, so you can imagine the crooked looks that we got from that little man (Coach Holtz) when we came back to school in the fall.

We were at practice one day during fall camp doing a kickoff return and I'm blocking on special teams. During the first kickoff the guy runs right by me and I don't block him. So we do it again, and I miss him again. I really could not block this guy. So we line it up and run it again and I don't block him yet again and I'm thinking, "Holy crap what's going on with me?" Holtz says to me, "I give you a job to do and you've got to do it. Well, everyone, go have a good practice. Tatum come see me after practice." So I go back to practice completely pissed off and am knocking people out to make up for it. I go to Coach Holtz's office after practice and his secretary Jan asks me, "Tatum, what are you doing here?" and I reply, "I dunno, I can't block." I go in to Coach's office and he's sitting there smoking his pipe. He says to me, "I know you were recruited by Georgia Tech, Tennessee, and UNC. I've got transfer papers to these schools right here." I push the papers right back at him and tell him that I am willing to do whatever he wants me to do. If he wants me to work on my blocking, I'll work on my blocking. And Coach Holtz agreed. He put me on probation and I was under his surveillance. He made a point to make sure that I did not play defense in any games that season. I only got to play on special teams all year. Man did I want to transfer. I played less my sophomore year than I did my freshman year and he did it deliberately. I spoke with Coach Davie about it and he wanted to put me in but told me if he did he'd get fired.

For the rest of the year I terrorized my own team.

So what did I do? For the rest of the year I terrorized my own team in practice. I'm sure they were thinking, "What is wrong with this angry guy right here?" I went through that year and then my mom came up to South Bend for the Stanford game. She only came up for one game a year and he didn't even play me once that entire game. I went into Coach Davie's office at 6:00 am Sunday morning and I was at my wits end. "Let me tell you, things are going to change or I'm outta here." He told me to keep doing what I'm doing. My mom came all of the way here and I didn't even play once. That really hurt my feelings right there. And I took it out on my teammates in practice. Heading into spring practice it was me and Bert Berry and that upcoming *year (my Junior year) was supposed to be my year. It was a nasty spring, you want to talk about head-banging. We were the most head-banging players on the team. We were trying to outdo each other. No one even knew what was going on but they saw the product we were putting out there and our junior and senior years were just awesome.*

When most guys arrive at Notre Dame ready to play football, they have a pretty good idea what is going to be expected of them to be successful on the team. But what so many of them don't realize is that there is much more to college, and to Notre Dame, than just football. You're on your own for the first time, you are responsible for getting yourself to class, completing your work, keeping up your grades, all on top of the rigors that are collegiate football.

It was tough trying to balance everything. The toughest part about it was getting into a routine that worked. Getting into what worked for me. Time management was a skill I had to learn. Instead of waiting until the evening, I needed to go ahead and knock out homework earlier in the day instead of watching the Young and The Restless. It was all about time management for me. I went to college not liking to write and then I got to college and realized that writing was one of my best skills. I had a lot to say, but I didn't know that I was a talented writer until Dr. Holly Martin saved me. She was an academic advisor for the freshman class back then. Now she's the Assistant Dean of Freshman Studies. She was all sweet with these glasses, Mary Poppins-like, but she was tough once she got you into that office. She was the female Hulk. She got so upset with you when she thought you were under achieving. She knew how to reach the students and get them to perform at their best. She got you to perform in the classroom like you did on the field. (Tatum studied Sociology at Notre Dame.)

Professional Career

After Tatum spent four years terrorizing not only his opponents but his fellow teammates as well, he was absolutely confident that he was ready to take his skills and talents to the next level and play football in the NFL.

I was drafted in the third round of the NFL draft, the 87th pick. Bertrand Berry was drafted 86th to the Colts. I stayed in South Bend and watched the draft by myself. I kicked my roommate Nate out of the apartment because I didn't want to be around anyone while I was watching the draft. Nate was an Air Force ROTC nerd studying civil engineering. Talk about yin and yang. Back then the draft was terrible and it took so long for each pick. I ordered Papa John's pizza, took a nap, woke up, saw Renaldo get drafted, saw more guys get drafted in the second round including Marc Edwards. I really didn't think I was going to get drafted until the second day. I tested really well at the combine. I tested at the safety level for a linebacker position. I'm sitting there watching the draft when I get a call from a friend of mine. I immediately tell him, "I can't talk right now! I'm waiting for my draft phone call!" I got off the phone and shortly after that I got a call from Jimmy Johnson and the Dolphins saying that they were going to take me at the 89th pick at the end of the third round and I really believed him because I knew he liked small explosive linebackers. I was so excited about the opportunity to get to move to Florida after four years in South Bend, Indiana. I always wanted to live there because it has sunshine 12 months out of the year and I could cookout and go to the beach all year round. It was somewhere around pick 65 or 70 when he called.

The phone rang again and this time it was the Carolina Panthers asking me if I wanted to be a Panther. You betcha!! I want to come home. They told me that they were going to take me at the 87th pick and that's exactly what they did. I've never been so overcome with emotion until that very moment. I didn't expect to go on the first day. It was like all of the hard work, the tough classes, overcoming injuries, everything, it all finally paid off. Getting drafted into the NFL was icing on the cake. My whole plan for my life was that as long as my parents didn't have to pay for my college education, things were going to be great. That was the best gift I could give back to them. All of that was going through my head as I was getting drafted to the Panthers and so it was completely overwhelming.

Tatum was well equipped with the tools that he gathered during his four years of learning on the Notre Dame Value Stream and was ready to sail the high seas of his next adventure: NFL linebacker.

The best part of playing in the NFL was that you're going against the best of the best. You never have to second-guess your competition because there are no mismatches. They are the top of their craft, all of them. When you're going against players like Jerome Bettis, Troy Aikman, Barry Sanders, having to cover guys like that in practice you're thinking to yourself, "Are you kidding me?" Talk about being a kid in a candy store.

Playing in the NFL and being on a losing team.

The challenging part was the job aspect of playing in the NFL and being on a losing team. I lost more in the first two years in the NFL than I had lost in the previous six or seven years of playing football. I wore my emotions on my sleeve back then, and there was no sugar-coating of things for me. I've learned now that if I'm really upset, I shouldn't say anything at all. But back then we'd lose games back-to-back and then we'd go kick it and drown our sorrows. It was not what I was used to at all. From my previous experiences, if things were not going right on the field, you'd be embarrassed to show your face off of the field, in public. But it wasn't like that. There were a lot of veteran players who told us to not take your work home with you. There is enough stress in this business, and if you take it home with you, you will only make things worse.

My greatest highlight from my time in the NFL is kind of a weird highlight, but it's who I am. We played the Dallas Cowboys on a Sunday night. It was the primetime night game and my dad is from Texas. I have a lot of family in Texas and a big number of them came to the game. We were playing against the likes of Troy Aikman, Emmitt Smith, Daryl "Moose" Johnston, and Michael Irvin; and we beat them in primetime on Sunday night. Even though our season was not going right, that was a huge win for us. I ended up tearing the ligament in my thumb that game and had to have my first surgery as a result of the injury. It was on a special teams play on a punt and I got tangled up with another guy. I got up and as I'm running back to the sideline I felt something flapping against my wrist. When I got to the sideline and tried to rest my hand on my hips, my left hand kept sliding off and when I looked to see what was going on it was at that point I realized I had done something bad to my hand. I could take my thumb and push it all the way back to my wrist because the ligament was totally detached from the bone. They did X-rays during the game and told me that I'd have surgery the next day. In the meantime they put a cast on it and they put me back into the game. After we beat Dallas, I partied with my teammates. That whole experience of winning in primetime was awesome. The four days following surgery were not awesome though. I had never felt pain like that before. I felt every pulse in my body. I called my trainer at 4:00 am and said, "There is no way I am waiting until 6:00 am for pain medication. I'm coming to you right now."

I played for four years in the NFL, three seasons in Carolina. At the end of my second season with Carolina I had what would turn out to be a career ending injury to my shoulder. I rehabbed for seven months going into the offseason and in my first "practice" back during my third season I re-injured my shoulder and sat out the rest of the '99 season. The next year, in 2000, I joined the Tampa Bay Bucs in March and was there until the last cuts in September. I stayed down there for a few extra months because I loved Florida so much, but it started to wear on me. I realized that my body just could not compete any longer; that my time in the NFL was over. At that point I hung up my cleats.

When football has been the prime focus of your life for so long, making the transition to the next phase of your life is not always straightforward. Some guys have a pretty good vision of what goals they want to pursue in post football life, but for many there is a great feeling of loss and that void is difficult to fill. The Notre Dame Value Stream helps to clear your head and define a vision for the road ahead.

Following the end of my NFL career I chilled out for a while, contemplating what to do next. I took a management trainee position with PN&B Marketing in North Carolina and then after that I opened up my own branch, JK3 Unlimited, in Fayetteville, North Carolina with a partner for a year. Then my partner decided one day to empty the accounts and up and move to Texas, leaving me with a bunch of angry employees. Then I decided to relocate to South Carolina to open up another branch.

All I was able to salvage after the hurricane were two of my helmets.

In 2003, I went into sales with Lincoln-Mercury-Subaru and began selling cars in Fayetteville, North Carolina. I just seem to have a way of talking, and sales seemed like a natural fit for me. But that was a very up-and-down business because it was a commission-based position. Then I thought to myself, "I have a Notre Dame degree. I'm supposed to have all "up" months." I had just had a child in 2002 and needed a position that would support my family. So in 2004 I moved to New Orleans and started working for Allstate in Metairie, Louisiana. You talk about the hook-up that was a great job and a fantastic city. I lived and worked there for Allstate until Hurricane Katrina hit in 2005. All I was able to salvage after the hurricane were two of my helmets. I lost all of my photos and jerseys – pretty much everything I had. That was a humbling experience for me.

Allstate relocated me to Charlotte, North Carolina post-Katrina, which was great for me because that was where my son was. I was hoping to be much more involved in his life, living in the same town and everything, but unfortunately due to unforeseen circumstances things did not work out that way. Then a friend of mine, Dante Jones, who played for the Steelers, was coaching high school football and asked me to be his linebackers' coach in South Charlotte at Providence High School — I absolutely fell in love with the job. I rearranged my Allstate schedule so that I could make practices every day. I coached high school ball for a few years when I got an opportunity to join Charlie Weis' coaching staff at Notre Dame. In 2008 I was an offensive quality control coach, in 2009 I was a defensive quality control coach, and then Bryant Young joined me. When Weis left Notre Dame, I got the opportunity to coach at Seton Hall and we had three pretty bad years so at the end of the third year it was time for me to move on.

Today

At that point I decided it was time to head back into the business world. I had new personal goals and needed some stability in my life which coaching does not often bring. Now I'm in Chicago at Allstate's main hub and I'm settling down. It's time to hang up the whistle and the cleats and explore all of the opportunities in front of me in the business sector.

Kinnon Tatum is enjoying a successful career with Allstate in Chicago, and is concerned that not enough former professional athletes experience a comfortable retirement primarily because of lack of information.

Kinnon Tatum

As a person who was lost and has clarity and direction now, I have some great information for you. Would you like to learn more about what I'm currently doing with Allstate? Are you interested in become serious about your savings and retirement planning? I invite you to explore the most liquid, tax-free options available today. For more information regarding your savings and retirement planning you can contact Kinnon Tatum at: ktatum97@alumni.nd.edu

Kinnon Tatum's Lessons from the Notre Dame Value Stream:

- Focus on the bottom line and not on the in-between.

- Focus on the now, the today. The in-between is glorified, the scholarship is glorified; it's the wow factor.

- The self-promotion for student-athletes starts so early these days with the internet and social media. Find out what really makes you happy, what really makes you a person, and concentrate on that.

- Don't be the loudest person in the room but make people miss you when you are gone.

- Be as humble as you can. Life has too many twists and turns.

- Let your work speak for itself at the end of the day. You see people play 8, 9, 10 years in the NFL who you never heard of when they were in college. If people focused more on improving their skills and letting their work speak for itself instead of tooting their own horn all the time they'd enjoy their career a whole lot more.

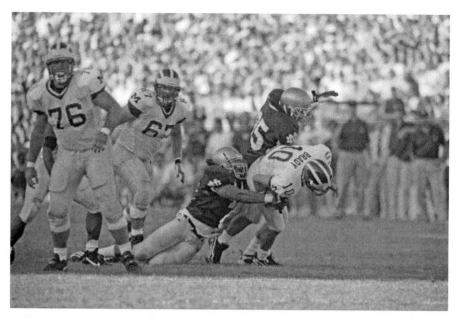

Notre Dame vs. Michigan, 1998. Notre Dame football player Kory Minor (#4) tackles Michigan quarterback Tom Brady with the help of Antwon Jones (#85). Photo by Gordie Bell. (Photo courtesy of Notre Dame Archives.)

CHAPTER TWENTY FOUR

The Business, Career and Life Coach

Kory Minor

*H*ow does a humble, hard working, salt of the earth kid go from living in laid back Southern California to moving 2,000 miles across the country and playing football in the frozen tundra of South Bend, Indiana? Kory Minor, hearing some stern advice from his mother while on Notre Dame's campus in the dead of winter, left behind his sunny California days and began his journey to play football for the Fighting Irish. During his tenure at Notre Dame, Kory totaled 245 tackles, over 40 tackles for loss and 22.5 sacks. When he stepped foot on campus in 1995 he was in good company, joined by fellow freshmen Mike Rosenthal, Jerry Wisne, Jarious Jackson, Jamie Spencer, Autry Denson, Bobbie Howard, Benny Guilbeaux and Jimmy Friday. Adjusting to the academic rigors and climate of Notre Dame was no easy feat for Kory — however, he did it with great determination, graduated with a degree in Marketing from the Mendoza College of Business, and set out to begin his NFL career. Now a successful motivational speaker, life and career coach, and author, Kory's path has taken several twists and turns since his NFL days. This is Kory Minor's story.

Since I was six years old I had a dream to attend and play football at Notre Dame.

Ever since I was six years old I had a dream to attend and play football at Notre Dame. Every Saturday morning I would sit and watch Fighting Irish football. I would be there for hours watching them play. Every time they scored, I scored. I would run around our apartment (Kory and his sister Koi were raised by their mother who was a single parent) and celebrate. The neighbors downstairs would come up every week and tell my mom, "Please get Kory to settle down!"

Notre Dame typically brings its top recruits to campus during the weekend of the football banquet at the end of the season. Kory's high school (Bishop Amat Memorial High School) was still playing in the California high school playoffs and he was unable to make his recruiting visit that weekend. Instead, Kory made his recruiting trip to Notre Dame in the middle of January.

It was freezing cold that weekend and there was a fair amount of snow on the ground.

The ND recruiters did their best to shield Kory from experiencing the South Bend cold.

When I got to the airport I saw Coach Mike Trgovac and told him, "There is no way I am coming here, it's too cold." And he told me, "No, no, no, just give us the weekend." They backed the van right up to the airport, opened the door and I went from inside the airport straight into the van; never touching the outside at all. In fact, I never even went outside until my hosts (Cliff Stroud, Renaldo Wynn and Shawn Wooden) took me out Friday night. The coaches and recruiters did their best the entire weekend to keep me as heated as possible.

My mom came with me on my recruiting trip and she was so excited about the opportunity that was in front of me. She was so gung ho about it. We were getting ready to be transported from the stadium to the academic advisors office when my mom asked the recruiters if they could give us a minute and let us walk on our own. This was our come to Jesus moment. We are standing there, outside of touchdown Jesus, when my mom says, "You see that over

*there? I can buy you a winter coat, but I can't buy you a Notre Dame educa-
tion. I can't afford this. Take advantage of this full ride opportunity that
Notre Dame is offering you."*

Kory committed that weekend. That's not to say that other schools didn't try to
lure Kory away from Notre Dame. USC, UCLA, Washington, Tennessee and
Miami were all in heavy pursuit of Kory's talents.

> *As a top recruit, there was a lot of pressure being put on me by many differ-
> ent colleges. Early on in the recruiting process the NCAA came to my house
> and spoke with me about what I could and couldn't do during the recruiting
> process. That is very intimidating for a young man.*

> ### *Notre Dame was my strangest recruiting trip.*

> *Cliff Stroud was my host for my trip. Notre Dame was my fourth recruiting
> trip. I had one more planned after Notre Dame (UCLA) but I cancelled it
> after my weekend at Notre Dame. For the record, Notre Dame was my
> strangest recruiting trip. Renaldo Wynn and Shawn Wooden took me out and
> their car broke down. It was negative 800 degrees and snowing and here I
> was outside helping change the tire. But I realized the opportunity that had
> been placed in front of me and I took it. My first year at Notre Dame, I must
> have talked to my mom four times a day. At one point I broke down and told
> her I wanted to come home. What was her response? "I bought you a jacket,
> suck it up."*

The Notre Dame Years

*We all have greatness inside of us. It's those who pursue their greatness that
spark magic, but you have to be willing to play big. ~ Kory Minor*

At many Division I schools the athletes, especially the football players, are secluded
from the rest of the student body. They live in "athlete dorms," they are in classes filled
with other student-athletes, and when they are not in football meetings, practices or
training table, they spend most of their downtime with their fellow teammates; never
to experience the rest of the student body. This is not the case at Notre Dame. The
Notre Dame Value Stream makes sure that its students receive a diverse experience
during their time at Notre Dame starting with living in dorms populated with non
student-athletes. Some of the Notre Dame football players still room with fellow athletes, but Kory Minor wanted to make sure he got the most out of his Notre Dame
education, both inside and outside of the classroom.

> *I wanted to experience people I didn't normally deal with all of the time. My
> best friend on the football team was James Spencer, and he and I were insep-
> arable through weights, training tables, and practice. But when we weren't*

doing football I wanted to live with people who didn't play sports, who were just average guys. I wanted some of that to rub off on me. I wanted to be around people who I could appreciate, who I could learn from and who could make me a better person.

Freshman student-athletes in any sport at a Division I school have their fair share of challenges. But for freshman football players at Notre Dame, the pressure to succeed is even more intense. The decision whether or not that freshman is ready to play is a tough one and is often a topic of debate among both collegiate coaches and players.

Why make a guy wait to play if he can help the team today?

I think that decision is up to the coaches and the players. If a player can perform on the field AND in the classroom academically, then they should play regardless of whether they are a freshman or not. You want to play the best 11 guys in every situation. Why make a guy wait to play if he can help the team today? When I went to visit the University of Washington, they were pretty deep at the linebacker spot and made it very clear to me that while I had the potential to be great I probably wouldn't start right away. But my feeling was if I could beat everyone out I should play right away. When I got to ND I was told that if I progressed, I would play. That helped me make my decision. As I was getting ready to start my first game as a freshman, I was sitting at my locker thinking, "Oh my God, I have arrived." Robert Farmer came over to my locker and said, "Kory, are you starting?" and I replied, "Yes." Robert said to me, "If you're starting, you're starting for a reason, because you deserve it." He may not have known it at the time, but what Robert said to me made a huge impact on me. It changed my whole thought process. It helped me regain focus and took away my jitters. Those few simple words were huge for me.

Minor had indeed arrived and from the moment he stepped on the field as a freshman at Notre Dame his football career was filled with many shining moments.

Off the field, my favorite football memory was my mom speaking at the Friday night pep rally before my final home game against Louisiana State (LSU). She walked to the podium and surprised me and the filled to the brim Joyce Center crowd with a moving "thank you" to the Notre Dame community for taking care of me during my four year stay at the University.

Kory sat there in the first row of players' seats, with tears of pride streaming down his face as he listened in appreciation of the moment he was experiencing. That night his collegiate journey was nearly complete.

***I can't even put the feeling into words, what it was like hearing the
WHOLE stadium cheer your name.***

*On the field, my favorite memory took place in a game against Ohio State my
sophomore year. I was on a blitz from the left side (the press box side). It was
a perfect call. I got to the QB Stanley Jackson, had him by the neck and
knocked him down. It brought a fourth down for the Buckeyes. We got off the
field to punt and I could hear the whole stadium chanting, "Kory! Minor!"
about six or seven times. It gave me chills. It was an insane moment. I can't
even put the feeling into words, what it was like hearing the WHOLE stadium cheer your name. It was absolutely unforgettable.*

Minor had been brought to Notre Dame to play for head coach Lou Holtz, but
during his time at Notre Dame, Coach Holtz retired and Kory finished his tenure
under head coach Bob Davie. While each coach had his own strengths and weaknesses, it is still bittersweet to not be able to finish for the man who brought you
there in the first place.

*It is impossible to compare Coach Holtz to Coach Davie. You're talking about
a Hall of Fame coach in Lou Holtz. He had so many principles that he
shared with us that we could apply to our lives. When he came to my house
to recruit me, he told my mom, "Your son will leave you a boy and you will
get him back a man." He had great leadership qualities both on and off the
field. His nurturing way, his commitment to excellence, his values; he is one
of a kind. Holtz and Davie coached two entirely different ways*

Professional Career

With four years of Notre Dame football under his belt and a marketing degree in
hand, Minor was ready to set out and prove his worth as a NFL player, but the
road proved rocky and the waters rough. The Notre Dame Value Stream was
there to guide Minor along his journey and steady his ship through the tumul-
tuous waters he experienced in his transition from college football to the NFL.

The pain of going the second day really made me the person I became.

*My NFL draft was absolutely horrendous. I shouldn't have watched the draft.
In my house, we always had a draft party every year, with pancakes, steak
and eggs — it was a huge deal for us. But my draft day was rough. It was a
tremendously humbling experience going in the 7th round. It made me work
hard, focus, and made me even more determined to be successful. There were
people who went ahead of me that I thought should not have gone ahead of
me, but the pain of going the second day really made me the person I became.
It developed a great deal of character in me. I was the no. 2 ranked outside*

*linebacker in the country going into the draft, was a starter all four years,
and a starter as a true freshman. How did I not get drafted higher than the
7th round?*

Reaching the pinnacle of playing in the NFL is the number one goal of any collegiate football player. But many of them get there and find out that it was not
what they expected or hoped it would be. This is where athletes like Minor are
fortunate to have the Notre Dame Value Stream in their back pocket to help
them appreciate the success that they've achieved, and also to recognize when the
journey is over and it's time to chart a new course.

> *I played for four years in the NFL. I was drafted by the San Francisco 49ers
> and then went on to play for the Carolina Panthers from 1999-2002. The
> game didn't tell me to go, but when they wanted to trade me to Cleveland, I
> didn't want to go. It was time for me to use that degree I earned from Notre
> Dame. The high of playing in the NFL was most definitely playing with such
> high caliber athletes. Getting to play with Jerry Rice and Steve Young at the
> 49ers was tremendous. The men that I played with in the NFL were awe-
> some. Those game day experiences, you can't make those up. I will never for-
> get that. The camaraderie that we had in the locker room was what kept you
> going week after week. The highlight of my NFL career was without a doubt
> the big hit I made on Monday Night Football against the Green Bay Pack-
> ers. What were the lows of my time in the NFL? The entire 2001 season. We
> started off the season on the road at Minnesota and dominated them that
> game winning by a score of 24-13, and then we went on to lose the rest of the
> games that season, finishing the season 1-15; that was rough.*

Some young men who come to Notre Dame to play football see ND as merely
another football school, as a means to reach their goal of pursuing a career in the
NFL. But whether or not they understood the true essence of Notre Dame before
they arrived, they all leave with a deeper understanding due to the Notre Dame
Value Stream. Our Lady's University provides for all of Her students, athletes and
non-athletes alike, and She prepares them to face anything that life puts in front
of them. They may have landed at Notre Dame ready to play the game of football, but they leave Notre Dame ready to play the game of life.

> *My biggest challenge was realizing that I could compete in the classroom with
> all of the brainiacs at ND. I had a 3.5 grade point average as a student in
> high school but when you get to Notre Dame it's a whole different level. I
> knew I could compete on the field, but I never thought I'd be able to compete
> off of it. I remember on my first day in class a guy raised his hand and asked
> a question and all I could think was, "What did he just say?" At that point*

I was not sure if I'd make it. I didn't understand what one of my peers just said, how could I compete with him in the classroom? I called my mom and said, "It's going to be a long four years."

Then I realized that my education was all about my mental state. If I could compete and be successful on the football field, then I needed to believe that I could do it in the classroom as well. I learned time management and how to balance football with my studies. Once I did that, I became the student my mom always knew I could be. Notre Dame helped me learn how to network and meet people. It helped me to become a man. You left your home, were on your own and were responsible for getting up each day, going to class and football practice, getting your work done; you didn't have anyone telling you what to do. My time at Notre Dame even helped me to become a better Christian. It gave me the framework and mindset to be my best in whatever I did.

Once Minor realized that his time in the NFL had come to a close, he set off to use the Notre Dame degree he worked so hard to attain, and with the lessons he learned from the Notre Dame Value Stream he took the first step towards his next adventure.

I've always been told if you can master two skills you can do anything. One, how to sell yourself; and two, how to market yourself. My first career path after the NFL was working for an insurance company, Northwestern Mutual Life, in North Carolina, doing sales and client services. I did that for a couple years and got really good at it. I became okay with hearing the word "no," and worked in partnership with my wife. Eventually, we decided we wanted to move back to California and the Northwestern Mutual Life office in Los Angeles was too long of a commute for us, so it was time to do something else. I went to see Coach Holtz and his wife in South Carolina, I told him my wife and I wanted to move back to California, and that I was looking for a new job opportunity. He recommended me for a sales position working for this wine company, E & J Gallo Wines, and I did sales for Gallo for three years. By this time I had been bitten by the entrepreneur bug big time and wanted to start my own business. From Gallo wine I transitioned into the pizza business. I started as a general manager with Dominos for six months after which I became eligible to buy my own store. I went on to develop my franchise business operating five Dominos Pizza locations and employing over 80 workers. I did this until 2012.

Today

In 2012 Minor decided it was time that he took complete entrepreneurial control of his future and launched his own business.

In 2012, I founded my company, Kory Minor Industries, a personal development and training company to get people (both individuals and organizations) "off the sideline and into the game," with a focus on winning every day. I do a lot of sales training and keynote speaking, I coach people in their personal lives and/or in their businesses/careers and I love what I have been able to do in this personal development space.

Get Off The Sideline And Get Into The Game

Kory is the CEO of Kory Minor Industries (KMI), a training and development company for individuals and organizations specializing in helping clients to Get Off The Sideline And Get Into The Game, by fostering the concept of WINNING every day.

I wanted to write a book for a while and I had compiled all of these notes and I decided I could really help people. I wanted to keep it football themed and that's how I came up with the title of "Make a Touchdown of Your Life." I wanted to share my story, things that I did, what I overcame. I believe everyone has greatness inside of them. Most people just don't know how to pursue it. So many people have amazing talents; they just don't know how to apply them. And that's what the book came to be: me giving people the tools they need to win, to give them confidence. The thing about me is that I'm just really "real." One of my coaches told me I was just too darn humble, that I never tell anyone about what I've accomplished unless I am asked. I do this because I want people to like me for me, and then they can find out about the rest of me later. With my new company and the book I'm trying to open up a little bit more about my accomplishments.

Play Like a Champion Today

In addition to helping companies and individuals find success, Minor is also involved with Notre Dame's *Play Like a Champion Today* foundation: *Working with Coaches & Sport Leaders to Shape a Positive Sports Culture for All Young People.*

Kory Minor

I absolutely love what Play Like a Champion Today is doing. They are teaching people to respect the game, whether you are a parent, player, coach or referee; respect the game. I came aboard with the foundation five years ago, and I've been helping out with camps all over the country. The next one is in September. I have been back to Notre Dame for Play Like a Champion Today's annual meetings, and their message is something I feel very passionate about. The game of sports is life. Be accountable to your team first and not yourself, in order to develop better character.

Minor currently lives in Southern California with his wife Lisa, and their three children, Ilyana, Noah and Julian.

Kory Minor's Lessons from the Notre Dame Value Stream:

- Be yourself… don't try to be anyone else.

- Embrace the moment. You're only in college for four or five years, live in it every day because eventually it will be over.

- Network, connect with alumni, your fellow students, and don't be afraid to network and use your name and what you've done to make connections.

- Enjoy the journey. Those four or five years of college go by so fast. Live in it, embrace it, and most of all find a way, every day, to make someone else's life that you come into contact with better.

Portrait of freshman Notre Dame football player Tim O'Neill, 1999. Notre Dame University Photographer. (Photo courtesy of Notre Dame Archives.)

CHAPTER TWENTY FIVE

The Author and Financial Trading Manager

Tim O'Neill

*S*ome kids instinctively know they are going to become a teacher, a doctor, or a fire fighter; and some kids instinctively know they are going to one day play football at the University of Notre Dame. Tim O'Neill was one such kid. He dreamed of playing football at Notre Dame and all of the traditions and rituals that accompany the mystique that is Notre Dame… tapping the famous "Play Like A Champion Today" sign on the way out of the locker room, running out of the tunnel into Notre Dame stadium, and of course that hallowed moment when your cleats hit the cushion to the tune of thousands of screaming fans. How does a 5'6", 165 running back from the heart of Wolverine country manage to get the Notre Dame football coaches to take note of him and eventually earn a scholarship position on the Fighting Irish football team? Take a walk with me along the journey of a walk-on who just wouldn't give up. This is Tim O'Neill's story.

Tim O'Neill grew up in the heart of Michigan Wolverine country but always carried a torch for the Fighting Irish.

> *My family history is the same as many other kids who follow in the footsteps of parents or siblings who also attended Notre Dame, and I grew up with a great love of the University. My brother, Mike, went to Notre Dame and was a walk-on full back under Coach Holtz and played behind Rodney Culver and Jerome Bettis. He didn't play much, as you can imagine. My father also went to Notre Dame, he graduated in 1961; my grandfather graduated in 1926, and my great grandfather graduated in 1906. That's one impressive Notre Dame Legacy ahead of me and as you can guess I was pretty brainwashed when it came to ND. My wife and I were married in the basilica at Notre Dame, my parents were also married in the basilica and my grandparents were married in the log cabin chapel by the grotto. Notre Dame is a very special part of our family history.*

Don the golden helmet.

With the deep affinity that O'Neill has for Notre Dame, he always wanted to don the golden helmet and play football at the University of Notre Dame.

> *There was no other place that I wanted to be. It honestly was a dream come true to attend Notre Dame, to walk on to the football team and eventually become a scholarship player. It was really special.*

O'Neill was a pretty decent football player in high school, but at 5'6" and 165 pounds there were no schools offering him a scholarship to play college football.

> *I took a trip to the University of Michigan but they didn't give me an offer. I knew my only opportunity was going to be to walk-on somewhere and prove myself. I thought about maybe going to a Division II or Division III school but my parents always taught me to dream big. I put a video together along with a letter of recommendation from my high school football coach, John Walker, and sent it off to a bunch of colleges and universities. But the only response I really wanted was from Notre Dame. I received a call from Coach Bob Chmiel, the recruiting coordinator under Coach Holtz. I answered the phone half asleep and heard on the other end, "Hi, this is Coach Bob Chmiel and we'd like for you to come to Notre Dame and walk on the team." I really had no idea exactly what that meant but I got my physical and joined the team after classes had started my freshman year. I will always be grateful to Coach Chmiel for the opportunity.*

The Notre Dame Years

O'Neill secured a spot as a walk-on but that came with no promises of playing time and no scholarship; but they liked what they saw and he made the team.

> *There were 105 players at fall camp that year and only myself, Matt Sarb, and John Crowther made the team as freshman walk-ons after classes had started. We recruited ourselves to be at Notre Dame because we wanted to be there. We worked summer jobs to help finance our education and we were there because we truly loved the University.*

The Notre Dame Value Stream teaches early and often that hard work and perseverance almost always pay off.

> *I had five amazing years at Notre Dame and I have absolutely no regrets. I can look back and honestly say that I wouldn't have done anything differently and that I gave 100 percent. I worked harder as a Notre Dame football player than I had ever worked in my life, both physically and mentally. It was full of ups and downs, successes and failures, along with the inevitable disappointments when you thought you were going to get playing time and didn't; but in the end it was absolutely worth it.*

A walk-on member of the Notre Dame football team is a unique experience. Competing at Notre Dame is already difficult, but working twice as hard to prove your worth and earn a spot on the team while keeping up with your rigorous studies is a challenge.

Every Play Every Day; My Life as a Notre Dame Walk-on

> *While I was at Notre Dame, I started writing a journal to document my experiences as a walk-on for Notre Dame. When I started writing (during my sophomore year), it was more of a diary at first, a reflection at the end of each day. During my fifth year I wrote a lot more. Finally, a few years after graduation, I got around to compiling the entries into a book and publishing my story. I didn't write it to make money, I wrote it because I truly believe in its message: to not underestimate yourself and your dreams and what you're capable of doing. The book is called "Every Play Every Day; My Life as a Notre Dame Walk-on" and I'm fortunate that it is now in its second printing.*

Yes, life is often hard. And yes, there are days when you're going to want to give up. The Notre Dame Value Stream gives a needed boost when we think we can go no further.

> *I wanted to portray a realistic look at the experiences of a Notre Dame walk-on and the sacrifices that it takes to follow your dreams and go after what you want. In order to succeed you often times have to give up some fun things, but*

in the end it was absolutely worth it. I didn't drink my entire time at Notre Dame, but that was my personal choice. I didn't want to be working out and sacrificing my body during the week, only to break it down and have to start all over after the weekend.

As if being a walk-on isn't challenging enough, O'Neill had the added twist of playing under two different head coaches and having to learn two systems. Both men had their own talents and strengths, and very different coaching styles. This was the time for the Notre Dame Value Stream to step in and show Tim that every situation, no matter how challenging, has positive results.

When everything fell into place for me it was under Coach Willingham so I will always have an affinity for him. He was a walk-on at Michigan State and so he valued the walk-on role and could identify with what we were going through as walk-ons. Coach Davie saw me practice every day. I was running the scout team offense against our first team defense every day and I know he respected my attitude and approach to practice every day. He had me speak at the Stanford game pep rally my junior year and I will always be grateful to Coach Davie for that opportunity.

Coach Willingham changed my life forever by giving me a scholarship to play football at Notre Dame.

Coach Davie and Coach Willingham had very different personalities but they both had positive qualities that they brought to the table. Coach Willingham changed my life forever by giving me a scholarship to play football at Notre Dame. After the football banquet, Coach Willingham would be there until 1 am signing autographs. He was always the last person to leave from events. That's who he was. On the flip side, he always felt the media didn't belong in his business; his players and coaches were most important to him and who he cared about. He would get down and do the workouts with us. We respected that. But, we could also see when he wasn't getting the results on the field the pressure on him increased greatly. He started out 8-0, ranked number three in the country and then it just fell apart from there. It's all about results in college football. That's the reality. You have to win. You have to have integrity. And you can't only excel in one area; you have to excel in it all. I have stayed in touch with Coach Willingham as well as Coach Buzz Preston, my running back coach. They've always been good about lending a helping hand if you need it or sending you a congratulatory message on your marriage or new baby. They never forget their players.

In a perfect world you would expect a coaching staff to treat their players, from walk-ons up though superstars, firmly, but fairly. However, this isn't a perfect world, and like any parent who has more than one child, there are always going to be favorites who receive preferential treatment.

> *I don't think they intentionally treated us differently, but that being said, I think you definitely had to earn their respect and rightfully so. They were invested in the guys they had recruited, guys whose homes they had visited and talked with parents. On the flip side of the coin, I think college football in general is a meritocracy. If you are the best person for the job then you should play. It's definitely hard to get playing time as a walk-on but it's not impossible. Take a look at Joe Schmidt, it's definitely possible. There were guys I looked up to who were walk-ons who had earned significant playing time like Anthony Brannan, Jonathan Hebert, and Jeremy Juarez, and I tried to emulate their work ethic. I don't want to make it sound like there was a bias towards scholarship players, but as a walk-on you have to work harder in order to get your chance. Once you get the chance, then it's all on a level playing field and all you can really ask for is to be given that opportunity.*

In addition to the rapport between the coaching staff and their players, there is also a dynamic between walk-ons and scholarship players. O'Neill explains how the players interacted with each other and how the team truly was a cohesive unit, an all for one, one for all mentality.

> *I think they looked at us as a football player. If you were a good football player they respected you. If you were lacking in talent, then they viewed you that way. I didn't look at the scholarship players any differently. We were all equal and working towards the same goal, to win all of our games. In that respect we were one team. That's how we approached it. Some of my best friends at ND were scholarship players. There was no dichotomy in the locker room. I think they respected us more because we had to work hard in order to maybe get a chance to play. They respected the fact that we weren't on scholarship and were still going through everything they were going through.*

I didn't want to be Rudy.

The Notre Dame Value Stream truly creates a bond between its student-athletes like no other. When you're a walk-on football player at the University of Notre Dame, you had better be ready for the Rudy comparisons.

> *I had heard of Rudy. I had watched the movie and loved it. When people hear you are walking on at Notre Dame they inevitably make that comparison. I didn't want to be Rudy, though; I wanted to be Emmitt Smith or Barry Sanders. I wanted to win the Heisman. And in my mind, I truly believed I was capable of achieving those things. That's how I approached every day of practice, every game, and every day of the offseason, that if I got*

my chance, my opportunity, I would be ready for it. During my freshman year at Notre Dame I didn't play one play, but I think I earned the respect of the coaching staff. I would be the opposing team's starting running back and go against the first team defense every day and I took pride in that. My first opportunity came my sophomore year when I got two carries against Arizona State. Then in my junior year I played in one game where Coach Urban Meyer put me in against Navy in the Citrus Bowl. He put me in as a wide receiver, even though I didn't normally play wide receiver, but he wanted to reward me and I will always respect him for that.

It's very difficult to stay positive when you don't get much playing time.

Just when you think you can't go on, the Notre Dame Value Stream picks you up, dusts you off, and gives you the strength to push forward.

Then Coach Willingham came in and that was my final year at Notre Dame. I really felt that it was my year and that the hard work of the previous four years had finally paid off for me. The week before the kickoff classic, Coach Willingham called me into his office and told me I was going to play that year under a full scholarship (He also offered scholarships to two of my teammates that same day, Chad Debolt and Jason Halvorson). That was one of the best days of my life. That was a very powerful moment. It proved to me that if you want something bad enough and make the necessary sacrifices that you can do anything. You're always hoping to be rewarded but you don't always get it. A lot of my walk-on friends and teammates didn't get the opportunities that I got. They put in the work, and that doesn't take away from their hard work, but it doesn't always end the way you think it should.

I started on special teams on the punt block team my senior year and had nine carries at tailback for 74 yards. It was not record breaking but it was awesome for me. It didn't matter that it was against Rutgers and we were up by 40 points, it was my opportunity. We started out ranked number three in the country that year, but lost three of our last four games and finished 10-3.

Professional Career

The Notre Dame Value Stream doesn't only guide you during your time at Notre Dame and give you the strength to continue when you think you can go no further, it also presents opportunities to you that you never thought would be possible.

I graduated from Notre Dame in 2003 and in 2009 I heard about the try-outs for a Notre Dame alumni football game versus the Japanese national team that was going to happen in Tokyo[4], coached by Lou Holtz and Tim

Brown. I was 29 years old at the time and trained for 7 months to make sure I was going to make the team because they were only going to take 50 guys. I viewed this as a once in a lifetime opportunity, to be able to play one game for Coach Holtz. What an honor. [4]

I was seven years old when I went to my first Notre Dame game with my dad, which was the Notre Dame vs. Michigan State in 1987, and Tim Brown ran back two punt returns for touchdowns in that game. I went home after that game and sent a letter to Tim Brown, asking him if he'd sign his name on this paper and send it back to me. He sent it back to me postmarked from Dallas, Texas, during one of his breaks from school, and it read, "Best Wishes, Tim Brown # 81." I kept that on my wall all through school. I ended up making the alumni team and got to go to Japan and play the Japanese national team. Tim Brown was the wide receiver coach and that was the position I got to play for that game. Being a part of that was such an amazing experience. I was able to take my future wife to Japan and she was able to see me play football for one game since she had never seen me play in college. It was almost surreal to me. It's one of the highlights of my life. I can see why Coach Holtz was such a successful coach. Tony Rice was 40 years old, and I was 30 years old and Coach Holtz coached us like it was the Super Bowl. He demanded excellence from us. He was there to win and you had better be there ready to win, too. Hearing him speak for a week at practice was worth everything.

Today

When you go to school at a magical place like the University of Notre Dame, you never want your time there to come to an end, but as we all know too well, nothing lasts forever. O'Neill's time being molded by the Notre Dame Value Stream not only prepared him for his time on the football field, but also for his time off the football field and for his journey beyond the hallowed ground that is Notre Dame.

I studied finance at Notre Dame with a minor in theology. I really enjoy finance, but I really enjoyed theology, too. I knew that I wanted something that was fast paced, challenging and a meritocracy like I experienced at Notre Dame. I interned at Lehman Brothers in New York City on the financial side of Wall Street. It wasn't on the trading side and I wasn't generating revenue for the firm, which is where I really wanted to be. I applied for various trading

---

Notre Dame alumni beat Japan: http://sports.espn.go.com/ncf/news/story?id=4355370

jobs with a lot of Wall Street firms that were recruiting, got an interview with Salomon Brothers and got a job in the sales and trading analyst program. I spent a year doing mortgage sales in Chicago and a year in high yield and credit default swap trading in New York.

When I was in mortgage backed sales in Chicago I had a great mentor in John Russell, who was a Notre Dame graduate and a good mentor to have. He took me under his wing and I worked there for two years and still ask him for advice. Most recently I am in Houston, Texas. I came to Houston with Citigroup in their commodity trading group. Currently, I am a managing director at Sequent Energy. Sequent Energy is one of the top natural gas marketers in the United States and I manage our financial trading exposure in the Western and Midwestern United States, I work with a great and talented team of individuals, led by our president Peter Tumminello. I wouldn't have had the opportunity to do what I do without the lessons I learned as a Notre Dame football player. It set me apart in interviewing. It helped me get my foot in the door and once I got my foot in the door I didn't let anyone slam it on me.

No journey is ever smooth or completely trouble free, but the bumps we encounter on the road tend to change us. As an undersized football player, O'Neill had to shine a little brighter to prove that he truly was a contender and the Notre Dame Value Stream helped him to achieve his goals.

Tim O'Neill and his family.

For me, I think my biggest challenge was overcoming the stereotype of being undersized. People have it in their mind that you have to be a certain size to play football, and for me in particular, running back. Overcoming the perception that my size was a disadvantage only made me better. On one hand I was smaller, but on the other hand I was harder to tackle. I was also quicker which made me more difficult to catch. I worked hard to be on equal footing with the other running backs that were bigger than me.

Tim O'Neill's journey with the Notre Dame Value Stream gave him faith and confidence in himself to keep him afloat on the stream.

Tim O'Neill's Lessons from the Notre Dame Value Stream:

- My advice to current student-athletes would be don't underestimate yourself, your goals, and what you're capable of achieving. There are going to be a lot of times when you are discouraged, when you think the coach doesn't like you, when you're being picked on.

- Stay the course, work hard, and good things will happen. It may not happen in the time frame you think it will happen, but if you stay focused and believe in yourself you will get there in due time.

- Don't let other people's expectations of you define who you are. Always have higher expectations for yourself than anyone else.

Portrait of Notre Dame football player Chris Yura, 1999. Notre Dame University Photographer. (Photo courtesy of Notre Dame Archives.)

CHAPTER TWENTY SIX

The Green Clothing Manufacturer

Chris Yura

*G*rowing up in the midst of the sprawling Appalachian mountains of West Virginia, one would think the only school looming on the horizon for Chris Yura would be West Virginia University. But when his beloved Mountaineers played the Fighting Irish in the 1988 national title game, it was another school that caught Yura's eye — Notre Dame. Yura was a USA Today honorable mention prep All-American, ranked 73rd among the top 100 national players by the Chicago Sun Times, and a Kennedy Award winner as the West Virginia player of the year in 1997. Chris decided to follow the mystique and lore of the Notre Dame Fighting Irish to play fullback on their squad and enrolled in the College of Arts & Letters. What does a Fighting

Irish bruiser do with this varied background? He founded SustainU, a company that produces athletic wear and collegiate apparel made completely from recycled materials. What path takes a young man from playing fullback and earning a sociology degree at Notre Dame to producing a green clothing line in West Virginia? This is Chris Yura's story.

I remember the first time I saw Notre Dame play, it was in the national championship game in 1988 when I was 8 years old. I grew up 20 miles outside of Morgantown and we didn't have cable television (in fact, we only had two channels growing up), but we did get the national title game. I remember how excited everyone was that West Virginia University (WVU) was in the national title game, but even more than that, I remember how excited everyone was that our opponent was Notre Dame. After that game Notre Dame took on a whole new life for me. ND wasn't just a football school, it was a legendary place. I respected Notre Dame very early on in every aspect. Being from a small state I learned very quickly that in order to be noticed by colleges I needed to work harder than everyone else and produce on the field. The mountains in West Virginia were a great tool for me. They were great for agility and training leg strength. I trained in the woods and was lucky enough to excel at the high school level and began to receive offers from colleges including Notre Dame. I was one of the first players from my high school football class to commit. Notre Dame called and made me an offer right after signing day in February of my junior year. My home state was not happy with me. My older brother Jon was a linebacker for the Mountaineers and everyone thought I would follow in his footsteps when, in my junior year, I was named the best player in the state. When I committed to Notre Dame I received some pretty cruel backlash from the state. Players would punch me when we were piled up after a play. People in the crowd held up angry signs. Even some of the parents made comments to me about my decision. Notre Dame just meant so much to me I could not imagine going anywhere else and it did not matter to me what they thought.

The Notre Dame Value Stream is powerful. We may not recognize it, but it is exactly what grabs hold of us and leads us toward the Lady Full of Grace perched atop the golden dome.

The first time I went to campus I was in awe. I remember going to camp at ND after my sophomore season and that's where I first received some recognition from the coaching staff. Sitting in front of the Joyce Athletic and Convocation Center and watching these huge guys show up for camp left quite an impression on me. I wasn't really all that big or anything but I worked extremely hard and made them notice me. The Notre Dame coaching staff

cares about getting the best players they can get and about getting quality stu-
dent-athletes who will do something after college. Fortunately for me I per-
formed well enough at camp and was offered a full ride to the school. Driving
home my dad and I were both in awe. Did that really just happen?

The Notre Dame Years

One of the things that makes ND so great is the diversity amongst the student body.

The friends that I made at Notre Dame were from all over the country. Many
of us came in as freshman not knowing a single soul. One of the things that
makes ND so great is the diversity amongst the student body. The only other
football player at Notre Dame who was from West Virginia was Bobbie
Howard. I met Bobbie at the football camp I attended at ND when I was in
high school. Bobbie graduated before I was a freshman. He made a big
impression on me. He was very excited that there was a kid from West Vir-
ginia at camp. He was very welcoming and was a great advocate for the Uni-
versity, as well as being a great representative of the state of West Virginia. He
left big shoes to fill but it was a tremendous experience. Notre Dame becomes
something that is always a part of you. Every time I go back to campus I feel
very connected, as if I had never left. There is a real emotional connection to
the University. I care as much about ND now as I did when I was there.

Once you accept the challenge that comes with going to Notre Dame, you antic-
ipate all of the memories that will fill your scrapbook, each one better than the
next. But you don't truly realize how lucky you are to be at a place like Notre
Dame until you reflect back years later.

Nothing truly prepares you for that moment.

It is extremely hard to select one memory as my best Notre Dame football
memory. There are so many moments that you remember. The first time I
walked out of the tunnel and onto the field at Notre Dame Stadium; that
was incredible. It was quite an accomplishment to get the opportunity to play
as a true freshman; to get the chance to play in the home opener "Kickoff
Classic" against Kansas in 1999. You get such a sense of awe seeing the fans,
the spirit of the crowd, walking out of the tunnel, the feeling of being on the
field for the first time, and knowing the responsibility of what you have to do.
I don't think I ran faster in all my life as I did on that opening kickoff. But
at the same time you are so nervous. A few short months ago you were play-
ing with high school kids, and now you are facing guys who have three and
four years under their belts. You've been training in camp and feel prepared
for the job, but nothing truly prepares you for that moment.

We were undefeated my senior year going into the Florida State game (on the road in Tallahassee). On the first play of the game Arnaz Battle caught a touchdown pass. Putting points up on the board so quickly like that and beating FSU at home to remain undefeated was an unforgettable moment for sure. From a game perspective, that was my favorite game. So many people thought we were untested and to go into Tallahassee like that to beat them was incredible. There are plenty of little memories that stay with me as well, like the fake punt against Boston College to get the first down, but everything about that FSU game was memorable. And not all memorable moments were winning ones. Such as when we played Nebraska, stayed with them the whole game, but then lost in overtime. Even though it was gut wrenching to lose on one play like that, we knew we had played our hearts out and gave it our all – that's something I'll never forget.

A lot of my favorite Notre Dame memories are off the field. The weight room was one of my favorite places, one where I felt the most at home. Such wonderful friendships were forged in the weight room — Gerome Sapp was my workout partner my freshman year. We had 6 am workouts, and we had to be there 10 minutes prior to the start time or we'd be punished. I lived out in Carroll Hall, so in order to be up and ready in time to walk all the way across campus I had to get up at 4:40 am and leave the dorm at 5:20 am. All of my roommates were sleeping because they didn't have class until 8 am. The mental toughness that is created from those situations, the friendships that are formed, the relationships with the coaches (my favorite strength coach: Mickey Marotti); those last a lifetime. They are not just your teammates or your friends, they are individuals who will sacrifice for you to make you successful, and you would do the same thing for them, no questions asked. It was a big contrast for me compared to what I was used to in high school. What I saw at Notre Dame was there weren't any stars - we were all equal and all on the same level. We didn't really feel a great deal of competition, but rather we all worked together towards what either became everyone's success or everyone's failure. I really felt that I was a part of a cohesive unit, I felt that we were working together as a team, and that was a really amazing thing. A lot of Notre Dame players were the best player from their high school, city, or state; it was pretty much up to them to carry the load prior to college ball. But at Notre Dame we played as a team. The commitment level in high school was not across the board. At ND, everyone worked so hard, no individual stood out – we were a united front. Hard work with a group of people all buying into the same concept creates such a strong brotherhood and camaraderie - win or lose you all become successful.

It was really important to the coaches that every player knew they were an equal. Whether you were a first string quarterback or a walk-on, everyone's effort and contribution was extremely important and a high level of production was expected from everyone. By doing this you eliminate the egos. If you let yourself not perform to your highest level you not only let yourself down but your teammates as well. I think training in this manner translates well onto the field. We had first round draft picks come out of that team, but for us as a team we never looked at anyone as a "star." And those guys never felt they were better than everyone else. If I blocked for Julius (Jones), I was just as happy as if I was making the running play myself. It is a refreshing feeling. In so many sports the focus is on the individuals. Football really is a team sport. You can see how one person's block can either make a play happen or make a play NOT happen. Our coaches were very adamant in pointing this out, to make everyone see that everyone needs to do their part in order for a play to work. This was drilled into our heads and it was a huge takeaway for life after football. If you work for a company, every person's job is crucial to the company's success. In my business, some days I spend my time on the phone on conference calls, and some days I spend my time on the line tagging and bagging t-shirts. Both jobs are equally as important. There is no hierarchy here; we all need to pitch in to make this work. When you manage people like this, your employees see that they are an important part of the process even if all they are doing is packaging t-shirts for the consumer.

A big part of the Notre Dame experience as a student-athlete is your relationship with your head coach. And often the man that sat in your living room wooing your parents with what his school had to offer turned into a completely different person the first time you stepped out onto the practice field, leaving many student-athletes wondering, "why did I come here?" Something that is completely out of the student-athlete's control is coaching turnovers. You came to a university to play for one specific coach, and then while you are there they leave to pursue other opportunities. On top of rigorous academic responsibilities, as a student-athlete the Notre Dame Value Stream makes maneuvering this turmoil more manageable.

He was a super engaging guy.

I only got to play for Willingham for a year. From an engagement standpoint he was a super engaging guy. He was invested in all areas of the team. He would come out and run and catch balls at the beginning of practice. He brought in assistant coaches who formed a great supporting cast for him and who really supported and cared for us. My time with Coach Willingham was very positive and I'm glad that was my last season. We had so many great players on that team. I had some elbow injuries during my sophomore year and started dislocating my elbow repeatedly and so I was limited as to how productive I could be. At that point blocking was my biggest strength. To be a fullback and have your left arm taken away from you causes you to have to relearn how to do things. I could no longer take a handoff. This was another great learning experience for me: know your role. Know what your role is and that it is important. Take the limitations that you have and do your best. For me it was to block - that is what I did to help the team. Coach Davie was the same way, he wanted production. In order to be productive you have to find a way to stay on the field. We had a great coaching staff that helped me find a way to stay out on the field.

I really liked Coach Davie a lot, too. He played at Youngstown State and he was familiar with kids from West Virginia and the way that we were raised. Kids from West Virginia may be from a small state, but it is a small state made up of strong individuals. I remember the first day he came in. He said, "I don't want fine china, I want Tupperware." That statement really stood out to me. I knew exactly what was required and expected of me. I needed to stay healthy, or get healthy, so that I could be productive. For me, his attitude towards toughness was spot on because he expected excellence and he rewarded excellence. So did Coach Meyer. He wanted you to be the best player you could be. It was proven time and time again on the field: if you were willing to work hard and be productive you were going to get a chance to play. They switched me from safety to fullback and special teams after my freshman year. I spent a lot of time with Urban Meyer working on special teams. He saw my work ethic and what I could offer the team; that I would do whatever it took no matter what my size. Size really is a relative thing and leverage is the name of the game. That group of coaches really knew how to bring out the best in us. I respected Coach Davie as a person and I really enjoyed playing for him. Having two years with Coach Meyer helped me develop a great deal as a player. He likes guys who are willing to give 110 percent all the time and it's a great mindset to have heading into the rest of your life.

Effort is a choice, talent is not.

Effort is a choice, talent is not. I love being able to look back at a situation and being able to say that I did everything that I possibly could have done. There never was a day when I didn't. Knowing that is extremely satisfying. I have no regrets. No "woulda, coulda, shoulda" moments. And I take the same approach to my business. There are days where you have disappointments, but as long as you worked as hard as you could have then you will still have peace with the situation. Having that internal determination helps when you face *the road blocks and keeps you humble in your successes. I've been in business (SustainU) for seven years now and we've grown so much, but all of the disappointments we've been through have been great learning lessons. Even if it doesn't work, as long as you've given it your all, it's all good.*

It's like a mountain; just take it one step at a time. If you doubt yourself at the beginning, you've already failed.

Our strength coach, Mickey Marotti (currently at Ohio State), would always push us until we could go no further. Push us so hard that it would take away our mental limitations. If you have no gauge as to when you've reached your goal, you just keep going. It's a great tool to be used and be taught. It can be taught if you're willing to give the effort no matter how great or small your talents. My dad was a child psychologist for years and then went into forensics. He knew no limits.

Student-athletes who come to Notre Dame expect to excel at everything. Both on the field and off, they know how to push themselves and those around them to be the absolute best they can be. This is not easy, by any stretch of the imagination, and this is where the Notre Dame Value Stream comes in. It is there to lift them when they fall, to support them as they succeed, and to direct them down the correct path when a fork appears in the road.

You are not just asked to compete on the field but in the classroom as well. I really enjoyed that challenge, academically, to be put in the same classes as kids who had this incredible intellect – kids who were at the top of their high school classes. The minute I stepped onto the field at Notre Dame I got so much faster because the competition was so much faster. My brain had to evolve to being faster and quicker. In the classroom the same thing happened. You are suddenly in class with these very bright students and they push you to get better and better. I remember feeling that everyone else knew so much more than I did academically. I asked my roommates what their SAT scores were and they had these crazy high scores. I had never even heard of anyone scoring so highly on those college entrance exams. We had a great tutoring network at Notre Dame and I found myself becoming more studious and organizing my time better. I learned that I enjoyed writing, which I had never done much of previously. I did better than I had ever thought possible and it was only the first semester my freshman year. I evolved so much in the classroom.

You need to be a Notre Dame man, there is no separation between who you are on the field and who you are off the field. You are a student-athlete.

They held us to the same high standards academically that they held us to athletically. They had the infrastructure and support system in place to make this work. If you have enough talent to get into Notre Dame you will be successful both on and off the field. For me it was a challenge, but I was more than ready to accept the challenge. I became a much better person based on the people with whom I surrounded myself. This really set me up for success in life not just after football but after Notre Dame. The smarter the student-athlete is off the field, then the smarter they are on the field. If you learn the strategy in the classroom, it absolutely translates onto the field because football is such a strategic, thinking game. This made us a better team all-around and helped us to perform better on the field. I think that is such a huge part of the concept of the student-athlete at Notre Dame. I hope they never stray from that mantra. Notre Dame does a great job at setting up its student-athletes for success both on and off the field, because let's face it, football does not last forever and you need to have something to fall back on after your football career is over. Notre Dame does a great job of choosing people who will represent the school well both on and off the field. You need to be a Notre Dame man, there is no separation between who you are on the field and who you are off the field. You are a student-athlete, it's all one being, and that is very unique about the culture at Notre Dame especially when you look at what other schools expect out of their student-athletes.

Professional Career

Our Lady's University does many things well, but one of the things She does best is prepare Her young men for life beyond the golden dome. She equips you with everything you need to handle the ups and downs that are life. She teaches you to trust that the Notre Dame Value Stream will not lead you astray, and that you're ready to make the big decisions.

Like anything in life, I don't think anyone knows where they are going to end up. You end up where God wants you to be. I definitely believe there is a purpose behind all things. All of the experiences I had leading up to Notre Dame, being at Notre Dame, and life after Notre Dame all somehow fit together. Ever since I was a kid I wanted to be a strength coach. I attended a training camp that was held at WVU back in the 1980s and I got this training booklet and did the workouts every day from when I was 12 years old. I loved that part of football. It was impactful to me and you always want to be impactful to others in your life. When I graduated from Notre Dame I wanted to go on and get my master's degree, but before that I decided to go into personal training for a while. I got a job at the Four Seasons hotel in Miami through an alumni connection. They did a cheesy promotional photo of me, in a tuxedo shirt with a dumbbell in one hand and a glass of champagne in the other, which ended up running on the front page of the Miami Herald. As a result of that photo I got a call from Ford Modeling and was offered a job modeling in New York City. When I was at ND, the guys used to tease me that I looked like an Abercrombie model, but then when you get approached like that to model in New York City for a top modeling agency, what could the guys say? It was crazy.

Moved to New York City to model for Ford Modeling agency.

I didn't know anything about modeling but I knew I wanted to get as many life experiences as possible and wasn't sure if I really wanted to pursue strength coaching so I seized the opportunity and moved to New York City to model for Ford Modeling agency. I thought to myself, "Why not?!" I learned about all different walks of life, I learned what it was like to live in a big city, and I got the chance to volunteer with charities in the city, which exposed me to urban poverty. I also learned a great deal about the fashion industry. I began to see the relationships between clothing and people. I thought about "The Shirt" back at Notre Dame. How the money raised from "The Shirt" project does so much good for students in need at ND. How clothing has this unifying effect on people. You see it in many other things like pink breast cancer awareness clothing. What I was also seeing is that sourcing and materials were coming from third world countries, exploiting people and using materials that were harmful to the earth. So even though "unifying" clothing was doing good things (i.e. breast cancer awareness and "The Shirt"), it was being harmful as well. What if clothing could be more sustainable? What if you could make clothing and help people in the process? I began to do some research into how clothing was made and what happened to the factories in the Carolinas after NAFTA. In 1997, 40 percent of the clothing we wore was made in the United States. Now it is around 2 percent.

I started to wonder what happened to these vacant factories. I did some research in the New York City Public Library and at the Fashion Institute of Technology Library, learning about what fibers would be better to use, how to produce clothing with less chemicals, fewer pesticides in the cotton, without using child labor. I started to learn about all of the environmental impacts from the production of clothing. Being from West Virginia, a coal state, I saw the aftermath of the coaling industry. It is something I've cared a lot about since I was a kid because I love the state I am from. West Virginia is one of the prettiest places on earth with incredible natural beauty, but when the extraction of natural resources is not kept in balance, it can produce very negative effects for the people and environment. I also was exposed to the reality of poverty in the United States from an early age and wanted to find a way to create jobs in my home state with an environmentally progressive mantra. I started to see potential in the clothing industry to create jobs domestically with innovation and more sustainable fibers. The light bulb went off and I felt that this could be a great business idea and something I could bring back home.

And just like that a fire is lit inside of you: the Notre Dame Value Stream veers your course and sets you on a new path.

This could be really great, could create jobs, and make a difference.

Living in New York City, I was in disguise as a model while trying to start a clothing business. I started making contacts and cold calls: Can I come work in your factory? Can I learn more about your business? I moved to North Carolina and worked in a factory putting labels in t-shirts. I started learning about recycled fibers and where 100% recycled fibers could come from. I learned about all of this cool technology and that there were a lot of domestic resources that I could tap into. The Appalachia/Tennessee/Carolina region had so many resources. I got some really great breaks, wrote a business plan, got some interns from West Virginia University to help me out, moved back home into my parents' house in 2009 (right when the recession hit) and told my mom and dad that this could be really great, could create jobs, and make a difference. They knew I was going to work hard and give it my all. My dad had been let go from his job, so in order to help me get the capital that I needed to start my business they took out a third mortgage on their house and I started buying the materials to make one single shirt.

A university group who does education in sustainability became interested in what I was doing and was willing to buy 1,000 shirts from me if I was able to make them from recycled products. The challenge was on and it worked. With the help of interns who are now a part of my full-time staff, who were willing to take a chance and learn this domestic apparel business, I was able to take on the investment, have paid off the lien on my parent's house, and have been in business since 2009. I truly believe that God has a plan for you; you just have to trust that you are where you are supposed to be. A green clothing line in the state of West Virginia? Come on! I knew that there were vacant factories out there and that people wanted to work — especially in these regions. The people who lost their jobs at the factories in the Carolinas and Tennessee, they didn't want to lose their jobs. The work had been shipped off to China and the Dominican Republic and they had no say in the matter. There is so much greed in the fashion industry. What if you took away the greed and replaced it with principles that matter and with sustainability? That is exactly what we did in creating SustainU.

Today

License to sell Notre Dame apparel.

In 2009, we sold 10,000 shirts that first year, and in 2016 we will be selling over half of a million. This will create more green jobs and just keep giving back. People have realized that once we ship jobs overseas we become a shell economy, so growing jobs domestically is very important right now. Our recent contract with Major League Baseball is a testament to the increased demand of Made in the USA Products. The biggest honor for me was when we got the license to sell Notre Dame apparel. The licensing department at Notre Dame has been extremely helpful to me in supporting my cause. They've been behind me completely. I held off on reaching out to them until we were strong enough as a business to support the demand of the Notre Dame family, and that the business was where we wanted it to be before we put it in front of the Notre Dame alumni and fans. I am so proud to be able to make a 100 percent recycled, USA Made Notre Dame t-shirt. People are really tuned into what we are doing as landfills are becoming full. And it makes sense because we can actually make things from these recycled products and create jobs all at the same time. To be able to make something in America out of recycled materials is incredible. To be able to make this with environmental stewardship makes so much sense for us.

We should not be exploiters of this world. We should all be looking into how we can reinvest in the infrastructure that we have abandoned. We only have two percent of people in the United States wearing American-made clothing so we have a lot of room for growth. This is very exciting for me. How does this become scalable? How do we grow? The scaling of all of this has been a lot more feasible than I ever imagined. As we produce more our price becomes more affordable. We have a very unique offering in today's marketplace but I hope that more clothing companies get into this market as well. As other companies are looking to enter our market, we are being looked to for advice and counsel. So many people don't know that there are companies in the United States that CAN do this. It is a very exciting time for me. Lots of challenges are ahead but it's the perfect time to invest back into the American economy. Being able to make Notre Dame products is the icing on the cake for me. I stand for the same values and principles as the University that I love. As an alumni and a former football player, I want to be able to give back to the school which gave me the tools to get where I am today.

Chris Yura and Amanda Vance

Football is an amazing medium, but what else are you in school for as a student-athlete? Football was a way for me to get where I am today. People in my company make fun of me because I use so many football analogies (all the time), but everything we learned on the field is all relatively the same in terms of how you go about the challenges in your life. Notre Dame prepared me for not only talking about the glory days of football but also to be a productive person in society.

Check out Chris' sustainable clothing line at SustainU.com and forndbynd.com

Chris Yura's Lessons from the Notre Dame Value Stream:

- If you are not taking a class right now that you feel really passionate about, find one. If there is a topic that you do feel passionate about, look and see where that could potentially lead you to your future. I can point exactly to the classes in my sociology major that sparked the ideas that have led me to where I am today.

- If you don't have a class like this, then change your schedule - find it and see where your passion might lead you further in life.

- Whatever job you end up in, you should feel passionate about it. I know guys who make a lot of money but are miserable because they hate what they do.

- If you have passion for what you do, you will be successful in life and you will be impactful on others.

Notre Dame vs. Navy, 2002. Notre Dame football player Courtney Watson (#33) makes a tackle. Photo by Jim Atkinson. (Photo courtesy of Notre Dame Archives.)

CHAPTER TWENTY SEVEN

The Fire Extinguisher

Courtney Watson

*B*eing a student-athlete at the University of Notre Dame is no Sunday stroll in the park. The rigors of classwork alone are enough to send students into fits of panic, not to mention all of the other demands and time restraints that go along with playing a varsity sport. Our Lady's University excels at drawing the caliber of individuals who shine under this special brand of pressure. Courtney Watson was just this sort of student-athlete. Not only did he excel both on and off the field during his time at Notre Dame, he also spent an entire year serving on the student senate, representing his dorm Zahm Hall, as well as shining on the courts of Bookstore Basketball. Watson left Riverview High School in Sarasota, Florida as a standout running back, rushing for 1,220 yards on 133 carries and scored 15 touchdowns his senior year in high school, and went on to become one of the most productive linebackers during his time at Notre Dame. In Watson's senior year at ND he led the team with 90 tackles in just 10 games, was named a first-team All-American by ESPN.com and was ranked as the 17th best middle linebacker nationally by The Sporting News which propelled him into a NFL career with the New Orleans Saints. After surviving not only the ups and downs of NFL life, but Hurricane Katrina as well, Watson heard the call to become a public servant. How does a standout athlete from Sarasota, Florida, end up following the call to public service post football? This is Courtney Watson's story.

Gold helmets and Touchdown Jesus.

I wasn't really interested in playing football at Notre Dame until I met Coach Urban Meyer. The only things I knew about ND were gold helmets and Touchdown Jesus. Coach Meyer took me through an education process of what Notre Dame is all about from the time I met him until the time I got there. Being from Florida, where a ton of kids go on to play football for a school in the state or at an SEC school, I decided to take a leap of faith and follow the opportunity that I was being offered by Notre Dame. I let my academics and football skills take me somewhere I normally would not have gone. I played both football and basketball in high school and the only time that I could get away to make my recruiting visit to Notre Dame was while the students were on winter break and barely anyone was on campus. My student host was Tony Fisher and I also spent time with Terrance Howard, Brock Williams and Jabari Holloway.

I really hit it off with the guys on my recruiting visit. We were similar in a lot of ways. They told me if I came to Notre Dame I would walk away with a great college experience, I would be pushed academically to achieve success in the classroom, and that unlike many other schools Notre Dame did not have "football dorms" and the athletes were not separated from the rest of the student body. This was a big selling point for me but I didn't completely realize this until I was a student at ND. By not spending all of your time with other football players you gain so many more collegiate experiences. You get a chance to make lifelong friends outside of this little bubble of football. That's very rare at most big-time football schools. I was able to sit around my dorm, make friends with people who were different from me, from different parts of the country. They were interested in me and I was interested in them and they truly inspired me.

The Notre Dame Years

Watson's peers and fellow dormmates were an inspiration to him. One of his favorite moments from his time at Notre Dame involves the overwhelming support his Zahm Hall classmates gave to him.

> *Off the top of my head the first thing that comes to mind is when I got to speak at the pep rally before the Michigan game (it was either my fifth year or my senior year). At the time I was on the student senate and my Zahm Hall guys were seated front and center at the pep rally. They all made signs with my headshot from the football program on them. There were 50 or 60 of them chanting "Senator Watson" through the whole pep rally… no matter who was speaking (including through Coach Willingham's speech); until it was my turn to speak, of course, and then they got quiet. On the field my favorite memory would have to be playing (and beating) Florida State in Tallahassee. Being from Florida I had a ton of family and friends at the game and I also had an interception. To play that well, to beat FSU on their home turf, that was such a high for me and for the whole team. There were very few games that I remember being nervous before, having butterflies, and not being able to control my emotions. This was one of those games.*

During his time at Notre Dame Watson played under two head coaches, Bob Davie and Tyrone Willingham. A head coach change adds to the stressors already felt by a student-athlete at Notre Dame. This is where the Notre Dame Value Stream teaches student-athletes to be flexible and fluid and to learn to adapt with the changes placed in front of them. Student-athletes who can flow with great changes can achieve great success.

Management styles

> *The biggest difference that I noticed between the two coaches was their management styles. Coach Willingham was a delegator. His management style was looking at the big picture. He let his coaches do more of the teaching and day-to-day instruction. Once he and his staff decided on the game plan for the week and what we were going to be taught, he was a macro manager. Coach Willingham understood that there was much more to being Notre Dame's head football coach than the day-to-day coaching.*

> *Coach Davie was more of an X's and O's guy. He was very hands on in the every day process. Because of the Coach Davie style of "micro" managing there was a lot of back and forth and changes made to the game plan during the course of the week. Sometimes when you micro manage like that you can get tunnel vision on certain things and forget about everything else that needs to be done. Coach Davie was one of those mad scientist type of guys. You could*

lock him in a room for 12 hours and what he'd emerge with would be noth-ing short of brilliant... Coach Davie didn't want to deal with all of the global head coaching responsibilities; all he wanted to do was coach football. Unfortunately there is much more to the job than just that. They were both able to get results. They each just went about it very differently.

Watson took advantage of many opportunities that Notre Dame had to offer, including participating in the esteemed tradition of Bookstore Basketball.

I participated in the Bookstore Basketball tournament for three years. My team won the tournament twice and we made it to the final four three times. Carlyle Holiday and Justin Tuck were both Division I basketball recruits (in addition to football) out of high school and neither one of them can say that. I loved playing Bookstore Basketball. I loved playing basketball growing up, even more so than playing football probably. I quit football for a while in high school to focus on bas-ketball until my coach (who coached both teams) told me that I was an idiot and that I needed to go back and play football. Basketball was always my first love. I always played on a Bookstore Basketball team with guys in my dorm. It was never a super team, but we played all year round and had a really great time. We played a lot of pickup games at the Joyce Center together. It was really important to me to go out and play with the guys that I lived with. We built a great camaraderie living and playing ball together. Bookstore Basketball is such a remarkable thing — I love how the student body comes out to support all of the teams. It was a great way to end spring football and celebrate the arrival of spring on campus. I always explain to people how our dorms acted as our fraternities and sororities on cam-pus.

In addition to participating in Bookstore Basketball, Watson also took advantage of yet another opportunity at Notre Dame which very few football players are able to participate in due to the level of time which must be devoted to it: Stu-dent Government.

Student Senate Representative

Prior to moving into Zahm Hall I heard a lot of bad stories about the dorm from some of the upperclassmen on the football team, but I absolutely loved living in Zahm. I loved my roommates. The guys were crazy and completely nuts, probably because everyone said the guys who lived in Zahm were crazy and nuts and they were trying to live up to the reputation. You know, the day before first semester finals start, the guys run through LaFortune and the sec-ond floor of the library wearing, um, bells. Yeah, those are Zahm guys. Not only were they crazy, but they voted for me to be their student senate repre-sentative. The year they voted me to the student senate they had a legitimate candidate; he had posters, gave speeches, was on the ballot. Then two days before the election my buddies convinced me to run. We got a bullhorn and walked around the night before the voting and told people to vote for me/write my name in on the ballot... and I won. Those crazy Zahm guys!

I'm not sure I realized going into it how much of a time commitment was required when you were on the student senate. We would meet every Tuesday. There was one person from every dorm on the senate, plus a president, vice president, and secretary. It was my job to represent what the guys from Zahm wanted regarding the different issues that the student senate was discussing. It was really cool. I would do a weekly meeting in the dorm to tell them what we talked about at the last senate meeting and what was up for discussion at the next one. It was really fun and I wished I could have done it again but time wise, it was tough. Tuesday was our long day of football practice and in order for me to go to the senate meetings I would have to miss part of the team meeting and the first part of practice. Coach Willingham was okay with that for one year but I didn't want to push my luck beyond that. It was an amazing experience. It was nice to be part of something bigger and to see how the student senate went about getting things accomplished. All of the student activities on campus that are not sponsored by a specific group, they are all put on by the student senate. At first I had no idea they did so much. I really got to see the inner workings of what happens on campus.

Watson's journey through his Notre Dame football career was filled with ups and downs. Fortunately for Watson, he had the Notre Dame Value Stream to guide him through the rough waters and show him that every dark cloud has a silver lining. Watson talks about the highs of the 2002 football season compared with the lows of the 2003 season.

They are very similar for me. When you have those highs, you try to keep everything in check, so it is really not that high. And the same goes for the lows. You try to take everything in stride, regardless of how good or bad it's all going, and you work hard every day to get even better. You are always focusing on the next year; the next season. But at the same time, to have those highs and to have them at Notre Dame... that was incredible. I'd rather have those highs at Notre Dame than anywhere else. I haven't been there in almost ten years, and we didn't win a national championship, but the teams I played on are remembered as if they had. At most other schools you don't get remembered unless you won a championship. We didn't realize at the time that our team was going to go down in Notre Dame history. It made me incredibly proud when they compared our team to the 2012 team, they compared me to Manti Te'o. We are considered one of the great all time defenses at ND.

If all difficulties were known at the outset of a long journey, most of us would never start out at all. ~ Dan Rather

Professional Career

And then, just like that, one journey ends and the next one begins.

About an hour time difference but it seemed like a week.

My NFL draft wasn't supposed to be very stressful, but of course, it was. It didn't need to be, but it was self-inflicted. I had a good idea as to what round I was going to be drafted in, just not which team. I had family over to the house and I was feeling pretty comfortable. For me it was going to be a celebration regardless of where I went. It started out mostly as family being with me watching the draft but as the day wore on more and more people came over. I knew I wasn't going to be drafted in the first round. There was a chance that I would be drafted in the middle to end of the second round but more likely at some point in the third. The problem was that me and my agent thought I would go ahead of certain other linebackers, so when people like Boss Bailey and Teddy Lehman came off the board before me my mood started to change. I really thought that I would go before them and they were coming off the board much earlier than we had anticipated. It was another 20 picks before I was drafted. That was only about an hour time difference but it seemed like a week.

You had to submit two different phone numbers for the draft and so I had two phones sitting in front of me. It got to the point where I had people checking to make sure the phones were working. I was sure that there must be something wrong with my phones. I was frustrated and completely distraught. I went into the back room and just closed the door. I had to separate myself from what was going on. Calm down. Talk myself back into reality. When the phone rang I ran out to get the phone and it was Jim Haslett from the New Orleans Saints telling me they were going to draft me, and then I heard everyone out in the front room screaming because it was at the bottom of the TV screen. My dad and mom and my aunts all jumped on top of me on the bed. It was a great feeling.

Playing in the NFL is a dream come true for so many young men coming out of college, but it can also turn into a nightmare in just a heartbeat. The advantages that Notre Dame student-athletes have include the experiences and development they received, and how the Notre Dame Value Stream prepares them to deal with the hardships they will inevitably face in their lives ahead.

The low for me was not the first time I got cut, but the second time I got cut, because at that point I pretty much knew that was it; my NFL career was over. You don't get much lower than that. The highs? Every game that I was able to go out there and play, to do what I had wanted to do my entire life; that was a high for me. I'm not a person who gets all jacked up before a game, but to have that feeling, to know this is what it's like to accomplish a lifetime goal, that was huge. Every time we went to a new city, a new locker room...every Sunday was better than the Sunday before. Those feelings were just the best feelings for me. It was the entire experience. There are only a select group of people who can say they graduated from Notre Dame and went on to play in the NFL, I am in that select group.

Most NFL athletes experience ups and downs during their pro football careers, but very few of them actually live through a hurricane. During Watson's time with the New Orleans Saints he lived through Hurricane Katrina.

Post-Katrina was crazy. It was tough because a lot of people don't remember that you couldn't even get back into the city after the hurricane hit. Even if you didn't have any damage to your material things you couldn't get back in to get them. First you couldn't get in to the city at all. Then they were letting people in but only during the daytime. Very quickly we realized, even though they were letting people back in, the city should not be open at all. There was no trash pickup. They had curfews set up to help prevent looting and vandalism. Marshall Law was in place. The National Guard was there, armed, sitting on top of Humvees. Gangs were fighting for territory. There were shootings every day. The NFL sends us back there and we had to live like that. I was renting in New Orleans and my home was in Florida so I had to find a new place to rent in a decent area... which just didn't exist. There was just random crime all the time. The NFL and the Saints did a great job at putting a band-aid on the dome but the city was in absolute chaos. It was very sobering to see. It was an experience like no other. It was sad to see how many people not only lost everything they owned, but loved ones, too. The whole experience was crazy. You could go weeks at a time and it would not come up... but even now, every time it comes up, it completely takes me back there and I can remember it vividly.

Watson made the most of his time in the NFL, after all the NFL stands for "Not For Long." When the time came to move on, Watson wasn't exactly sure what his next steps would be.

During my first year after I was cut from the NFL I pretty much worked out in the hopes that someone would pick me up. I tried to stay in shape and showcase my talents but no one expressed any interest in bringing me back to the game. I didn't want to do that for two or three years. After one year I knew it was really over. There are always younger guys coming out of college who can do it faster, better, and cheaper. So at that point I knew I was truly retired. I didn't really know what I wanted to do post-football. I planned on playing in the NFL for ten more years than I did so I was not prepared for the transition into my next career. While I was playing in the NFL I had opened a restaurant back in Florida. My dad was running it and I was just kind of helping out, but I knew I wanted to do more than that.

Today

It's been the best decision that I've made since my decision to go to Notre Dame.

I ran into a few guys I went to high school with who were firefighters, one friend who was a fire chief, and I decided I wanted to learn more about what it took to be one. I signed up for the academy to see if it was something that I wanted to do. I knew I had a great degree from Notre Dame but I didn't want to have a 9-5 job; that just wasn't for me. The further along I got in the academy, the more I knew this was where I belonged. I loved the crazy schedule; I loved being outside, working with the guys as a team. I really took to it and have not looked back since. I finished the academy in a year, and some medical schooling as well, and I got hired by a firehouse within three weeks. I started in July of 2009 and I still absolutely love it. It's been the best decision that I've made since my decision to go to Notre Dame. I get to use my business degree as I move up the ranks and my schedule allows me to do side work as well.

In addition to my work with the firehouse I speak to kids and sports teams and help out with their clinics here in the area. I have also developed a successful personal training business. I train young people/athletes, as well as doing personal training for individuals who are looking to get in better shape. My schedule allows me to do a lot of different things. I can give back to the community while I further my career. One of my long-term goals is to get more minorities into civil services — both firefighting and the police. Where I grew up you were either really smart and went to college, or you really didn't have any direction regarding your future. You don't have to go to college to go into civil service. It's a really good thing for kids who either can't afford to go to college or don't feel like college is a good fit for them. I want to create awareness within minority groups about the opportunities available to them in civil service. It's a great way to have a career and be able to give back to your community.

There is a tremendous amount of carryover from football to working in a police department or at a firehouse. Instead of being in a locker room you are in a fire station, but you still have to work together as a team, and you still need to be prepared for the situations you are going to face even before you face them. You have to already know how you are going to react. Especially in dangerous situations, if you are not prepared, a life or death situation could go wrong very quickly. For those of us who played sports, we have developed a skill set that works very well in this sort of career, that's a skill set that many people don't have.

Life is full of challenges, which can be perceived as a bad thing, but being challenged from an early age can set us up for success as we progress through life.

Being a student-athlete at Notre Dame was quite a challenge. If you cannot manage your time well you will not be able to succeed in both the classroom and on the field. I've heard from talking to other guys who I played with in the NFL that they felt the NFL demanded so much of our time. If you don't come from a place such as Notre Dame where that is the norm, you are going to struggle. At Notre Dame you are taking a real class schedule alongside your peers who are very smart. You have to manage class, practice, games, media request. You've got to eat and try to have a social life, too. Notre Dame taught me how to juggle all of the demands that were put upon my time.

Courtney Watson and his daughter.

Being a red shirt freshman was great for me. I knew I was not going to play that first year, but that if I showed up on time and worked out I would have chances. That year gave me an opportunity to transition into school and the rigors of Notre Dame. If I had been like Julius Jones or Gerome Sapp and had played as a true freshman it would have been a lot more difficult for me. I took the year to learn about myself, about being away from home, and how the system worked. I got myself into a groove and was more than ready to play the following year. My freshman year in Zahm, each section had a flag football team. The games were at night during the week and I played in every flag football game with my freshman section. This helped me stay in shape while I was red-shirted. What I learned is that when there are so many demands on your time, when you actually have some free time, you should do your best to fill it with something you like to do. When you have a free hour, take advantage of that free hour and use it well because you never know when you're going to have another one. As a red shirt freshman, I went from being a starter in high school to being a whipping boy and stuck on the sideline at Notre Dame. Playing flag football with my Zahm dorm mates gave me an opportunity to be out on the field, having some fun playing football, which is all I ever wanted to do!

Courtney Watson's Lessons from the Notre Dame Value Stream:

- Try to get engaged in non-football activities while you are in school. It is a great chance to go out and meet people who will become life-long friends. There is more to life than just football. Mingle, meet people who can support you in the non-football aspects of your life.

- Take advantage of all opportunities put in front of you in college. Get engaged and be involved. I worked in the Zahm hall cafeteria on Sunday nights cooking pizza and selling soda. It was awesome to be an integral part of the dorm and have a chance to really meet and get to know people. I went to college to get an experience and I wanted to take advantage of everything I possibly could.

- If you are unsure about what goals you would like to pursue in your future or you don't know what you want to do "when you grow up," consider a career in civil service. For example, if college is not a good fit for you check out the opportunities that a career in civil service can offer you and give back to your local community at the same time.

Notre Dame vs. Michigan State University (MSU), 2004. Notre Dame football player
Matt Shelton runs with ball. Photo by Clement Suhendra.
(Photo courtesy of Notre Dame Archives.)

CHAPTER TWENTY EIGHT

The Property Guru

Matt Shelton

*S*ome of us land at Notre Dame because it has been our lifelong dream to attend - or play football - at Our Lady's University. Some of us find our path drawn towards Notre Dame because of a significant influence in our life. And some of us find ourselves signing a letter of intent with Notre Dame because we simply trust all that it has to offer. That third option is exactly how wide receiver Matt Shelton found himself playing football for the Fighting Irish. During his tenure at ND, Shelton totaled 47 receptions for 890 yards and seven touchdowns, while averaging 18.9 yards per catch. In 2005, he graduated with a degree in Marketing from the Mendoza College of Business. Now a successful commercial real estate broker, Shelton's journey has had a stunning landscape. This is Matt Shelton's story.

> *My ending up at Notre Dame had a lot to do with luck. One of the Notre Dame recruiters was in Memphis talking to high school coaches in the area — ND has a great "farm system" in Memphis if you will. One of my high school coaches told the ND recruiter (along with other Division I recruiters) that he needed to come to Collierville to see me in person. As a result of my coach going to bat for me, recruiters from several schools came to Collierville to see me play. I was being recruited by Ohio State, Vanderbilt, Arkansas, Memphis, Ole Miss, and of course, Notre Dame. I really hit it off with the recruiter from Notre Dame and so that moved it to the top of my list.*

The Notre Dame Years

Following all of those recruiter visits, how many schools did Shelton take official visits to?

> *Only one: Notre Dame. When it came time for me to start taking my official visits, the unthinkable happened: during the fifth game of my senior year I tore my ACL. Pretty much every school that was recruiting me tucked its tail and ran. A few kindly called and wished me well, but most ran. After an ACL, nobody knows if a kid is really going to ever recover. What attracted these colleges to me was my speed, and there was no telling whether or not that would ever come back. And then I received the call from Bob Davie letting me know that Notre Dame's offer was still on the table. Coach Davie said to me, "I don't care if you ever step on the field again or not. You will graduate with a four-year degree from Notre Dame." That spoke volumes to me that the University was willing to stand behind its offer and support Coach Davie's actions. After that phone call there really was no question in my mind, I was going to Notre Dame.*

During the 2004 season, Shelton's 87 yard receiving game against Michigan State, and most notably the 33 yard catch which was play number five in the top 10 Notre Dame plays that week on WNDU, is one of the biggest plays for which Shelton is remembered. But one of his favorite Notre Dame football memories is that classic moment "when the cleats hit the cushion."

> **The trainers wrapped up my leg and my coaches put me into the game so that I could get my one catch and I broke the record even with my torn ACL.**

> *I guess I have two ND football memories that are very special to me. The first is running out of the tunnel and onto the field for the very first time. It was simply breathtaking. After the preseason grind of two-a-days, being away*

from home for the first time, getting used to being a student and the whole college experience, it's definitely an unforgettable moment, an unforgettable feeling. Right about at that point the doubts start crossing your mind as to whether or not you can actually play football on such a big stage as Notre Dame Stadium. And then you run out of the tunnel, onto the field to 80,000 screaming fans. You are overcome with goose bumps and everything melts away. I still get goose bumps when the team runs out of the tunnel. My next favorite ND football moment is from the Insight.com Bowl. I tore my ACL at practice on Christmas day just prior to the Insight.com Bowl game. I needed one catch for better than negative seven yards to break the record at Notre Dame for most yards per catch during a season. The trainers wrapped up my leg and my coaches put me into the game so that I could get my one catch and I broke the record even with my torn ACL. I will never forget that moment. I ran off the field and could not even feel my arm because the hit on that catch was so crushing.

My favorite off-the-field memory has to be time spent with the guys in the locker room. The incredible bonds that you make with the guys in the locker room prior to, during, and after games; they stay with you forever. I miss going out and playing football, but I really miss the camaraderie of the team. Hanging out, getting to know each other, goofing off, and having fun; that is what I miss the most.

A big part of playing football at Notre Dame is the travel. Especially for kids who have not traveled much, travel is a major highlight. And then there are those chance opportunities when the travel brings a young man back to or near his hometown. Returning to your hometown as a star football player at Notre Dame is an exciting experience for any young man, just as it was for Shelton. This is the perfect opportunity for the Notre Dame Value Stream to show these young men how to carry themselves on a prime stage and be the best representative they can for Our Lady's University.

Our trip to play the University of Tennessee was my favorite road trip game. Going home (even though Knoxville is six hours away from where I grew up); playing in that stadium which holds 100,000 screaming fans. It was so loud, the lights were so bright, and it was just such a great experience playing in my home state. The Tennessee fans treated the players and the Irish fans with great hospitality. Playing on the road is awesome, but playing on the road in your home state is something that is really hard to describe. You run out of the tunnel and they are booing you and you learn to really focus yourself and feed off of that energy.

Like any journey, the sailing is not always smooth and the road is often filled with speed bumps and potholes. Playing football at a Division I school is not always the seamless journey that one might expect. Most people see a student-athletes' time at school in simple terms: you commit to a college coach and then you learn, develop and play under him for four years. Ask pretty much any football player at a Division I school and he'll tell you this is the dream rather than the reality. What was it like for Shelton to play under several coaches at Notre Dame?

> *Speaking of what it was like to play for Coach Willingham and Coach Weis, I have to mention that I am writing a book myself. I am at about 55,000 words right now. My book details my experiences of playing for Coach Davie, Coach O'Leary, Coach Willingham, Coach Baer, and Coach Weis. How many people can say that they played under five different coaches at Notre Dame? When I played under Coach Willingham I still had a lot to learn. I still had a lot of work that I needed to put in order to become a better football player. By the time Coach Weis got to ND, I was a better player and already had been given a chance to prove myself. I was already groomed, had proven myself on the football field, and was recovering from ACL surgery and a staph infection that almost killed me. Coach Weis was much more lenient with me than he was with most of the other players. He really treated me like a son.*

Being a student-athlete in any sport at any Division I school is a challenge. But playing football at a school like Notre Dame where the time commitment to the sport itself is overwhelming and the academic standards are top tier, it is easy to find yourself lost in the crowd. You start to get that feeling of being surrounded by the crowd and yet very alone, when the Notre Dame Value Stream steps in to show you that the work is not unachievable and that success is within your reach.

> *I played football and ran track in two of my seasons at Notre Dame. Running track was great for me because it was great speed training and additional conditioning for football. Adding track to the fold didn't really change my workload much as a student-athlete at ND. I was still going to be training during the offseason so it might as well have been within a second sport. Offseason training for football is just as important as preparation during the regular season. If you don't train hard enough during the offseason then you are not ready for the grueling schedule that you have to face during the regular season. Track was very run-heavy so I didn't work out as much with the football team as I otherwise would have. It really wasn't difficult to play those two particular sports at ND. In fact, it was very beneficial to me and the other football players who were running track with me.*

Without the academic support the University gave us - freshman year of studies, making us go to class, study hall, meeting with our academic advisor - I probably would have failed out of school.

One of the most difficult transitions of my life was from high school to college. I didn't understand the concept of time management as well as I thought I did. Notre Dame made us go to study hall four times a week and without that and the rest of the academic support which the University gave us - freshman year of studies, making us go to class, study hall, meeting with our academic advisor - I probably would have failed out of school. Study hall was crucial to my success. If I had gone back to my room instead of study hall, and had been given the choice between studying and going to bed at night, I would have definitely gone to bed. Study hall forced us to get our work done and use our time wisely.

Professional Career

They may not admit it but every Division I football player dreams of playing football in the NFL. They've done the work, they've put in the time, and now they hope to shine at the next level. But so many times, just when their future seems as clear as it can be, their path is altered and a new journey begins. This is when a Notre Dame student-athlete is fortunate to have the Notre Dame Value Stream help them steer though the uncharted waters and embark upon their new journey.

I thought I was going to be drafted in the late rounds of the NFL draft or at least by the last round. The Indianapolis Colts called to say that they would have drafted me if they had a pick in the last round (which they did not). I wonder how many other guys they said that to. In the situation I was in, though, it's not a bad thing to be undrafted. Suddenly the tables are turned and if you have several teams looking at you, you get to decide. The Colts were offering me more money but I knew 98% of the offense currently playing with the Patriots and so I decided to sign with New England.

Getting my shot in the NFL was an amazing experience. Coming from a school like Notre Dame with the level of guys who I played with on the team, and who we played against on a weekly basis, it wasn't as big of a jump from college to the NFL as it had been from high school to college. Football in college was a full-time job and you get to the NFL and it's just a full-time job again. The difference is that you're working 60 hours per week in the NFL instead of 40 hours per week in college. By the time I got to the NFL I had already gone through four knee surgeries, a back injury (I had to wear a back brace for months to allow my stress fracture to heal), and a staph infection. I pretty much got hurt right away after arriving in New England and was put on injured reserve. I was a Wes Welker-type of player and was drafted by New England the year before Welker got there. I'm not saying that I would have been the next Wes Welker, but I definitely had an amazing opportunity in front of me had I not gotten hurt. I was just physically worn out by the time I got to the NFL.

You grow up spending your whole youth and young adulthood wanting to play football and then when it's taken away from you, you are kind of lost. That's when the transition and transformation begins.

My first job post football was doing day trading. I had the opportunity to work for a small company where I learned how to work the day trading industry. It was during the tail-end of the market crash and I was given five million dollars to "play" with. Seeing that it was at the tail end of the market crash we did quite well and increased our holdings by 20-25% because we were able to buy-in at a low price. Even though I was successful at day trading I quickly learned that I needed a career that has more interaction with people on a daily basis. So then I decided to try my hand at sales and I used the Notre Dame network to get a sales job. I called a friend who knew of a company that was hiring and I moved back to South Bend and took a job in Medical Device Sales for Arthrex. I did sales for two years and really loved it, but didn't love the weather in South Bend so much. After two years with Arthrex I was presented with an opportunity to move to California and do pharmaceutical sales for OcuSoft and I jumped at the chance to head west and enjoy some warm weather.

After a couple of years at OcuSoft I found myself searching for a career I could be passionate about, a passion I once had with football. Finding this needle in a haystack has not been easy and yet I stayed optimistic that lightning would strike me twice. Strike twice it did with commercial real estate. Through networking I was able to reconnect with an old friend who had an opening at his company, Continental Funding Group. My interest was piqued, so I got my real estate license in California and now I am a commercial real estate mortgage broker. I specialize in securing debt and equity financing, sourcing, underwriting and managing commercial real estate investments. I focus on numerous property types including: retail, multifamily, office, industrial and hospitality. I have found the perfect career for me, a perfect mix of numbers, human interaction and passion.

Today

The Notre Dame network made my transition from football to the business world 100% easier. Being able to lean on the network, whether you are transitioning from football to the business world or from sales to engineering, it's the same: to have a network that is in every city in the country is absolutely phenomenal.

When I'm not busy facilitating deals and working with my clients, I am working on finishing writing my book. I am trying to strike the right balance of good with juicy. I don't want to put Notre Dame in a bad light, but there are some conversations that should be had, should be known, but it's all about how you tell them. At the end of the day, I want to keep Notre Dame in a positive light.

Matt Shelton

The University did so much for me. When I was recovering from ACL surgery during my senior year at Notre Dame I got a staph infection. I didn't truly realize how bad off I was. I lost 25 pounds in a week and a half, was barely eating a bite of food a day, and was running a fever of 105 degrees. When I finally was taken to the emergency room one of the doctors almost let me go home. Instead they decided to put a picc in my arm that went straight to my heart and I got Vancomycin twice a day. While I was being treated for the staph infection I started putting down all of my thoughts, documenting my experiences from high school through my current point at Notre Dame. I continued to document my story through the rest of college and the NFL, recording the ups and downs, the injuries, and everything that I experienced along my journey. Fortunately for me the night I went to the emergency room Dr. Michael (Mike) Yergler was on call. He was the one who realized how sick I really was and recognized the urgency to save the graft in my knee. He had me taken into surgery and spent two hours flushing out my knee, which is what ended up saving my ACL repairs, and Dr. Mike most likely saved my life. My plan for finishing my book includes interviewing some other players and adding their thoughts to mine. They may either contrast what I'm saying or agree with it, but I feel it's important to add their thoughts to what I already have documented.

Matt Shelton's Lessons from the Notre Dame Value Stream:

- Stick with it. You see a lot of student-athletes who commit to a team and then de-commit before signing day arrives. If you have a chance to play a sport at Notre Dame, do it. It's a LIFE decision, not a COLLEGE decision.

- Stay there. Just because the first year is tough, don't leave. Fight through it, own your decisions, and it will be the best decision you will ever make.

- Third, soak in every moment you have during your time in college. When it's gone, it's gone, and life will never be the same again. You will always have memories that other people don't — make sure to cherish those memories.

Notre Dame vs. Pittsburgh, 2009. Notre Dame quarterback Evan Sharpley throwing the ball. Photo by Ian Gavlick. (Photo courtesy of Notre Dame Archives.)

CHAPTER TWENTY NINE

The Trainer of Athletes

Evan Sharpley

*W*hen you grow up in Marshall, Michigan, you spend your time dreaming of the day when you'll don the maize and blue for the Wolverines of Michigan and shine as a quarterback in the Big 10 conference. But as fate would have it, when Evan Sharpley reached high school and began to make some college visits he realized there was more to school than just football. At this point he redirected his focus and began to search for a school that could fulfill all of his needs: academically, athletically, spiritually and socially. It didn't take long for Notre Dame to emerge from the pack as the best school to develop him in all aspects of his life, not just football. Though Evan's journey may not have turned out exactly as he had planned, he has grown wise beyond his years. He developed not only from coaches' instruction and classroom teaching but also from real life experiences, and matured into a man ready to help other young men and women on their journeys through life. How did Evan go from future Wolverine to quarterbacking the Fighting Irish? This is Evan Sharpley's story.

If you can talk with crowds and keep your virtue, Or walk with Kings— nor lose the common touch, If neither foes nor loving friends can hurt you, If all men count with you, but none too much; If you can fill the unforgiving minute with sixty seconds' worth of distance run, Yours is the Earth and everything that's in it, And—which is more—you'll be a Man, my son!
~ Excerpt from If, by Rudyard Kipling

I was born in Pontiac, Michigan, and when I was about one year old my family relocated to Marshall, Michigan. Growing up in the heart of Wolverine country, I always imagined myself lacing up the spikes and donning the maize and blue of Michigan. We 100% hated Ohio State in my house, but there certainly wasn't any love for Notre Dame in our household either! But once I started making recruiting trips my eyes began to open and I realized I wanted more out of college than just football. I wanted to find a school that could offer me an education, spiritual development, social interaction, as well as an excellent football program. After visiting a few Big 10 schools, Notre Dame very quickly rose to the top of the pack as one of the few schools who could offer me everything I was looking for. College was always more to me than just football. I always promised myself that if I didn't get an offer to play football somewhere that I would go to college on an academic scholarship. I wanted to be at a college where I could not only get what I needed academically, but also spiritual guidance and personal development. I wanted a school that could offer me not only an excellent football program but an excellent baseball program as well. Notre Dame was the only school where 100% of those things could happen.

As a student-athlete, choosing a college based on regional proximity or local support may sound like a good idea but Sharpley decided to take a different route. He did ample research and due diligence before committing the next four years of his life to just any school.

I attended camps at Iowa, Purdue, Michigan and Notre Dame. I knew I needed to get on these various campuses and perform well at camp to be noticed. I also visited Michigan State along with some other Big 10 and MAC schools. I was heavily recruited by several Ivy League schools but they didn't give many scholarships. I enjoyed the process of getting recruited even though it was stressful at times. Once I got the offer from Notre Dame, I felt very much at peace and knew it was where I needed to be. I also knew once I committed I wasn't going to change my mind. Even when there were major coaching staff changes during that offseason (Coach Tyrone Willingham resigned following that season's college football bowl game and Notre Dame hired Coach Charlie Weis), I knew the University would bring in a qualified coach. I know it's so cliché, but it's true … Notre Dame is a "four year decision for a 40 year future." I don't regret my decision to attend and play football at Notre Dame one bit. It's been great to see the path that it's taken me on, from Marshall High School to where I am now. Quite amazing.

When I made my recruiting trip to Notre Dame, Kyle McCarthy and I took our visit together, and quarterback Brady Quinn was my host. Only 12 guys signed with Notre Dame due to the significant coaching changes that were going on. The incredible thing to me is how so many guys take their visits to Notre Dame during the winter and don't run away screaming!

The Notre Dame Years

You've put in the time and hard work and you're now a quarterback at the University of Notre Dame. And then you get to experience, first hand, the lore and mystique that is Notre Dame football. Truly unbelievable.

That's what you play the game for.

Throwing my first touchdown pass during the Purdue game my junior year is definitely something I will never forget. I came in late in the third quarter when Jimmy Clausen got injured. That first drive down the field, I felt so confident in what I was doing, it was unbelievable. All of the hard work, the time, and the sacrifices, to finally see it all come to life, that's what you play the game for. I connected with Duval Kamara on a pass dropped into the back of the end zone. That's what you dream about.

But there are so many other moments. To be on the field for the 2005 Bush push play. The emotions of that game were so high. To go from thinking we had won to having it all taken away. Then there was the intensity of the high-scoring game against Michigan State in the rain that kept going back and forth between the two teams. And then of course the late touchdown pass from Brady Quinn to Jeff Samardzija in the game at UCLA. To go from playing small town high school football in Marshall, Michigan to being in Notre Dame Stadium in front of 80,000 screaming fans was quite incredible. The camaraderie of being a part of the team regardless of whether you were playing or not was unforgettable. My time at Notre Dame was filled with so many wonderful and amazing moments and experiences. Learning

from a guy like Brady Quinn, both on and off the field, was a very impor-
tant part of my experience at Notre Dame. Being behind him for two years,
someone who had so much success on the field and who represented the Uni-
versity so well off the field, I patterned my game and work ethic after him.
Hopefully I was able to do the same thing for the guys who played behind me.

As a Notre Dame football player and student-athlete, you arrive at school bright-eyed and filled with hope and promise. The journey that you envision and the journey you experience, however, can be quite different. This is where the Notre Dame Value Stream guides Our Lady's young men to see their true path and achieve their ultimate potential.

I was recruited by Coach Tyrone Willingham, who resigned following Notre
Dame's bowl game appearance. The University hired Charlie Weis to be the
next Notre Dame head coach. Then during my sophomore year the head
baseball coach left Notre Dame to go coach the LSU baseball program. All of
this change was extremely difficult for me. Coach Paul Mainieri, the Notre
Dame Baseball coach, was instrumental in getting me to come to Notre
Dame. He told me, "Listen, Evan. Even though Coach Willingham and his
staff are no longer here, all of the reasons why you wanted to come to Notre
Dame are all still there. Yes, the coaching staff has changed, but the Univer-
sity will go out and hire a great football coach and you still have the acade-
mics and faith development." Coach (Paul) Mainieri was one of those people
who you wanted to be around. It was definitely a challenge to have to get
used to being around new coaching staff in both football and baseball. It
tested my attitude and the effort that I was going to put into my game on a
daily basis.

He did not know how to develop us as men.

From a professional standpoint, Coach Weis did an excellent job at teaching
us the game of football, and helping us to bring our game to the next level.
For that I am very appreciative. He came from a great background and a suc-
cessful NFL career. He knew how to teach us the X's and O's, how to develop
us on the field, but he did not know how to develop us as men. That was
where I felt there was something missing. To go from being recruited by some-
one of such high character as Tyrone Willingham, to someone like Charlie
Weis who was trying to run a pro style program at the college level was quite
an adjustment.

A balance between sports, academics, faith and a social life.

The time you spend in college is a formative time of your life where you are
steered and guided into who you are going to become later in life. Coach

Willingham really knew how to do that. To have a father figure like that throughout college, that didn't happen with Coach Weis. That was not his mentality or approach as a coach. Coach Weis came from a pro style mentality where everyone was paid to be there, to a college environment where players needed to be coached, mentored and guided; he needed to adjust his coaching philosophy and he did not. He will even admit that was his downfall. Some coaches are made to connect with their players, and some are not. We needed to be nurtured; there was more to college than just football. I felt all too often that things were out of balance in my life during my college years. Sports have always been important in my life, but you need to be able to find a balance between sports, academics, faith and a social life.

To the casual fan, Notre Dame is nothing more than another football school. But to those who attended Our Lady's University or know someone who did, it is so much more than just another football school. For a student-athlete such as Sharpley, football was definitely an important part of his time there. But it is only one fraction of the whole that is Notre Dame.

I played three sports in high school and two at Notre Dame. Very quickly you learn how to balance your time in a wise fashion, but even so it took me a couple of years to master that at Notre Dame. Playing two collegiate sports and keeping up your academics at a school like Notre Dame is no easy feat. It took time to figure out how many friends I was going to have and how often I'd get to hang out with them, how much time I needed to spend studying, along with the time that I had to spend at practice, in the weight room, watching film, training table, and at team meetings. All of the time management skills and structure that sports provided in my life is still very prevalent in my life and I am very grateful for that preparation and how it still benefits me today. As far as goal setting goes and the career moves I've made so far, that structure has been very helpful in guiding me to make the right decisions. I try to pass that along to the athletes that I work with because it is so lacking today. To help the kids who don't have goals or things to look forward to, and to guide them towards a positive future. During your freshman and sophomore years of college, it's a huge wakeup call. I struggled with some depression sophomore year; that along with what I was dealing with on the football team, and breaking up with my girlfriend. Sophomore year was quite a struggle for me. I made some good decisions and I made some bad decisions, too, but it was a great learning experience for me.

As a quarterback at Notre Dame your number one goal is to get your opportunity to shine and to make the most of it. But unfortunately getting that chance is not as easy as it sounds. It involves more than just working hard and being successful. Often it involves circumstances that simply cannot be controlled. During his time at Notre Dame, Sharpley determined that whether you get that opportunity or not, you can still shine.

I contemplated leaving Notre Dame.

After going through summer workouts and practice and not getting named the starting quarterback, I was pretty heartbroken, and for me that was one of the most difficult moments of my career. I had worked so hard. I had never been so focused in all of my life. In the weight room, watching films, on the practice field; I thought I had done everything I possibly could have done and I still didn't get the starting position. We lost the first game that season (under Demetrius Jones), and then Jimmy Clausen started the second game as a true freshman. That was a very low moment for me. I contemplated leaving Notre Dame. I didn't feel supported by the coaching staff. I called my brother (who was a freshman at Notre Dame at the time) and he met me at the Notre Dame baseball field and he pitched to me. It was a hate filled batting practice.

It was a "fake it til you make it" time of my life. I knew my goals, and as important as they were to me, they didn't need to outweigh the goals of the team. I tried to put my bitterness aside and not share with the team. What was most difficult for me was that I felt that I could have helped the team. We were not a nine-loss team. We had a lot of talent on that team, including an awesome offensive line. For me, that was the hardest part of that season. That should have been my window, the beginning of my Notre Dame football career, but with Clausen coming in I did not get my chance. I did my best to control what I could, my effort, and I put in the best effort that I possibly could. And I did my best to control my attitude. My attitude wasn't always great, but I wanted my teammates to see that I could maintain a positive attitude and be a team player. I know guys still go through similar situations, but I would not wish it on anyone. I contemplated leaving, but I was already three years into my education and I knew that sports were not going to last forever. At some point, that piece of paper, that diploma from Notre Dame, would open countless doors for me, and that was my priority. 18, 19, 20-year-olds don't see life in terms of long-range goals. So many guys transfer because they don't see their future. Instead they want instant gratification. Very few guys go on to play professional ball, and even if they do even fewer actually make any money playing at the next level. It is so very important to get your education for when sports is over.

Why is Evan Sharpley #13 in our program, #3 on our depth chart, but #1 in our hearts? ~ Jude Seymour

Sharpley may not have won a Heisman trophy or a national championship during his time at Notre Dame, but he will go down in history as a beloved Notre Dame quarterback. Despite everything Sharpley went through at Notre Dame, he resisted the urge to transfer and graduated with his degree. So many young quarterbacks either transfer with the hopes that a big opportunity will present itself somewhere else or end up finishing their collegiate careers in a position other than quarterback. Fortunately for Sharpley, the Notre Dame Value Stream was there to support him when times were tough, and carry him through the rough waters.

These guys take it as a business decision.

I think in general, that's how the college landscape is today. It is upsetting to me that in the past 10 (or so) years there have only been three quarterbacks that started at Notre Dame and used up all of their eligibility at Notre Dame in the same position: Brady Quinn, myself and Tommy Rees. Dayne Crist didn't. Andrew Hendricks didn't. Everett Golson didn't. You would think that at a place like Notre Dame, that wouldn't happen. These guys take it as a business decision, though. If they can get positive playing time and some NFL looks by going somewhere else, they feel like they have to take that opportunity.

Professional Career

And then one day you are standing at that inevitable fork in the road trying to decide which path to choose. Which path did Sharpley choose?

During my fourth year at Notre Dame, following the baseball season, I really wasn't sure what I was going to do next. I had not decided at that point whether or not I was going to come back for a fifth year. I had not heard from a lot of MLB teams and my senior baseball season had not gone as I wanted it to; neither individually nor as a team. I was spending some time doing some soul searching about what I wanted next when I got drafted in the final round of the MLB draft. Getting the opportunity to pursue a childhood dream was awesome.

When you get drafted in the first round of the MLB draft, you get a bonus in the 5 to 10 million-dollar range. I got a one thousand dollar bonus and bought myself a MAC book.

I played professional baseball for three years and won championships on my first two teams. It was awesome being a part of a winning experience after not winning in baseball or football at Notre Dame. I loved being around

*guys who knew how to win. It was a dream come true to be able to play pro-
fessional baseball, but you really have to love it to live that kind of lifestyle.
Long bus trips, not a lot of food, not a lot of pay. You need to have a great passion for the game of baseball to live that way for a long period of time. I
promised myself that when the time came to move on that I wouldn't be
standing on that baseball field saying, "why am I still here?" When my baseball career didn't pan out, I decided to move on.*

Today

*During the off-seasons of my professional baseball career I spent my time
working as a youth director at my church. When it was time to move on from
baseball, I got in touch with a fitness facility in Elkhart (Indiana) and was
hired on as a manager at the fitness center. I worked there for a year and a
half and then that opportunity ended. That was God's swift kick in the butt
to say, "your time is done here." With the support of my wife, I opened my
own performance facility in Elkhart. I am my own boss; I create my own
schedule, create my own culture and get to teach life lessons while I train athletes. I am training quarterbacks as well. It is very rewarding to be able to do
the work that I do. To help people athletically as well as to impart some life
lessons along the way. I am also able to bring my dog (Bulldog: Coco) to work
with me every day, which I absolutely love. What I say goes. I set the rules at
the facility and I have a lot of fun doing what I do at work every day.*

I get to interview former players and tell their stories.

Evan Sharpley and his wife.

*I've also, surprisingly, gotten some media gigs
along the way. I feel as though I bring a
unique perspective to covering sports after
having played it at a very high level. I started
writing for the South Bend Tribune, and on
(radio station) WSBT I started hosting my
own radio show; first during home games,
and now during home and away games. I get
to interview former players and tell their stories, and I get to interview some of the
younger guys to give fans a glimpse of the
next generation of players. I started writing
for Irish 24/7 at the beginning of 2015 and
I write between four and six articles a week; analyzing coaching, covering
what to expect in the coming season, and recruiting. I have been analyzing
the next cycle of recruits, helping out with recruiting camps, breaking down*

film, and giving feedback on current players. It is a great opportunity for me to stay closely involved in Notre Dame sports in a low stress environment. I don't have to make the cut. I don't have any pressure to win. All I have to do is share my knowledge and expertise. It's a win-win situation for sure.

Follow Evan Sharpley's sports analysis at 247 Sports: www.247sports.com/User/Evan-Sharpley13

Evan Sharpley's Lessons from the Notre Dame Value Stream:

- Find the balance in your life as quickly as possible. For me it was sports, academics, spiritual and social… making sure they are all in proper balance. If one is out of balance, another will falter along with it.

- Lean on the support staff at Notre Dame. They are there to help keep you accountable.

- To the players who aren't playing as much as they should/want to: control your effort and your attitude. It is much easier to look yourself in the mirror when you can do that and not be bitter with life. You can't control your teammates, your coaches, your friends, your girlfriend; but you can always control your attitude.

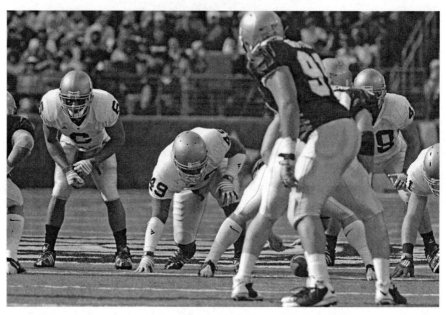

Notre Dame vs. Navy, 2008. Notre Dame football player Toryan Smith at the line of scrimmage. Photo by Quentin Stenger. (Photo courtesy of Notre Dame Archives.)

CHAPTER THIRTY

The Builder of Men
Toryan Smith

*W*hat is a Notre Dame man? When I asked a friend and teammate of Smith's to describe who he is, he described Toryan as follows: "Toryan is as passionate as they come. What you see is what you get. Loyal to those he calls friends and family. He wants to impact those around him and create a positive change in the world. He isn't afraid to 'rock the boat.' He stands up for what he believes in. He is serious, but doesn't take things too seriously. He enjoys life." Toryan Smith, son of Charles Smith, a Georgia Bulldogs football player and assistant high school football coach at Rome High School, decided not to follow in his father's footsteps and play at hometown favorite UGA but to instead travel north and don the gold helmet of the Fighting Irish of Notre Dame. During his time at

Notre Dame, he impacted the Irish defensive and special teams squads as a hard-hitting inside linebacker who loved the contact and physical aspect of the game. What is Smith up to these days? This is Toryan Smith's story.

Some of us have an early connection with Notre Dame and our choice to follow the Notre Dame Value Stream and pursue an education at Our Lady's University is an easy one. But for others it is unexpected when the Notre Dame Value Stream appears in our life and carries us off on an unforgettable adventure.

The "40 years" pitch was what got me.

When I was making the decision whether or not I was coming out of SEC country, it really came down to the invitation that I received from Notre Dame. I was really sold on Notre Dame and what it had to offer. What was the biggest selling point? "Give us four years and we'll give you 40." The "40 years" pitch was what got me. Not only that, but I also felt so comfortable when I made my visit to South Bend, I knew it was where I wanted to be. I was so excited about going to Notre Dame that I literally could not sleep at night; that's what ND does to you. My host during my visit was Darius Walker, another Georgia boy; he helped to reassure me that the transition from Georgia to South Bend was doable. I received offers from every school in the SEC but my top four schools were Alabama, Florida, Michigan, and Notre Dame.

The Notre Dame Years

During his time at Notre Dame Smith played under Notre Dame head coach Charlie Weis. A former NFL coach, Weis brought a coaching style to Notre Dame that was at times viewed as unorthodox. Despite the criticism, Weis prepared his players for success on the field, and they loved and supported him.

It was a great experience playing for Coach Weis. He was a great X's and O's coach. He was an NFL-style coach and was very business-like in his coaching mentality and how he handled the ups and downs throughout the season. I think in Coach Weis' first two years everything really clicked. We had an experienced group of players and went to two BCS games. Then in Coach Weis' third year we had a new quarterback and a young team and went 3-9 and that is when the pressure started. For some reason we just were not able to deal with the ups and downs and the challenges that were put in front of us. Coach Weis did a great job at preparing us for life with his business-like style of coaching. I will always have his back because he gave me the opportunity to go to Notre Dame.

A football career at Notre Dame is filled with countless memories and moments that live in a player's mind forever. Often the most memorable times occur early in their college football career.

My best Notre Dame football memory was playing Michigan State in East Lansing my freshman year (2006). That year we played Michigan State on the road and came from 21 points behind to beat MSU. That's when I really felt the magic of Notre Dame. It was a big-time game and we had a quarterback competing for the Heisman; simply put, it was an epic game, an instant classic. I was just getting used to playing football, the hectic schedule, balancing football and class work. That game really solidified to me that I was an integral part of a big-time football program.

The other memorable experience that really stands out for Smith is his favorite road trip.

My best road trip experience at Notre Dame was playing UCLA at the Rose Bowl. We were having a rough season up to that point and hadn't won a game yet, but traveling to Los Angeles was unbelievable. We stayed at the Beverly Hilton, were living the high life in LA, and we upset UCLA on their home turf. It was the first win of our season, on ABC, and in primetime at the Rose Bowl. It was also my first start of that season. It was definitely a road trip I won't soon forget.

Football players at the collegiate level typically do not get to start their freshman year. You have to practice for a year, learn the ropes and earn your spot on the team before you ever touch the pigskin. In recent years while many coaches still prefer to redshirt their freshmen players, there are many occasions when a freshman is ready to start right out of the box. Smith gives his views on starting freshmen players.

It depends on whether or not the player is ready.

I think you can look at starting players as freshmen two ways. First, I definitely think starting players in their first year can be a positive experience. Most of all it depends on whether or not the player is ready. If they are ready to contribute, I see no problem starting them right away. In the long run, as a team you want to have enough depth that you don't HAVE to start players as freshmen. I think if your team is in the position that you have to start guys as freshmen, especially if they are not quite ready, then that can be a negative experience and you can be doing a disservice to your players and team. Being thrust into such a situation without the adequate preparation can be very damaging. There are so many expectations that a player is under to perform, to handle the pressure, and to succeed; not only from the coaching staff but also from the fans and the alumni. If they are not ready to handle those expectations, the resulting experience can affect their ability to succeed in the long run. If you look at a team like Alabama, they rarely start freshmen players, but that is because they have developed the depth that they need to not have to start them right away. That is the ideal situation for a team to be in. If they are ready, though, it can be an empowering experience.

Notre Dame is no walk in the park. And then add football onto an already rigorous schedule. The Notre Dame Value Stream carries its student-athletes through the rough waters and towards the calm seas of success.

My biggest challenge at Notre Dame was being able to balance academics and athletics all at once. You spent an endless amount of hours each week just preparing for football and then on top of that you had to add in 25-30 hours in the classroom, homework, studying for tests, and being expected to perform at a high level in both arenas. There is such a high standard at Notre Dame in both athletics and academics. Notre Dame would never let you jeopardize your academic goals in order to achieve your athletic ones. It was not a trade-off, it was not an either/or situation, it was always both. Most of the students at Notre Dame were either valedictorians of their class or big-time athletes. There were no tiny fish in the sea at Notre Dame. It was a very competitive environment all around.

Being able to perform under such high pressure and intense scrutiny really molded me into a person who can handle just about anything. If I can perform in front of eighty thousand people, being instructed by three different coaches, being hit by my opponent, then I can perform anywhere. Being able to handle all of that pressure and still perform prepared me to face just about any work situation placed in front of me. The hardest part of my day these days is waking up. If I can wake up, physically, emotionally, and mentally, I can accomplish anything. Notre Dame shaped me into the person I am today and this helps me take myself to the next level.

Professional Career

While every college football athlete dreams of taking their career to the next level, they also recognize that the odds are not in their favor. Smith recognized this and was ready to set out onto the adventure that is life.

I wasn't expecting to be selected in the NFL draft as I was predominately a backup player. I was not on the field with enough consistency for people to really see what I could do. I played through three different defensive coordinators and that didn't help either. I tried out at the Pro Day and had a few calls but couldn't get anyone to make an offer. At that point I just wanted to get into the business world and make something of myself. The whole process of trying out for the NFL was amazing. I got to go down and do some serious NFL training, really body-specific training. I learned a great deal about my genetic make-up and learned a lot about my body and how it works, what it can do, and I really enjoyed going through the NFL workouts. I also got to see another side of the NFL: the business side. You have to be able to ride the ups and downs, work through the pain, and maintain your sanity to survive and succeed in the NFL. What I also realized is that this applies to the rest of life as well. The NFL at its core is just another business like anything else!

After graduation I moved straight from South Bend to Los Angeles, California. That is where I wanted to go so I took a business management position with a tobacco company, my territory was in Ventura County and stretched from Santa Barbara to Santa Monica. My title was account manager and I was responsible for the entire business segment; I was 100% in control of the business. I was leery about selling tobacco but it was a good business. I negotiated the deals with the chain accounts and worked with the purchasing managers of stores like 7-Eleven, Circle K, Wal-Mart, and Albertsons to make sure our products were on their shelves. It was fun. I looked forward to doing it every day. And I loved living on the coast, I almost felt that I was cheating by living somewhere that the weather was so good all of the time.

In April of 2013 I decided to start a not-for-profit with some of my friends called the Bridges Society of America. It is what I really want to get into and so we've been spreading the word and are getting ready to eventually expand and launch it as a nationwide program.

Bridges Society of America (BSA) *is a Kansas City, Missouri based non-profit organization, wholly committed to developing the character of young men in Kansas City's urban center, as well as young men across the United States. BSA acknowledges and appreciates the myriad of challenges facing disadvantaged youth and recognizes the pivotal role male mentors play in fostering the development of qualities paramount to a young man's success in 21st century America. BSA's mission statement proudly pledges to "help young men in urban areas across America build professional and social relationships that help them achieve their academic and professional goals." The overarching theme is to employ a vast network of like-minded professionals in an effort to empower young men all over the country in creating their own destinies.*

Preparation is the key to success.

We are going into urban neighborhoods to connect young men with their communities. We are teaching them how to network in order to connect with their goals both academically and athletically. We're teaching them how to say, "Yes ma'am and no ma'am," how to pull their pants up, how to dress for an interview, how to place themselves in the best position, and teaching them how to play the game of life. It's all about presentation. You can set yourself apart from the rest by working with a career center and doing a resume. We are showing them how to strategically place themselves in front of others by being prepared. Preparation is the key to success in anything in life, both on and off the field. I want to focus on the kids because they are our future. If we can turn a kid around, we can make the world a better place for all of us. If we can get the top kids in the community to become role models, and teach them how to lead in their own community, we can reach kids that we might not otherwise reach. If we can get one kid, we can get five; and if we can get five kids, we can get twenty; the whole thing just snowballs! We're just trying to impact the community any way we can.

When your time is limited as it is when you're a student-athlete at Notre Dame, you learn to make use of every bit of your time. This is a skill that will be very useful when school and football are over and you're out in the real world. In addition to all of the work that Smith is doing with the Bridges Society of America, he is also involved with a College Football podcast network called HuddlePass. How did Smith get involved with HuddlePass?

Toryan Smith

One of my teammates was telling me about Hud-dlePass. He basically gave me the information and introduced me to CJ Bacher, a quarterback out of Northwestern University. Their goal is to have a site where former student-athletes can interact with the fans.

HuddlePass *is an interactive community for fans to connect with former student-athletes who wish to share and teach the game. Fans get an insider's perspective and behind-the-scenes access to their favorite teams. Join your favorite team's Huddle and start getting analysis from those who know the program inside and out.*

On most websites you have sportswriters who never gained a ton of playing experience covering the games, but at HuddlePass you are getting articles directly from former athletes and you are able to interact with them and get the story straight from the horse's mouth. My job is to get former Notre Dame student-athletes involved and to contribute to the website.

Toryan Smith's Lessons from the Notre Dame Value Stream:

- Definitely get to know your classmates. Quite frankly, these are going to be world leaders moving forward. The people we went to school with are people of outstanding talent and character and will change the world.

- Get involved, use the network; especially the alumni network because it is so vast. Become active in the alumni network even before you graduate. Right now I consult a bit with the alumni association as well as help the monogram club attract younger members. We're doing our best to get young people active in the alumni and monogram clubs sooner rather than later.

EPILOGUE

They've Only Just Begun

*I*f history is any indication, they truly have only just begun. The question is, in future generations, what greatness will this University mold, shape and breed - a president, a supreme court justice, a corporate CEO, a Nobel prize winner, a scientific researcher; the potential is limitless and the children of these Saturday afternoon gladiators will also be shaped by this tremendous mold. The unique nature of this "mold" is that it has the ability to change and adapt to the future and to the challenges that life will present; yet the mold maintains its solidness and foundation.

The foundation is Notre Dame and the values it instills in all who enter its historic gates and emerge with not only the best academic education, but also having experienced the thrill and education of life as a student-athlete at the greatest of Universities. The toolbox She provides Her student-athletes also provides them with mentors and resources needed to help navigate those moments in life when failures happen, as they inevitably will, and redirect them towards a path of success.

Whether they achieve All-American status or toil as a walk-on, never realizing that excitement of playing in a game, each athlete who graduates today and tomorrow from Notre Dame will leave behind their legacy as a student-athlete. What is most significant is the accomplishments and pride we observe as these student-athletes become men and what their mark on the world around them will be - how they will create families, how they will mold and shape their children and be impacted by their Notre Dame Value Stream experience. It has been my honor to be able to tell the stories of so many and I look forward to sharing the journeys and stories of many more. Not only Her Loyal Sons, but Her Loyal Daughters as well. Stay tuned!

Notre Dame alumna and author, Lisa Kelly (Photographer: Tracey Saraceni)

ABOUT THE AUTHOR

*L*isa had no choice but to love Notre Dame football. Ever since she can remember, Notre Dame football has been a part of her life. She learned her first colorful word at the tender age of three during the Notre Dame - USC game on a Thanksgiving weekend spent at her grandparents' house. She and her family made annual pilgrimages to Notre Dame to spend football weekends with her dad's college roommate and his family. Notre Dame football has always been an integral part of her life.

As a business major at Notre Dame, Lisa made sure she took advantage of three things in her four years. First, being a student of theology at the most renowned theologian Institution in the world. Second, studying English to support her passion for effective communications no matter her career direction. Finally, and most importantly, leaving this great University with a degree in business and a specialty in marketing. Armed with these tools she engages the world, continuing to use what she so aptly calls, the Notre Dame Value Stream.

Lisa began her professional career in the not-for-profit sector, working for the Better Business Bureau (BBB). She taught people how to be better-informed consumers and served as a dispute resolution arbitrator. She expanded her career horizons by branching further into her career field, working 13 years as a marketing professional in yellow page advertising. The fast-paced environment in an agency setting and the creative outlet energized her career.

In 2007, she took a leap from the advertising world and accepted a job with a marketing and communications company, Katey Charles Communications. Their specialty was web design and maintenance, and e-mail newsletter design and production. She knew little about HTML programming or copy writing, but was confident that she could learn how to do anything. She spent two amazing years working for Katey Charles and learned much about copy writing, web design and HTML programming. What she learned there was the stepping off point to where she is today.

When the economy took a downturn in 2009, Lisa, like so many others, was faced with a job loss. But such a loss with the right mental attitude turns into an opportunity. For Lisa, her loss turned into a marketing research position running in-house advertising, marketing and social media for a small company. She also took the lessons and skills she was learning and began her own blog. Blogging is hard work, taking patience and perseverance. Lisa's perseverance was the catalyst for a major life change.

In 2011, Lisa was contacted by an advertising agency on Twitter who was working on a contest sponsored by Volvo and the Big East Conference to determine the "Biggest Fan of the Big East Conference." She was selected along with 15 other alumni writers representing the 16 schools in the Big East Conference, to compete for the title of "Biggest Fan." As basketball is not really her forte, Lisa had to dig inward for this contest. After eight writing assignments, a trip to New York City for media day, a trip to her Alma Mater for the Notre Dame - Syracuse match-up and endless self-promotion on social media, Lisa rose to the top and was crowned the "Biggest Fan of the Big East Conference." In all honesty, Lisa never expected to win this contest, but the more she thought about it, losing really is not in her vocabulary. If you're going to do something, give it your all and shoot for the top.

Shortly after the contest, Lisa realized she was constantly defending Our Lady's University. People were quick to find the shortcomings of Notre Dame and those associated with it, and she really wanted to do something that would showcase all of the positive things that emerge from Our Lady's University. And that is how her first book, *"Echoes From the End Zone: The Men We Became"* took shape. Her first interview was with former tight end Oscar McBride. It was more like two friends catching up, but it was a wonderful walk down memory lane with Oscar and a discovery of how Notre Dame helped shape him into the man he is today. She realized that this was the beginning of something special. One interview lead to another. As she completed each interview, it was clear that a theme was emerging. Even though Lisa and these former players all came to Notre Dame from vastly different backgrounds, they all had similar experiences and each credited their time at Notre Dame and the Notre Dame Value Stream with playing a huge role in molding them into the people they are today.

Currently Lisa is a Digital Publishing Manager at Nestle Purina PetCare. Fifty plus interviews and a second book later, Lisa is still enjoying how wonderful it is to be able to share these positive stories about Our Lady's student-athletes. In Lisa's words, there are so many of these stories yet to be told and she hopes that you have enjoyed her journey through the lives of these Loyal Sons of Our Lady's University and the stories they tell. These two books only touch the surface. She looks forward to continuing the journey and sharing more remarkable stories of Her Loyal Sons, not only from football, but from other sports as well ... and maybe some of Her Loyal Daughters, too!